GREATLY EXPANDED

CORROBORATING EVIDENCE II

The Cleveland Torso Murders
The Black Dahlia Murder
The Phantom Killer of Texarkana
The Zodiac Killer

CORROBORATING EVIDENCE II

The Cleveland Torso Murders
The Black Dahlia Murder
The Phantom Killer of Texarkana
The Zodiac Killer

William T. Rasmussen

SUNSTONE
PRESS

SANTA FE

Sunstone books may be purchased for educational, business, or sales promotional use. For information please write: Special Markets Department, Sunstone Press, P.O. Box 2321, Santa Fe, New Mexico 87504-2321.

Library of Congress Cataloging-in-Publication Data:

Rasmussen, William T., 1948-
  Corroborating evidence ii : the Cleveland torso murders, the Black Dahlia murder, the phantom killer of Texarkana, the zodiac killer / by William T. Rasmussen.
     p. cm.
  "Chapters 1 , 2, 3 and comparison of quotes as well as the chronology of torso murders are identical to 'Corroborating evidence,' c2004 (ISBN 0865344922)".
  Includes bibliographical references and index.
  ISBN 0-86534-536-8 (softcover : alk. paper)
  1. Serial murders--United States--History--20th century. 2. Serial murder investigation--United States--History--20th century. 3. Trials (Murder)--Illinois--Chicago. 4. Heirens, William. I. Title.

HV6524.R38 2006
364.152'30973--dc22

                                       2006021927

Published in

WWW.SUNSTONEPRESS.COM
SUNSTONE PRESS / POST OFFICE BOX 2321 / SANTA FE, NM 87504-2321 /USA
(505) 988-4418 / ORDERS ONLY (800) 243-5644 / FAX (505) 988-1025

"No one knows what will be the fate of the child he begets. This weary world goes on begetting . . . and all of it is blind from the beginning to end. I don't know what it was that made these boys do this mad act, but I know there is no reason for it. I know they did not beget themselves . . . . We are all helpless . . . . But when you are pitying the father and mother of poor Bobby Franks, what about the fathers and mothers of all the boys and girls who thread a dangerous maze in darkness from birth to death? . . . I am sorry for all the fathers and mothers. The mother who looks into the blue eyes of her little baby cannot help musing of the end of the child--whether it will be crowned with the greatest promises that mind can imagine--or whether he will meet death upon the scaffold. All she can do is to rear him with love and with care, to watch over him tenderly, and to meet life with hope and trust and confidence, and leave the rest to fate."

"Everybody is a potential murderer."

—Clarence Darrow, from the trial of Loeb and Leopold, 1924

CONTENTS

ACKNOWLEDGMENTS

I would like to thank the Cleveland Police Historical Society; the Cleveland Police Department; Cleveland State University; Western Reserve Historical Society; the staff at the Cleveland Public Library; Marjorie Merylo Dentz, daughter of Detective Peter Merylo; Elizabeth K. Balraj, M.D. Coroner; Donna P. Allen and the staff at the Cuyahoga County Coroner's Office in Cleveland; Delmar Watson, Los Angeles Historical Archives; the Museum of Death in Los Angeles; my editor; my publisher, James Clois Smith Jr. at Sunstone Press; the staff at the Harold Washington Public Library in Chicago; Douglas Bishop, Attorney at Law; and Dolores Kennedy, author of *William Heirens: His Day In Court*.

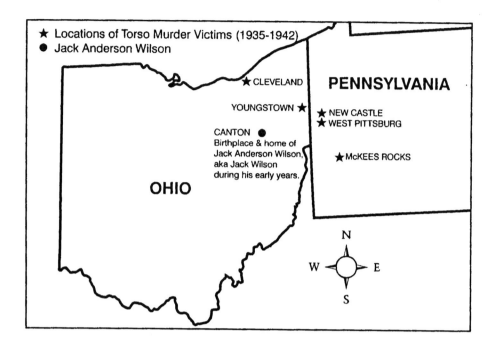

★ Locations of Torso Murder Victims (1935-1942)
● Jack Anderson Wilson

★ CLEVELAND

PENNSYLVANIA

YOUNGSTOWN ★

★ NEW CASTLE
★ WEST PITTSBURG

CANTON ●
Birthplace & home of
Jack Anderson Wilson,
aka Jack Wilson
during his early years.

★ McKEES ROCKS

OHIO

N
W — E
S

Date Murdered
★ Josephine Ross   6/5/45
  Frances Brown   12/10/45
  Suzanne Degnan   1/7/46

It is known that the
Black Dahlia is in
Chicago at times
during 1946

★
CHICAGO

ILLINOIS

INDIANA

●
INDIANAPOLIS
Jack Anderson Wilson
is in Indianapolis
Aug.-Sept. 1943

N
W — E
S

Maps Courtesy of Forton Graphics, Inc.

INTRODUCTION

Someone was killing, decapitating and dismembering other human beings for some unknown reason. A sadistic serial killer was on the loose but no one at the time realized it. The Great Depression had thrown millions of Americans into poverty and despair. Feeding a family, staying healthy and alive during these lean times was no easy task. Jobs, especially good-paying ones, were few and often out of reach for the average person. Thousands of men, down on their luck, put the responsibilities of the world behind them, became hobos and "rode the line." Some of these hobos, along with other unfortunates that fit a similar profile, became targets of one of the most horrific killers in the history of the United States.

From September, 1934, to August, 1938, a total of thirteen torso murders were committed in Cleveland, Ohio, by a psychopathic killer who became known to some as "The Mad Butcher of Kingsbury Run." In 1938, the torso murders in Cleveland "officially" ended. The torso killings were bad for business in Cleveland, so even though the killer was never apprehended, the authorities publicly announced that the torso killings had ended. That's one way to end a crime spree, just declare that it is over. It's obvious that a killer such as this would pay little attention to such a public utterance. On December 23, 1938, someone in Los Angeles mailed a letter to Cleveland's Chief of Police George J. Matowitz, claiming, among other things, to be the Butcher.

Between 1939–1942, New Castle, Pennsylvania experienced at least five torso murders similar to the murders committed in Cleveland. Was the same person or persons killing and dismembering individuals in Pennsylvania and Ohio? Was he traveling by train to and from the various locations in Pennsylvania and Ohio? Was he killing and dismembering his victims in railroad boxcars? Cleveland's detective Peter Merylo was convinced that there was one killer and he was doing just that. Killing and dismembering several bodies with decapitation and surgical skill, draining the blood from the corpse, according to one detective, would take a very rare, unique person. The odds of there being two killers with the same skill, intelligence, capability, stomach and sleuth as the Mad Butcher, operating in different states at times that never overlapped the Ohio killings, are very slim. A copycat killer might get away with a single representative killing, but not a series of nearly identical murders. Not every person, hell-bent on killing someone, has the fortitude to decapitate and dismember a human body and then completely drain the blood from the corpse and move the remains to a different location, where they were deposited. This takes a rare type of psychopathic killer with sadistic tendencies. One that, thank goodness, doesn't come along every day. If the other detectives who didn't accept Merylo's theory were correct in their assumptions, then there would have been at least three different persons who were committing murders in New Castle and Cleveland, all in the same manner as the Mad Butcher of Kingsbury Run. I submit that detective Merylo was probably correct in his evaluation that there was only one person, possibly with a subservient assistant, who was committing all of the torso murders in Pennsylvania and Ohio. There weren't two Jack the Rippers, two Zodiac Killers, two Ted Bundys or two Green River Killers, and there probably weren't two different Torso Killers. If the police agencies in each jurisdiction and the Federal Bureau of Investigation had fully cooperated in a concerted effort with a full exchange of information, the odds of apprehending the culprit would have been much greater.

Now here is where the plot thickens. What happened to the Mad Butcher of Kingsbury Run after 1942? I have a couple of theories and some clues that may shed some light on the identity of the elusive Butcher. I may be correct, but if nothing else the story is interesting and may lead to additional clues and evidence that could solve this mystery. One thing is for sure, if the Butcher was alive and not in prison or a mental institution in the decade that followed the Torso killings, he was still killing and dismembering somewhere. The question is, where?

The Case Against William Heirens

On June 5, 1945, a woman by the name of Josephine A. Ross was savagely murdered in Chicago. The Red Line, a passenger railway, was located near her apartment, where she was murdered. On December 10, 1945, Frances Brown was also murdered in her apartment close to where Ross lived. Her killer left a message written in red lipstick on her living room wall. The message read: "For heavens sake catch me Before I kill more I cannot control myself." Less than one month later, on January 6, 1946, 6-year-old Suzanne Degnan was kidnapped from her first floor bedroom of her parents' apartment on North Kenmore Avenue, strangled to death, dismembered, and her body parts discarded in the Chicago storm sewer system. A few months later a 17-year-old boy by the name of William Heirens was arrested for burglary in a nearby Chicago neighborhood. He was brutally interrogated by the police for his possible involvement in the Ross, Brown and Degnan murders. After being held in "protective custody" for over a month, he eventually signed a purported confession and pled guilty to the crimes. He was sentenced to three consecutive life sentences for the murders of Ross, Brown and Degnan and one year to life for burglaries and assaults. There has been speculation over the years that certain evidence may have been planted at the scene of the killings, including a "rolled fingerprint" that may have been lifted from Heirens' fingerprint card at the police station. William Heirens has been incarcerated in Illinois since 1946. There is something about this case that just doesn't seem to add up. The autopsy report and the police files on these cases have disappeared from the records department at the Chicago Police Department. Did William Heirens commit the crimes that he pled guilty to, or was someone else, someone more sinister, prowling the streets of Chicago at that time? The dismemberment of Suzanne Degnan took place four years after the last known torso murder in Pennsylvania and almost exactly one year before the Black Dahlia was murdered and professionally bisected in Los Angeles.

Georgette Bauerdorf, The Black Dahlia, Jeanne Axford French and Other Los Angeles Victims

On October 12, 1944, a young, pretty socialite by the name of Georgette Bauerdorf was found murdered in her apartment on West Fountain in Hollywood, California. Her killer left her body lying face down in her bathtub. She had been strangled and raped.

On January 15, 1947, the severed corpse of Elizabeth Short was discovered on the corner of 39th and Norton Avenue in Los Angeles. Elizabeth Short was known by her friends and others in her social group as the Black Dahlia. On February 10, 1947, the body of Jeanne Axford French was found near Grand View Avenue and National Boulevard in Los Angeles. Some of the detectives thought that whoever killed the Black Dahlia also killed Georgette Bauerdorf and Jeanne French, but who?

These murders, and other associated murders in Los Angeles between 1947-1949, have never been solved. Had the Mad Butcher of Kingsbury Run traveled to Los Angeles in the late 1930's, traveled back to Pennsylvania and then reappeared again in Los Angeles after 1942? Did he travel to Chicago in 1945-1946 and then relocate in Los Angeles between 1947-1949? The timing is right: a letter sent by someone in Los Angeles in 1938, to the Cleveland Chief of Police, indicated that he might have. Several other clues and documented evidence seem to be pointing in the direction of the Mad Butcher of Kingsbury Run as being the killer of the Black Dahlia and the other women in Los Angeles and Chicago. Was the person who killed the Black Dahlia, Josephine Ross, Frances Brown and Suzanne Degnan somehow connected to the Cleveland Torso Killer? The clues and evidence indicate that he may have been.

Chapter 1

THE TORSO MURDERS

New Castle, Pennsylvania; Youngstown and Cleveland, Ohio

In 1934, dismembered torsos and body parts of murdered victims began appearing in Cleveland, on a fairly regular basis. Many of the headless victims were never identified. The killer became known by a variety of names, including the "The Cleveland Torso Murderer," "The Head Hunter of Kingsbury Run," "The Mad Butcher of Kingsbury Run," and "The Mad Butcher." In each murder the killer used a sharp instrument similar to what a butcher would use when slaughtering an animal. The lower half of the first Cleveland victim, a female, showed up on September 5, 1934, found partially buried in the sand near 156th Street in Cleveland close to the water's edge of Lake Erie. It was determined that the torso had been in the water for approximately three months before it was discovered. Two weeks earlier the upper portion of her torso had been found on a beach thirty miles east in North Perry. Her killer had applied a preservative to the corpse "that turned the skin reddish, tough and leathery." Medical authorities later determined that the preservative applied to the body was either calcium hypochloride or chloride of lime. The woman has never been identified and to this day is known as "The Lady of the Lakes." Her limbs were skillfully removed except for the right arm. The butcher had missed this joint and completed the separation with a saw. In an apparent attempt to eliminate members of the medical profession as the killer, Cuyahoga County Coroner Arthur J. Pearce indicated, "No surgeon ever would have used a saw; he would have known how to manipulate a knife around the joint."

In an effort to locate and identify the Mad Butcher of Kingsbury Run, the City of Cleveland hired famed "Untouchable," Elliot Ness, as director of Public Safety in 1935. Prior to this time Ness had successfully battled organized mobsters, including Al Capone in Chicago. As it turned out the Mad Butcher was much more of a challenge to Ness than all the Chicago hoodlums combined.

The headless corpse of Edward Andrassy, a white male, described as Victim No. 1, was found on September 23, 1935, at the foot of Jackass Hill in Cleveland.

His body was found stripped, except for his stockings, completely drained of blood, emasculated and cleaned. A substance had been found on the body which "turned the skin reddish, tough and leathery." The authorities thought the killer may have tried to burn the body. "The head was found buried in the ground about twenty feet from the body; just enough hair showed above the surface of the loose earth to ensure the police would find it" (Note 1, p. 31).

Was the killer experimenting on the dead bodies with some sort of preservative?

Thirty feet away from Andrassy's body the police found Victim No. 2. He also had been emasculated. The severed genitals of both men lay in a pile next to the corpses. Found near the bodies were several pieces of rope, a railroad torch and a two-gallon water bucket containing crankcase oil. Dr Samuel R. Gerber, who succeeded A. J. Pearce as Coroner of Cuyahoga County, declared, "Appearances, together with certain findings, seem to indicate that the body, after death, was saturated with oil and fire applied. The burning, however, was only sufficient to scorch, hence the peculiar condition of the skin" (Note 1, p. 36). Each victim had been decapitated after his hands were tied, then stripped of clothing, and further mutilated. The presence of rope burns on one of the victim's wrists indicated he may have been conscious when he was decapitated.

Decapitated body of Victim No. 5, found July 22, 1936, on Cleveland's west side.
(photo courtesy of the Cleveland Police Historical Society)

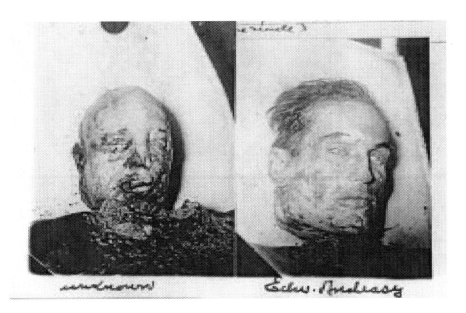

Decapitated heads of Edward Andrassy and Victim No. 2, found at the
foot of Jackass hill in Cleveland, September 23, 1935
(photo courtesy of the Cleveland Police Historical society)

On January 26, 1936, body parts, some of which were located neatly wrapped in half-bushel baskets, were discovered behind Hart Manufacturing Plant in Cleveland. The murdered woman was later identified as Florence (Flo) Polillo, "a part-time waitress, part-time barmaid, part-time prostitute" (Note 1, p. 51). She became known as torso Victim No. 3. It is curious to note that embedded in her skin were cinders and coal dust. An indention of a lump of coal was found in the lower portion of her torso. Had she been butchered in a coal bin?

Police photograph of Flo Polillo, Victim No. 3, taken approximately 1934 (photo courtesy of the Cleveland Police Historical Society)

Remains of Flo Polillo found behind Hart Manufacturing Plant in Cleveland, January 26, 1936 (photo courtesy of the Cleveland Police Historical Society)

On June 5, 1936, Victim No. 4 was discovered in Kingsbury Run. His head had been wrapped up in his pants and placed in a burlap bag. Drawn on parts of Victim No. 4's body were six tattoos: A butterfly on the left shoulder; the comic strip character, Diggs, on the surface of the left calf; crossed flags with the letters WCG on the left forearm; a heart and anchor also on the left forearm; a cupid and anchor on the outer surface of the right calf; and the names Helen and Paul on the right forearm. Investigators believed the dead man may have been a sailor.

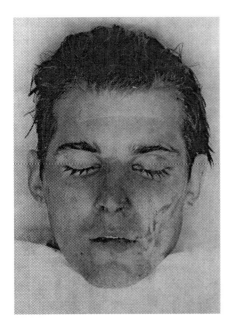

The head of the "Tattooed Man," Victim No. 4, located in Kingsbury Run, June 5, 1936 (Cleveland Press Collection, courtesy of Cleveland State University Library)

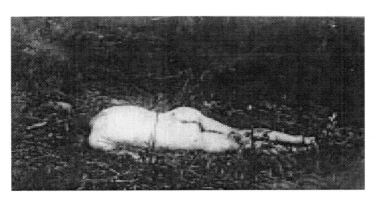

Remains of the "Tattooed Man," Victim No. 4, found in Kingsbury Run, June 5, 1936 (photo courtesy of the Cleveland Historical Society)

In June, 1936, in an area near New Castle, Pennsylvania, a couple of Pittsburgh and Lake Erie Railroad inspectors found the naked, headless body of a white male. Located near the body were pages from newspapers including a Cleveland newspaper dated August 30, 1933.

Victim No. 5 was found on Cleveland's west side, just south of Clinton Road, July 22, 1936, decapitated and lying about a hundred yards from the tracks of the B & O Railroad. The head and clothes were found approximately ten feet from the victim's body. Coroner Pearce indicated that, "The killer would have to possess the skill and anatomical knowledge of a surgeon to sever the head and body so cleanly" (Note 1, p. 71).

Sheriff O'Donnell, Detective Harry Brown, jailer Mike Kilbane & (stooped) Dr. E. F. Ecker
inspecting a tub used in a dismemberment by the Cleveland Torso Killer
(Cleveland Press Collection courtesy of Cleveland State University Library)
Also see chapters 2 and 3.
Sinks and tubs were used in the murders and dismemberment of victims.

Sometime in October, 1936, a decapitated body of a white male was discovered along the train tracks near Haverstraw, New York. The killer had used a saw to sever the head from the torso. Curiously, the New York Central runs past Haverstraw.

Victim No. 6 was discovered September 10, 1936. The head had been severed between the third and fourth cervical vertebrae. The killer had severed the torso about two inches above the navel between the third and fourth lumbar vertebrae. The stomach and both kidneys were cut in the process. Based on the method of amputations, it was determined that the killer had gained knowledge of anatomy as a medical student or as a butcher.

Cleveland detectives searching for body parts of Victim No. 6, September 11, 1936, in a stagnant pool near Kingsbury Run
(Cleveland Press Collection courtesy of Cleveland State University Library)

Storm drain at the end of Superior Avenue in Cleveland where a piece of Victim No. 6's leg was recovered (photo courtesy of Marjorie Merylo Dentz)

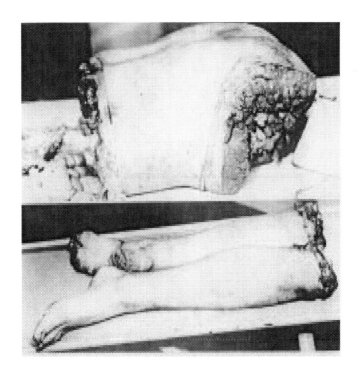

Body parts of Victim No. 6 found September 10, 1936, in Kingsbury Run near 37th Street (photo courtesy of the Cleveland Police Historical Society)

Throughout my study of the torso murders, Cleveland's Detective Peter Merylo seems to have offered the most probable analysis based on the known facts at that time. He determined that the Cleveland, New Castle and additional torso killings in Youngstown, Ohio, were committed by the same person or persons. Detective Merylo thought that similar murders during this time period in Pennsylvania and in Cleveland were committed by the same individual. He also determined that the killer traveled from one location to another by rail and may have used a boxcar as his laboratory to butcher his victims. Merylo also toyed with the idea that more than one person acting together were committing these crimes. Based on the known evidence, I concur with his conclusion. Elliot Ness also studied the idea that the New Castle and Cleveland torso murders might somehow be connected. He sent his assistant, John R. Flynn, to New Castle to investigate a possible link between the two locations.

Detective Peter Merylo (photo courtesy of his daughter, Marjorie Merylo Dentz)

Detective Peter Merylo searching for clues (and body parts?) in a Cleveland storm sewer. Notice the shovel and pick (by the boot of the standing detective) that were used to open the heavy sewer cover. This search for body parts in a sewer compares to the search for body parts in chapter 2. (photo courtesy of Marjorie Merylo Dentz)

Picture of New York Central freight cars near Kingsbury Run
(photo courtesy of Marjorie Merylo Dentz)

Detective Peter Merylo with Lieutenant Moffitt; Cleveland's Director of Public Safety and former head of the Chicago "Untouchables," Elliot Ness; Sergeant Massey; and Lieutenant Schanadam, October 19, 1938 (photo courtesy of Marjorie Merylo Dentz)

On May 5, 1937, the upper torso of Victim No. 7 was found located in the cold waters of Lake Erie just off East 30th Street in Cleveland. The killer had inserted a pants pocket inside the woman's rectum. The rectum had been stretched to accommodate the foreign object.

The skull of Victim No. 8 was located on June 6, 1937, under the Lorain-Carnegie Bridge in Cleveland. The head of this victim had been separated from the body and the torso had been placed in a burlap bag. The victim was later identified as a black woman named Rose Wallace. On the day she disappeared, according to witnesses, she left a laundry with a dark-skinned, white man named "Bob."

Cleveland police searching under Sidaway Bridge in Kingsbury Run
(Cleveland Press Collection courtesy of Cleveland State University Library)

On July 6, 1937, Cleveland police and the Ohio National Guard began searching the banks of the Cuyahoga River for body parts of Victim No. 9.

On July 9, 1937, the lower half of a man's torso was discovered floating in the Cuyahoga River. For the first time, drugs were detected in the body. Was the killer introducing drugs into the victims before killing and dismembering them? The drug was determined to be morphine. He left deep gashes in the thighs of Victim No. 10.

Cuyahoga County Coroner Samuel R. Gerber had speculated that the killer could be a doctor. If drugs were introduced, then this could explain why the torso victims were dismembered without showing signs of putting up much defense. The *Cleveland News* included an editorial in a September 12, 1936, edition:

> That this creature, sly, crafty inhumanly skilled in butchery is a menace to every man, woman and child who walks the streets of Cleveland does not have to be emphasized. Why these dead? Why the darkest of all Cleveland murder mysteries? He kills for the thrill of killing. He kills to satisfy a bestial, sadistic lust for blood. He kills to prove himself strong. He kills to feed his sex-perverted brain, the sight of a beheaded human. He must kill for decapitation is his drug, to be taken in closer-spaced doses. Yes he will kill again. He is of course insane.

In March, 1937, Coroner Gerber reviewed the known facts covering the first seven torso murders in Cleveland:

> It is particularly the peculiar dissection of the bodies which groups these seven cases together. All cases show that the heads were severed from the bodies through the intervertebral discs . . . by means of a sharp knife. Cases No. 3, 6, and 7 showed further that the bodies were cleanly dismembered at the shoulder and hip joints apparently by a series of cuts around the flexure of the joints and then by a strong twist wrenching the head out of the joint cavity and cutting the capsule. The torsos were further sectioned through the abdomen, the knife being carried in cases No. 3 and 6 through the intervertebral discs . . . . Case No. 3 (Flo Polillo) was further mutilated by disarticulating the knee joints roughly, fracturing the mid-portion of the bones of the lower legs and slashing the abdomen down through the pubic bones . . . All the skin edges, muscles, blood vessels and cartilages were

cut squarely and cleanly, apparently by a long sharp knife such as a butcher or heavy bread knife. There is relatively little hacking of the tissues and relatively few hesitation marks . . . . the direction of these marks indicate . . . a right handed individual . . . . (knife marks) indicate they were cut through anteriorly down to the vertebral spines and then the section completed from behind in all cases. The procedure followed in these cases suggests to us that the dissection was done either by a lay person, or persons, highly intelligent in recognizing the anatomical landmarks as they were approached, or else, as is more likely, by a person, or persons, with some knowledge of anatomy, such as a doctor, a medical student, a (male) nurse, orderly, prosector butcher, hunter or veterinary surgeon. (. . . the bodies may have been sectioned as they were, to facilitate transportation and disposition.)

On the afternoon of August 16, 1938, in a dumpsite near the southwest corner of Lake Shore Drive and East 9th Street in Cleveland, the torso of Victim No.11 was found. Shortly thereafter other body parts were discovered in the same area wrapped in heavy brown paper like the kind used by butchers. At 5:30 that afternoon a fellow by the name of Tom Bartholomew spotted the bones of Victim No.12 at the Cleveland dump site. The murders in Cleveland "officially ended" in 1938.

On December 29, 1938, a letter addressed to Cleveland's Chief of Police George Matowitz, dated December 23, 1938, was found in the dead letter office at the Cleveland Post Office. The letter reads:

Chief of Police Matowitz

You can rest easy now, as I have come out to sunny California for the winter. I felt bad operating on those people, but science must advance. I shall astond the medical profession, a man with only a D.C.

What did their lives mean in comparison to hundreds of sick and disease twisted bodies? Just laboratory guinea pigs found on any public street. No one missed them when I failed. My last case was successful. I know now the feeling of Pasteur, Thoreau and other pioneers.

Right now I have a volunteer who will absolutely prove my theory. They call me mad and a butcher, but the truth will out.

I have failed but once here. The body has never been found and never will be, but the head, minus the features is buried on Century Boulevard, between Western and Crenshaw. I feel it my duty to dispose of the bodies as I do. It is God's will not to let them suffer.

(signed) X

Whoever wrote the 1938 letter seemed to know that the killings in Cleveland were ending, at least for the time being.

On August 7, 1939, Detective Finnis W. Brown wrote Detective Merylo from Inglewood, California. Brown's letter is as follows:

He needed to direct attention away from Cleveland for a short time, so he evidently sent a letter, to be re-mailed from there. Then while all attention was focused on Los Angeles, he disposed of his dangerous evidence. I fully expected to hear of the discovery of another torso murder victim soon thereafter and sure enough, a short time later, part of a woman's body was found. Well, he is on his guard right now, but as time passes without discovery, he will gradually gain confidence in his ability to outsmart the police—and he'll try his luck again. For he must have heads for his experiment, and get them he most likely will. Best wishes. F.W. Brown #719 West Kelso St., Inglewood, Calif.

In 1942, Los Angeles detectives had tentatively identified the author of the 1938 letter as one Charles August DiVere, a quack doctor. No positive link was ever established between DiVere and the Cleveland Torso Murders. Whoever wrote the December 23, 1938, letter may have had access to information printed in Cleveland newspapers, but one has to wonder if someone in Los Angeles in 1938 would have read that the heads of the Cleveland and New Castle torso victims had been buried.

Copy of envelope mailed from Los Angeles to Cleveland Chief of Police Matowitz postmarked December 22, 1938 (photo courtesy of Marjorie Merylo Dentz)

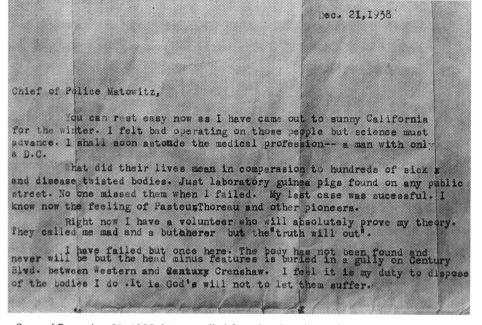

Dec. 21, 1938

Chief of Police Matowitz,

You can rest easy now as I have came out to sunny California for the winter. I felt bad operating on those people but science must advance. I shall soon astonde the medical profession-- a man with only a D.C.

What did their lives mean in comparasion to hundreds of sick and disease twisted bodies. Just laboratory guinea pigs found on any public street. No one missed them when I failed. My last case was sucessful. I know now the feeling of Pasteur, Thoreau and other pioneers.

Right now I have a volunteer who will absolutely prove my theory. They called me mad and a butaherer but the "truth will out".

I have failed but once here. The body has not been found and never will be but the head minus features is buried in a gully on Century Blvd. between Western and Century Crenshaw. I feel it is my duty to dispose of the bodies I do .It is God's will not to let them suffer.

Copy of December 21, 1938, letter mailed from Los Angeles to Cleveland Chief of Police Matowitz (photo courtesy of Marjorie Merylo Dentz)

The Cleveland Police Department has been unable to locate the files on the Cleveland Torso Murders. Fortunately, Detective Merylo was a very dedicated police officer. While in office he accumulated duplicate copies of thousands of notes and letters associated with the Torso Murders, which he studied at home after completing his shift at the department. I personally reviewed all of the known copies that were in Detective Merylo's care. In one of the letters, dated July 20, 1937, Merylo wrote a letter to Lieutenant Harvey Weitzel:

Sir

Reported for duty 8:30 a.m. and with Detective Zalewski, assigned to further investigate Torso Murders.

In reference to letter received by the department from North Hollywood, California, pertaining to the Torso murders, in which one suspect being mentioned, who is now employed at the Great Lakes Exposition, we checked up on this suspect from various sources unbeknown to him and will continue to do so until every angle has been thoroughly checked and a report will follow when the investigation is completed. We also located a woman with whom he made a date, but after a confidential inquiry, she could not tell us anything that would substantiate the information received in the letter from North Hollywood, California.

I further wish to state that we detailed ourselves at the exposition ground watching the movements of the suspect mentioned in the above letter, but up to this time have learned nothing that would warrant the arrest and detention of the suspect. Reported off duty at 6:00 p. m. Respectfully Peter Merylo, Det.

Detective Merylo wrote another letter July 20, 1937, to Lieutenant Weitzel:

Report on letter received from North Hollywood, California

Sir;

On July 10, 1937 a letter was received by this department in reference to the Torso Murders. The writer of the letter gave a detail of the suspect that is suppose to have been connected with the Great Lakes Exposition. It was considered at that time and still is until a thorough investigation proves otherwise that her information was very important. The writer refuses to sign her name but requested that we communicate with her through a personal column of the Los Angeles, Calif. newspapers. The Los Angeles Herald and Express. With the permission of Inspector Sweeny and Chief Matowitz the ad was inserted in said newspaper and the same ran for a period of one week. This transaction was accomplished through the Los Angeles Police Dept., and we were successful in receiving a reply through said ad which gave us the name of the person and additional information. On this date we received a bill from Chief of police, Los Angeles, Calif. In which he stated that he had paid the bill as instructed by our Chief's office which amounts to $9.24 and the same is attached. Respectfully, Peter Merylo, Det.

Detective Merylo determined that the suspect mentioned in the 1937 letter from North Hollywood was a 17-year-old boy, who's last name was "Wilson." Wilson was employed at the Great Lakes Exposition in 1936. Merylo also learned that the suspect's mother's name was Helen Wilson and his father was Walter F. Wilson. Merylo related this information to Lieutenant Weitzel. The 17-year-old boy was ultimately dismissed as a possible suspect.

On August 16, 1938, the severed head of Victim No.12 was found in a Cleveland dump site in a tin can, separate from the body. One of the New Castle torso victims' heads was found buried in the ground near the unburied body.

In the spring of 1950, a man approximately fifty years old was seen sunbathing for about twenty minutes each day close to East 22nd Street and Lakeshore in Cleveland. One day the man disappeared and did not return to his sunbathing activity. On July 22 of that year near the location where the man sunbathed a dismembered torso of a white male was found. The sunbather was thought to be the killer of the person later identified as Robert Robertson, a forty-year-old alcoholic from Boynton, Pennsylvania. Robertson had not been seen since June 12. Was the sunbather someone who soaked up the sun during the winters in "sunny California"? At the scene of this murder investigators found something new: two pages from a telephone book covering the letter "K" (See Chapter 3, page 79).

Similarities Between the Cleveland Torso Murders and the Pennsylvania Torso Murders

1. None of the timings of the murders overlap.
2. There was decapitation of victims in both states.
3. There was dismemberment of victims in both states.
4. All of the murders occurred in close proximity to railroad tracks.
5. The New York Central Railroad traveled to and from Cleveland and Youngstown, Ohio; New Castle and West Pittsburgh, Pennsylvania; Haverstraw, New York, and Chicago. The New York Central passes by Kingsbury Run.
6. In all cases there are similarities in the victim profiles.
7. In Cleveland, Edward Andrassy's severed head was found buried in the ground near his unburied body. One of the Pennsylvania torso victims' heads was located buried in the ground near the unburied body.
8. The Mad Butcher of Kingsbury Run used a saw to finish separating the shoulder of the Lady of the Lakes. A murder in New Castle in late 1939 mirrored the Cleveland torso murders. In the New Castle murder the killer used a saw or a knife with serrated teeth to remove the head from the victim's body. The killer of the victim in Haverstraw, New York, used a saw to sever his head from the body.
9. Bloodstained underwear was found near the victims.
10. Decapitation was "clean and expert" in each state.
11. Several of the victims' decapitated heads were never found.
12. Several of the murdered victims were never identified.
13. Several victims in both states were located in remote areas.

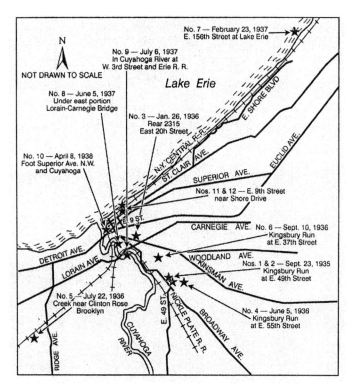

Cleveland Map 1: Location of Torso victims.

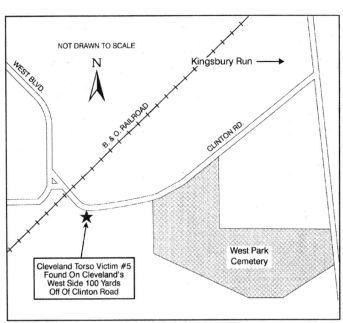

Cleveland Map 2: Location where Torso Victim No. 5 was found on Cleveland's West side.

Detective Peter Merylo kept a separate ledger on ten of the torso murders. His notes, courtesy of his daughter, Marjorie Merylo Dentz, include the following:

Torso Victim:
Case No. 1
Name Unknown
Address Unknown
Sex: Male   *Color*: White
Date Found July 23, 1935   *Duration of Death* 7-8 days
Approximate date of death July 15, 1935
Estimated age 40 to 45   Height 5 ft.6 in. Weight 160
Location found Kingsbury Run at East 40th Street
Parts Recovered Head, body
Parts Missing Left testicle
Neck Disarticulated mid-portion.
Body
Extremities Intact
Cut surfaces, soft tissues, Sharply cut, muscles retracted
Genitalia Left testicle excised (?)
Blood in Body ?
Contents of stomach
Identification marks two scars middle third right thigh one inch and two in
    diameter.
Cause of Death Decapitation

Torso: Victim:
Case number 2
Name Andrew W. Andrassy
Address
Sex male   *Color* white
Date found July 23rd, 1935   *Duration of death* 2-3 days
Approximate date of death July 20th, 1935
Estimated Age 28 years   *Height* 5 ft. 11 in.   *Weight* 150
Location found Kingsbury Run at east 40th Street

Parts recovered Head, body, genitalia

Parts Missing

Neck Disarticulated mid-portion

Body

Extremities	Intact (Rope burns on wrist)
Cut Surfaces, soft tissue	Sharply cut, muscles retracted
Genitalia	Scrotum and penis amputated
Blood in Body	Heart and large vessels empty
Contents of stomach	Recently ingested vegetable meal
Identifying marks	Appendectomy scar, small scar forehead, Gold-capped left upper lateral incisor tooth
Cause of Death	Decapitation

Torso Victim:

Case number 3.

Name	Florence Polillo alias Martin	
Address		
Sex	Female	Color white

Date found January 26, 1936

Approximate date of death January 23, 1936

Estimated age 42   *Height* 5 ft 5 in. *Weight* 160

Location found 2315-2325 East 20th Street

Parts Recovered upper and lower half of torso, four extremities

Parts missing head

Neck Disarticulated C4-5

Body Disarticulated L 3-5. Also longitudinal section

Extremities All extremities disarticulated also at the knee joints

Cut surfaces, soft tissues all surfaces sharply cut, no retraction of muscles. Few hesitation marks

Genitalia none veneris and symphysis incised

Blood in body Heart and large vessels empty

Contents of stomach

Identifying marks vaccination mark right thigh. Mid-line lower abdominal laparatomy wound

Cause of death Decapitation

Torso Victim:

Case number 4

Name Unknown

Address Unknown

Sex Male   *Color* white

Date found June 5, 1936   *Duration of death* 2-3 days

          June 6, 1936

Approximate date of death June 2nd, 1936

Estimated age 25   *Height* 5 ft. 11 in.   *Weight* 150

Location found Kingsbury Run, East 55th Street

Parts Recovered Head, body

Parts Missing

Neck Disarticulated C 1-2

Body

Extremities Intact

Cut Surfaces, soft tissues Sharply cut. Few hesitation marks

Genitalia Intact

Blood in body Heart and large vessels empty

Contents of stomach Small amounts of undigested food (Baked beans) in stomach

Identification marks Tattoo marks 1. butterfly; 2. Picture of Jiggs. 3. Hearty and Arrow. 4. Flag with "W.C.G." 5. Cupid and anchor. 6 Dove with "Helen and Paul."

Cause of death Decapitation

Torso Victim:

Case number 5

Name Unknown

Address Unknown

Sex Male   *Color* white

Date found July 22nd, 1936   *Duration of death* 1-2 months

Approximate date of death May 22nd, 1936

Estimated age 35-40

Location found Big Creek, Clinton Road, Brooklyn Village, Ohio, near Rayon Silk Mills.

Parts recovered Head, body

Parts missing

Neck Disarticulated C 3-4

Body

Extremities Intact

Cut surfaces, soft tissues ?

Genitalia?

Blood in body?

Contents of stomach

Identifying marks?

Cause of death Decapitation (?)

Torso Victim:

Case number 6

Name Unknown

Address Unknown

Sex Male   *Color* white

Date found September 10, 1936   *Duration of Death* 1-2 days

Approximate date of death September 8, 1936

Estimated age 25-30   *Height* 5 ft. 10 in.   *Weight* 145

Location found Kingsbury Run at East 37th Street

Parts recovered Upper half torso, lower half torso, thighs and legs.

Parts missing Head, both upper extremities, Genitalia

Neck Disarticulated C 3-4

Body Disarticulated L 3-4

Extremities All extremities disarticulated, also at knee joints

Cut surfaces, soft tissues Sharply cut, few "Hesitation" marks on neck. No retraction of muscles

Genitalia: genitalia amputated

Blood in Body Heart and large vessels empty

Contents of stomach Kernels of corn in stomach

Identifying marks None

Cause of death ?

Torso Victim:

Case number 7

Name Unknown

Address Unknown

Sex Female *Color* white

Date found February 23, 1937 *Duration of death* 3-5 days

Approximate date of death February 17th, 1937

Estimated age 25-35 *Height* ? *Weight* 100-120

Location found Lakeshore Boulevard at East 156th Street

Parts recovered Upper half torso

Parts missing Head, lower half torso, all four extremities

Neck Disarticulated C-7-T 1

Body Disarticulated L 1 (through body)

Extremities All extremities disarticulated

Cut surfaces. Soft tissues Sharply cut. Numerous hesitation marks on neck

Genitalia?

Blood in body blood clots in heart and large vessel

Contents of stomach

Identifying marks None except extremely flat breasts

Cause of death ?

Torso Victim:

Case number 8

Name Unknown

Address Unknown

Sex female *Color* Colored

Date found June 6th, 1937 *Duration of death* 1 year

Approximate date of death June, 1936

Estimated age 30-40 *Height* 5 ft. 0 in. *Weight* 100-110

Location found Cuyahoga River Basin, region of West 3rd Street Bridge

Parts recovered Skull, entire vertebral column, ribs and pelvis

Parts missing Bones of all four extremities

Neck Disarticulated C 4 C 5

Body ?

Extremities Apparently disarticulated at the shoulders and hip

Cut surfaces, soft tissues ?

Genitalia ?

Blood in body ?

Contents of stomach ?

Identifying marks Gold bridge upper left side cuspid 1st, 2nd bicuspid

Cause of death ?? Decapitation

Torso Victim:

Case number 9

Name Unknown

Address Unknown

Sex Male   *Color* White

Date found July 6th, 1937   *Duration of death* 2 days

     July 10th, 1937

Approximate date of death July 4, 1937

Location found Cuyahoga River region of West 3rd Street bridge

Parts Recovered Upper and lower halves torso, both arms, both legs, both thighs, both forearms.

Parts Missing Head, neck

Neck Disarticulated C 6 C 7

Body Body disarticulated L1 L2

Extremities Disarticulated at shoulders, hips, elbows and knees

Cut surfaces, soft tissues Sharply cut, hesitation marks on skin of out surfaces. Retraction muscles of neck. Body eviscerated.

Genitalia Intact

Blood in Body Blood vessels empty, heart excised

Contents of stomach ? Eviscerated

Identifying marks Blue pigmented cross on left leg. Two linear scars dorsum right thumb

Cause of death ?? Decapitation

Torso Victim:

Case number 10*

Name Unknown

Address Unknown

Sex Female   *Color* White

Date found 8th, 1936   *Duration of death* 3-7 da.

            May 2nd, 1936   27-34 da.

Approximate date of death January 5th, 1936

Location found Cuyahoga River, region upper West 3rd Street bridge

Parts recovered Left leg, thorax, abdomen, both thighs, left foot.

Parts missing Upper portion 2nd and 3rd cervical

Neck Disarticulated 12 T 1 L

Body Disarticulated L 1 through body

Extremities All extremities disarticulated

Cut surfaces, soft tissues Sharply cut, hesitation marks on skin of cut surfaces. Some retraction of muscles

Genitalia Intact

Blood in Body Heart and blood vessels empty

Contents of stomach Empty

Identifying Marks Old scar 4 inches long horizontally in right lower quadrant abdomen. Midline scar lower mid abdomen 5 inches long.

Cause of death ?? Decapitation

*A letter from Detective Merylo to Lieutenant Tozzel indicated that the torso victim found May 2, 1938, was a female and "her privates were cleanly shaved."

DEPARTMENT OF POLICE:CLEVELAND.O.
Bureau of Criminal Identification.

September 4th,1938

The following is the list of Murders - (TORSO) committed
in Cleveland,Ohio,evidently by a Homicidal Maniac.
- -

NO.- O - Torso of an UNKNOWN white woman found at the foot of East
156th,st,evidently washed ashore (buttock & thighs only)
on Sept.5th,1934

NO.- 1) - On September 23rd,1935 the nude bodies of two white men were
NO.- 2)   found on the side of a hill in Kingsbury Run,Cleveland,Ohio
they had been dead probably about four days when found.
The heads,penis,and testicals had been severed from the bodies
none of their clothing had ever been found. they were not
killed at the spot where the bodies were found,but no doubt
were brought there.
One of the men was identified by his finger printd but the
other was never identified (Identified as Edw.Andrasy of
5702 Storer Ave,Cleveland,Ohio.
There were no marks on either of the bodies,only at the neck
where the head had been severed and this was very neatly done.

NO.- 3 - On Sunday January 26th,1936 the Pelvis,Thighs and Right Arm
of a white woman was found in an alley back of 2315 East
20th,st,Cleveland,Ohio.
The head of this woman had been hacked away from the body and
was never found,also the legs and arms had been clumsily
hacked from the body.
This woman was identified by the prints of her right hand as
Florence Martin alias Clara Dunn alias Florence Polilla alias
Florence G.Sawdey she was married to an Andrew Polilla with
whom she lived in Buffalo,N.Y.for some time.
The remains were turned over to her relatives January 30,1936
and taken to North Girard,Pa,for burial.
This woman was a prostitute and a hard drinker.

NO.- 4 - On June 5th,1936 the headless body of a white man was found
in a place known as Kingsbury Run in Cleveland,Ohio,this place
is a ravine or gully close to the Nickle Plate Ry. The water
being about three feet to fifteen feet in depth.
This mans head was found about 200 feet from the body under
a tree wrapped in this victims clothing. He was never
identified and there were no marks on the body only at the
neck where the head was severed.

NO.- 5 - On July 22nd,1936 the Head body of a white man was found near
Clifton Rd,& Big Creek in Brooklyn Township a Suburb of
Cleveland,Ohio. The head had been very expertly severed from
the body,there were no marks of violence on the body only at
the neck. The head was found a short distance from the body
wrapped in the victims clothing and was under a low growing
bush, the place where this crime was committed is very isolated
and close to a railway tracks as have all of the others.
This man was never identified and all the bodies which have
been found have been stripped of the clothing after death.

September 4, 1938, list of first five Torso Murders in Cleveland prepared by the Cleveland
Police Department (photo courtesy of the Cleveland Police Historical Society)

On April 15, 1939, Detective Merylo made a request to Lieutenant Harvey Weitzel of the Cleveland Detective Bureau that the following letter be sent to the Baltimore, Maryland, Police Department:

Sir;

I respectfully request that a letter be sent to the Baltimore, Maryland Police Department asking them to furnish us with details of the human body found there dissected recently. What we particularly would like to know is, was the body dissected at the joints, did it appear that any other instrument than a knife was used to dissect the body. What was the condition of the parts found as to blood, was there any blood left in the veins? We understand the body was wrapped in the comic section of the newspaper. Will you kindly advise what newspaper and the date of same. Were the hands found, and if so can you send us fingerprints of same. In what section of the city was the body found? Since 1935, we have had in the city a series of so called "torso" murders, that is where the body has been found dissected and in most instances decapitated and the heads have never been found. Respectifully, Peter Merylo, Detective

Another letter of interest was received by the Cleveland Police Department in the late 1930s that was among the letters in the Peter Merylo file. This typed letter provided the following:

Chief of Police
Homicide Bureau
Cleveland, Ohio

Dear Sir;

Being particularly interested in discovering the identity of the Cleveland Torso Slayer for a long time. I thought I would write you my impressions on seeing the photo of Edward Andrassy. What he is sitting on appears like a bench used by a Professional Photographer. The back ground doesn't seem to be clear and may be disguised. What about doing a quiet investigation of places of this sort within a radius of a mile from the Run.

Its likely that this fellow may be one who hasn't a first class place. Just a small neighborhood affair. Hence the few pictures in the rear which may at first appear to be a private residence. Again, he may be and likely is a man of foreign extraction. Also, a former butcher or orderly who does work either on a full or parttime. In this manner he may get acquainted with the history of his intended victims. He also may do the strip tease stuff on the side. Would suggest getting a youthful plain clothes man or men do a round of these places by getting a few negatives developed. And in this way size up the owner there. There's an outside chance that it may be a woman with previous nurse experience. Again this party is likely to have a car. Also, a large developing lab situated in a spot of this kind could be a good blind. Persons in this line too get a large part of the News. Would advise to take your time as this person is crazy but no fool. Sincerely, Lewis Wilson Appleton, Jr.

Could this letter have been written by the Cleveland Torso Killer? He signed his name as Lewis Wilson Appleton, Jr. Perhaps he was sending a clue to the police: Lewis (Clue is) Wilson? The writer advised the police to "take your time." This may be of importance when compared to a note, referred to in Chapter 3, sent by the Black Dahlia Avenger, in which the writer wrote: "Go Slow Man Killer Says." Also note that this letter refers to a "former butcher" (See tip reported to Detective Orley May on page 96 in which the informant refers to Jack Wilson as a "former butcher").

Chapter 2

THE CASE AGAINST WILLIAM HEIRENS

Forty-three-year-old Josephine Ross lived in an apartment building at 4108 North Kenmore Avenue in Chicago's Edgewood District. An elevated passenger railway, known as the, "Red Line," is located within one block of her apartment. The train makes scheduled stops at Thorndale Avenue near her apartment. At 9:00 a.m. on June 5, 1945, after Josephine's daughter, Jacqueline, had gone to work, Josephine went to bed. When her daughter came home for lunch she discovered her mother's blood-soaked body lying on the bed. Sometime between 9:00 a.m. and 1:00 p. m. Josephine Ross was savagely murdered. Her throat had been stabbed several times. The killer had wrapped her head in a dress. The custodian of the apartment building and another tenant reported to detectives that they had seen an "unfamiliar, swarthy, dark-haired male in white sweater and dark trousers, seemingly without purpose, wandering through the building." Janitor Elmer Nelson estimated the stranger to weigh in at about 190 pounds; lodger Bernice Folkman called him slender.

4108 North Kenmore Avenue, Chicago, Illinois

Six months later, on December 10, 1945, the body of Frances Brown was found in room 611 at the Pinecrest Apartments, 3941 Pine Grove, in Chicago near the apartment rented by Josephine Ross and the near the Red Line. A large knife was found lodged in her throat, and there was a bullet hole in her skull. Her head was wrapped in her pajamas. Written in red lipstick on her living room wall were the words, "For Heavens sake catch me before I kill more. I cannot control myself." "The words had been written a full six feet from the floor and the hand that wrote them seemed to be heavy." The red lipstick message may have been written by a tall man.

3941 Pine Grove, Chicago, Illinois

Less than one month later, on January 7, 1946, six-year-old Suzanne Degnan was kidnapped from her parents' home at 5943 North Kenmore Avenue in Chicago and murdered. The Degnan family lived on the first floor, and the Flynn family occupied an apartment on the second floor. Suzanne's abductor may have placed a ladder against the side of the building and gained access through a first-floor window. The killer or killers left a ransom note behind in the girl's bedroom. The note read, "Get $20,000

46

reddy & waite for word. Do not notify FBI or police. Bills in $5's and $10's." On the back of the ransom note was a warning: "Burn this for her safty." Cecelia Flynn later recalled hearing two men talking in the street the evening of the abduction. She thought one of the men said, "This is the best-looking building around." Suzanne's body could not be found until an anonymous telephone call, by someone who was never identified, was received by the police. The caller directed the authorities to neighborhood storm sewers. The police immediately began searching and located the dismembered body parts of Suzanne Degnan discarded where the caller indicated they would be found. It was later determined that a basement washtub in an apartment located at 5901-03 Winthrop was the place where she was dismembered (Note 14).

On the night of the abduction a witness saw a woman carrying a large bundle in both arms in the vicinity of the Degnan home. "She got into what seemed to be an awaiting automobile where a balding man sat behind the wheel." Another witness recalled seeing a large dark man carrying a shopping bag near the Degnan house at the time of her disappearance. None of these individuals has ever been identified.

William Heirens at Vienna Correctional Center, Illinois Correctional Facility in 2004
(photo courtest of Dolores Kennedy)

A 17-year-old University of Chicago college student and part-time petty burglar by the name of William Heirens was at the wrong place at the wrong time searching for something to steal when he was arrested and eventually charged with the murders of Josephine Ross, Frances Brown and Suzanne Degnan. While in the custody of the Chicago police he was interrogated relentlessly for days, often brutally. He was physically beaten, kept awake, interrogated by several detectives, paraded past the electric chair on a daily basis and threatened with its efficiency. He was given sodium pentathol, had ether applied to his scrotum and was given a painful spinal tap. The five Chicago daily newspapers headlined the Heirens story 157 times over a ten-week period (Note 14).

He faced up to fifty years in prison for the burglaries alone. His attorneys strongly advised him to plead guilty, and his chances for a fair trial in Chicago had all but evaporated. Public sentiment towards his condemnation and political pressure were taking their toll on Mr. Heriens. He finally agreed to plead guilty, in his words, "so I could live." As an example of the interrogation methods that might have been used on William Heirens, consider the case of another earlier suspect in the Degnan murder, Hector Verburgh, the janitor at the Winthrop Apartments where Suzanne was dismembered. Mr. Verburgh was arrested under suspicion of murder. After his ordeal, Mr. Verburgh told reporters:

> Oh, they hanged me up, they blindfolded me. I can't put up my arms, they are sore. They had handcuffs on me for hours and hours. They threw me in a cell and blindfolded me. They handcuffed my hands behind my back and pulled me up on bars until only my toes touched the floor. I no sleep, I no eat, I go to the hospital. Oh I am sick. Any more and I would have confessed anything (Note 17, p. 52).

Following Mr. Verburgh's release from custody he was hospitalized for ten days with a separated shoulder. "Immediately following his recuperation, he filed a $125,000.00 lawsuit against the department. After the investigation the Verburghs were awarded $20,000" (Note 13). Author John Bartlow Martin wrote an applicable segment in *Butcher's Dozen and Other Murders:*

Several policemen whom I originally met professionally have become my personal friends; my wife and I visit their homes. A few weeks ago one of them startled my neighbors as he drove away by turning on a siren. The next I heard of him was a few days ago: an ex-convict had run amok in downtown Chicago and after being pursued by a couple of hundred cops had been trapped in a washroom in a railroad station, and my friend happened to be the man who killed him with a sub-machine gun. This was the first man he ever killed. He often told me he hoped he'd never have to kill anybody, and I called him up to see how he felt about it. He said he didn't know. 'It was just one of those things. He was in the washroom and couldn't get out any other way.' Some policemen like to kill criminals.

All policemen hate sex criminals and criminals who harm children. Many good cops hate all criminals, and in a truly personal way. I have sat in the little back rooms in police stations where prisoners are questioned and have watched a squad bring in a man, and their hatred and contempt is clear even in the way they close the door behind him. They seem bitter, affronted, outraged by his crimes. Frank Pape, a detective who figures in 'Cops and Robbers,' once told me how he had killed a murderer in a dark tenement the night before, and, shaking his head, Pape said seriously, 'He was a bad man, John, a bad man.' It was reproach. Another time Pape told me how he and other detectives had found parts of the body of the child, Suzanne Degnan. Pape has a couple of kids of his own. Though he, and the other policemen too, had worked on many cases, they were as horrified by what happened to Suzanne Degnan as any of the thousands of Chicago parents who woke up nights and looked in at their own sleeping children during the time that the murderer was at large. I remember Knifey Sawicki, a foolish kid who had spent his youth in reform schools and who one weekend killed a policeman and three other people: detectives pleaded to have fifteen minutes alone with him; the captain said correctly, "He's too hot—if you lay a hand on him you'll throw the case away." Sawicki had killed a cop who had a wife and two children and who was just minding his own business; Sawicki had killed him just because he didn't like cops. One can hardly blame the detectives who wanted to beat him up.

Police brutality is not as common as most people think but it is common enough. One team of detectives I know beat a confession out of a man and as soon as he was safe in the county jail he repudiated it and got a lawyer, who turned up a second man who also confessed to the murder; the first man was released and the second acquitted. The detectives had thrown the case away. I remember spending an evening listening to a detective (now dead) try to justify beating a prisoner. "Hanging her over a door," as he and the other cops call it—the practice of tying a prisoner's wrists behind his back, hoisting him off the floor so that his body hangs by the armpits from a door with his arms on the back of the door and the rest of the body on the front, then beating him across the stomach with a baseball bat. The woman they had just done this to had a previous criminal record and was the leader of a gang of stickup men who made a practice of going into a crowded tavern and pistol whipping or shooting the customers before emptying the cash register. They finally killed a good policeman who, on his way home, chanced to drop into a tavern they were holding up. My detective friend explained that through he was positive the woman was guilty he might have had a hard time proving it in court without a confession, that he had beaten her rather than take a chance on letting her go free to commit more crimes, that there was tremendous pressure on the case from the public and from higher police officials, that policemen in self defense can't afford to let a criminal get away with killing another policeman (the one alarm on the police radio that will bring every squad running is "Policeman needs help"), and that policemen never beat respectable people or ones of whose guilt they are in doubt. (This is almost true—you or I wouldn't get beaten up by the cops—but it isn't quite true, as has been shown. Cops are fallible.) (Note 18, p. 218-119).

Policeman have a sworn duty to "serve and protect," not to punish. In our system of justice it is the court's duty to hand out punishments to those who break the law. Pursuant to the United States Constitution, all men are presumed innocent until proven guilty. There is nothing contained in the Constitution that allows the police to inflict punishment on anyone suspected of a crime, no matter how outrageous the crime might be. To condone police activity that allows them the right to inflict punishment on those suspected of a crime undermines the foundation of our legal system.

William Heirens was in "protective custody" for over one month before he finally pled guilty to the Chicago murders in June, 1946. After he confessed, one of the five Chicago daily newspapers ran an article that read, "The Werewolf was in Chains." He received three consecutive life sentences and one year to life for burglaries and assault. He was spared the death penalty.

Following the murder of Suzanne Degnan, Chicago's Mayor Kelly received the following note: "This is to tell you how sorry I am I couldn't get ole Degnan instead of his girl. Roosevelt and OPA made their own laws. Why shouldn't I and a lot more?" (OPA stood for Office of Price Administration.) Keep in mind that during this time there was a nation-wide meat packer's strike in progress. Representative Jenkins, Republican from Ohio and chairman of the Republican Congressional Food Study Committee, was quoted in 1946, as follows: "The OPA is to blame for this strike which no one in the industry really wanted." Jenkins told the House, 'The single point at issue is an adjustment of meat prices so that the industry can afford to pay its employees higher wages." Senator Eastland (D. Miss) told the Senate a continuance of the meat strike would eventually make rationing of milk and dairy products necessary (Note 9). Could someone associated with the meat-packing industry or a butcher have something to do with the murder of Suzanne Degnan? The *Chicago Daily Tribune* reported on January 14, 1946, that "Police last night posted a guard at the home of Marion Isbell, wealthy restaurant owner and former top executive of the OPA, after receipt of two mysterious telephone calls at the home inquiring if there were any children there." The OPA agents did enter another murder in Chicago at about the same time as the Suzanne Degnan investigation because there were reports that the murder might have been the result of black market operations in meat. The head of the person killed was nearly severed.

In the investigation of the Degnan murder, certain members of the Chicago police department homicide division "believed that the kidnapper-killer must have driven a car the few blocks to the dismemberment; that carrying a 74-pound child through the streets would have drawn too much notice" (Note 14). Keep in mind that somehow the Mad Butcher of Kingsbury Run managed to dismember the bodies, often large bodies, in one location, transport and deposit the pieces in another location without being detected.

Several other women had been killed in Chicago during the previous six months immediately preceding the Degnan murder. In each case the body had been meticulously cleaned. In each instance the killer demonstrated a form of psychopathic cleanliness. I have already mentioned that the Heirens' case doesn't add up, and there may be a good reason for this. I would render a guess that whoever killed Josephine Ross, Frances Brown and Suzanne Degnan would have to be classified as an "organized killer."

Suzanne Degnan was kidnapped, a ransom note was left at the scene, and she was dismembered at a location other than where she was kidnapped. The killer used a basement tub and drain to complete the dismemberment. She was expertly dismembered. Her remains were discarded in nearby sewers. After the murder the Chicago Police Department, the FBI and every vigilante within fifty miles of Chicago had entered the race to find the killer. In other words, the heat was on, big time. So what was William Heirens doing at this time? Was he following the performance of an organized killer? Did he fit the part? I don't think so. William Heirens was a petty thief. He robbed houses, apartments and stores. He accumulated furs, men's suits, radios, utensils and guns. He got a thrill out of stealing things. On June 26, 1946, according to author Dolores Kennedy, Heirens was in the process of stealing a wallet from a third floor apartment of the Wayne Manor apartments on Wayne Avenue in Chicago. A neighbor in an adjacent apartment witnessed the theft of the wallet and yelled at Heirens. Heirens fled the building. Another tenant spotted Heirens and called the police. The police arrived, a scuffle ensued, and Heirens was hit on the head with a flower pot. He was arrested, and the rest is history. Now you have to ask yourself, does this sound like an organized serial killer or a 17-year-old kid who was on a mission to commit another robbery? Had William Heirens been an organized killer he would not have risked apprehension by stealing a wallet from an occupied apartment building at a time when all of Chicago's police force was looking for the murderer of a six-year-old child that had been brutally killed and professionally dismembered. With this in mind, remember how meticulously the killer of Suzanne Degnan acted to complete the kidnapping, murder, ransom note, dismemberment and disposal of her body. I will say it again: The case against William Heirens just doesn't add up.

The kidnapping, murder and dismemberment of Suzanne Degnan may have been patterned somewhat after the famous kidnapping case of Colonel Charles A.

Lindbergh's 20-month-old son on March 1, 1932 and if it was then it is possible that the killer knew it would cause a sensational response from law enforcement and the media, which it obviously did. If this was a motive then again William Heirens does not fit the profile. Someone like the Cleveland Torso Killer would relish the publicity.

In comparison to the Lindbergh case consider the following: Suzanne Degnan's kidnapper may have used a ladder to gain access to an occupied residence. In the Degnan case the person responsible kidnapped a small child, left a ransom note demanding $20,000, requested the bills be in $5's and $10's, and killed the child in a manner that would shock the nation. The kidnapper in the Lindbergh case used a ladder to gain access to an occupied home, kidnapped a small child, left a ransom note in the child's nursery demanding "50,000$, $25,000$ in $20 bills 15,000$ in 10$ and 10,000$ in 5$." On March 12, 1932, the kidnapper increased his ransom demand by 20,000$.

It is also interesting to note that:

1. The Cleveland Torso Killer may have killed a man in October, 1936, in Haverstraw, New York, along a railroad track. Coincidentally, Haverstraw is located within 60 miles of Hopewell, New Jersey, where the Charles Lindbergh mansion was located and the Lindbergh kidnapping took place.
2. The Reading Railroad tracks pass by Hopewell, New Jersey, not far from where the New York Central Railroad line ends in New York.
3. A ladder was used in the Lindbergh case to gain access to an occupied house.
4. A ladder may have been used in the Degnan case to gain access to an occupied house.
5. The ransom note in the Lindbergh case read in part, "Have 50,000$ Redy . . . "
6. The ransom note in the Degnan kidnapping read "Get $20,000 Reddy . . . " (The word "reddy" has been written "ready" in the book *William Heirens: His Day In Court.* Arthur C. Becker, noted musician scholar indicated in 1946, that the spelling was "Reddy." I am not exactly sure how the killer spelled this word.)
7. The Lindbergh ransom note demanded in part 5$ bills and 10$ bills.
8. The Degnan ransom note demanded bills in 5's & 10's.
9. In the Lindbergh kidnapping case a small child was kidnapped and killed. The murder shocked the nation.

10. The ransom note in the Lindbergh case also read: "We warn you for making anyding (sic) public or for notify the polise the child is in gute care."

11. A note written in the Black Dahlia case read, "We're going to Mexico City-catch us if you can. (signed) 2k's" (See chapter 3).

12. In the Lindbergh case the ransom note was found on the window sill of the nursery.

13. In the Degnan kidnapping case the detectives speculated that the wind blew the ransom note onto the floor from her bed. The ransom note was found in her bedroom.

The events in the life of William Heirens can be found in Dolores Kennedy's book *William Heirens: His Day In Court*. I would recommend her book as a background to the following summary of the Heirens' confession and for a review of the disputed trace evidence used against William Heirens. The entire text of Mr. Heirens' confession can be found at the end of this book. I would like to summarize the text of Mr. Heirens' confession and then show that what he confessed to doing was nearly physically impossible. In the "confession" he admitted:

1. Murdering and kidnapping Suzanne Degnan early Monday morning January 7, 1946

2. Cutting up her body and depositing it in different storm sewers in the neighborhood

3. Cutting her up with his knife

4. Depositing the knife on elevated train tracks

5. Walking North and boarding the Jackson Park Express at Grandville "L" Station after the murder and dismemberment

6. Arriving at school (University of Chicago located at 57th and Ellis) at 6:00 a.m.

7. Not going to bed and staying up and studying

8. Having previously been in the vicinity of the murder scene in an apartment of a man named Gold located just to the north of the Degnan home

9. Not having observed the Degnan home while at the Gold apartment

10. First observing the Degnan home at 2:45 a.m. on the morning of January 7, 1946, never having observed the house before

11. Finding a ladder but not yet knowing where he was going to "burglarize"

12. Feeling "dizzy"

13. Entering the Degnan home through a window
14. Having a flashlight with him
15. Shining the flashlight in the direction of the person in bed
16. Strangling the person in bed
17. Carrying the 78 pounds of dead weight down the ladder, and out with no idea where he was taking this dead person (Suzanne's weight was reported as 78 pounds in the Coroner's Report)
18. Proceeding to the alley and turning north, and from there not knowing what happened
19. Taking the child to a basement of an apartment building on Winthrop Avenue
20. In the basement of the apartment house, writing the ransom note after discarding all of the body parts down separate neighborhood sewers
21. Not remembering cutting up the body
22. Claiming that the knife he used was carried in his "regular coat pocket"
23. Washing the tubs after dismembering the body
24. Then washing the knife
25. Not remembering he got into the basement of the apartment where the body was cut up
26. Having no light in the basement apartment
27. Carrying the body 150 feet from the Degnan home
28. Not remembering cutting the head off
29. Not remembering cutting the torso, the body, the arms and legs off
30. Not remembering where the head, left leg, torso or buttocks and right leg were found
31. Noticing the open window at 2:45 a.m.
32. Coming down the alley a block and a half or two blocks from where the knife was thrown next to the "L" station and burning his coat
33. Remembering that the reason he burned the coat was that there was blood on a sleeve
34. Remembering that he had a gun on him and that it was a .32 caliber
35. Remembering that he had a wire in his coat pocket that he always carried with him
36. Remembering that after depositing the body parts he went back to the apartment where he had dismembered the body of Suzanne Degnan, washed the tubs and his knife, and wrote the ransom note

37. Going back to the Degnan home and leaving the ransom note in her bedroom (The police thought it was on the bed and it was blown by the wind. This would mean that Heirens must have reentered the bedroom to leave the ransom note on the bed. Could the ransom note have been left on the window sill and been blown onto the floor?

39. Taking the ladder away from the window and leaving it in the alley

40. Going south across the lawn at the Degnan house to Kenmore, north on Kenmore until he reached Glenlake and to the alley beside the elevated where he disposed of the knife and sheath

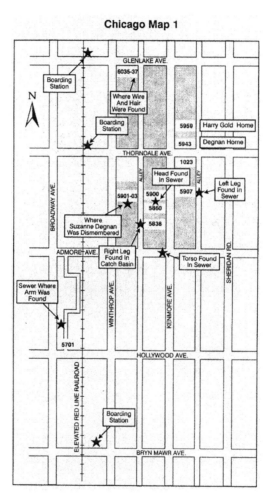

Map with the locations of Suzanne Degnan's murder, dismemberment and disposal of her body parts

According to the William Heirens' "confession," he was "dizzy." Later in his "confession" Heirens acknowledges that he had consumed six shots of alcohol earlier that evening. He entered the Degnan house, a house he had never seen before this night, at 2:45 a.m. When he carried Degnan's dead body out of the Degnan home, he had no idea where he was taking her. Miraculously, within a block of the Degnan home, he found an occupied apartment building with a basement that he could access without being noticed, that had tubs and running water in working condition that could be used when he dismembered Suzanne's body. Then, with the aid of a single flashlight and a knife he carried in his jacket pocket, he performed an anatomical feat by expertly dismembering a human body, cutting off a head, legs, arms and buttocks. During this entire process he only managed to get blood on the wrists of his jacket. Then he took separate body parts, in the middle of the night, to separate storm sewers in the neighborhood. He opened the extremely heavy, iron sewer covers with his bare hands and deposited the body parts, each time moving farther away from the place of dismemberment.

Photograph of heavy iron storm sewer cover where one of Suzanne Degnan's legs was found January 8, 1946

The arms were the last parts to be deposited in a sewer near Hollywood and Broadway Streets, near the elevated train. Close to this point is a boarding station. At this sewer the "confession" indicated that Heirens dropped a heavy sewer cover and injured a finger on his right hand. According to the "confession," Heirens then returned to the place where the body was dismembered, and with his injured finger on his right hand he washed the tubs, cleaned his knife, wrote a ransom note, put oil on the ransom note to obliterate any clues, and then returned to the Degnan home and left the ransom note in the bedroom because "he didn't want her parents to worry." Once he left the Degnan residence, he made his way back to a boarding station further west of where he had originally gotten off the train. To top this off he stopped on the way back to the University of Chicago, after performing what must have been one of the goriest dismemberments of a human body in Chicago's history, and had donuts and coffee. When he arrived at his dorm room, he began studying. According to Heirens' "confession," he went from a bumbling thief to bumbling kidnapper to a calculating murderer all in the same evening.

The body parts were located, after an anonymous telephone call tipped off the police, in separate sewers throughout the Kenmore/Thorndale neighborhood. The Heirens "confession" indicates that William Heirens used his fingers to open the sewer covers. In another part of his "confession" Heirens indicated that he used the butt of his pistol to pry open a sewer cover. Chicago street sewer covers are very heavy. They are intentionally constructed that way so that people cannot lift them off the sewer hole and create a hazard in the middle of a street. Lifting a heavy, cold, iron sewer cover without the necessary and proper tools, would be literally impossible for most people. It may be possible for an extremely strong person to lift a sewer cover, but if one is dropped or mishandled, someone in this populated neighborhood would probably have heard something. Once the sewer covers are removed, the dirt and grime embedded near the rim of the sewer cover become separated. When the covers were replaced, there would have been obvious indications that someone had removed the covers. "Detectives Lee O'Rourke and Harry Benoit had noticed that the ground surrounding the sewer in the alley behind a building on Winthrop had been disturbed. They lifted the sewer cover, and peering into the blackness, saw a blond head on top of the sewer muck" (Note 17, p. 44). It may have taken both of the detectives to lift and replace the heavy sewer cover. I spoke with three members of the Sanitation Department for the City of Chicago, and they all indicated that it would be very difficult if not impossible for someone to physically lift the sewer covers without the aid of a proper tool. It is extremely difficult to see anything down one of these sewers, let alone some object submersed in sewer muck. A concerned citizen in the neighborhood might have noticed the disturbed ground near a sewer cover and, not wanting to get involved, for good reason, made an anonymous telephone call reporting that the girl might be found in the sewers. If he reported that "body parts" could be found in the sewers, or that the police should look in "sewers" instead of a "sewer," I would suspect that the caller knew a little more about the murder than an ordinary concerned citizen. It is interesting to note that the direction of the catch basin and sewers from the basement where the dismemberment took place appears to be from Winthrop to Admore to Hollywood, close to the elevated train track. Just down an alley, beyond the location of the storm sewer where the arms were found, is a boarding station for the Red Line at Bryn Mawr. The logical direction the killer took after the dismemberment is away from the basement apartment and away from the Degnan residence. That is not the route Heirens indicated he traveled.

The Heirens "confession" does not make much sense for a number of reasons:

a. In order to successfully carry out this type of crime it would seem logical that the perpetrator would have had to preplan his movements and have access to secure locations in advance. It would also seem that the killer would have intended to kidnap, murder, possibly sexually assault her body after she was dead, dismember her body, and dispose of the body parts in separate sewers, long before the kidnapping took place.

b. The kidnapper would have had to know where the room was that he could use to dismember the body before she was kidnapped.

c. The kidnapper would have had to have the necessary expertise and tools to complete the dismemberment. It is a major undertaking to expertly dismember a human body. "It's a hell of a job to remove a human head anyway," according to an unidentified homicide detective present at the autopsy of Edward Andrassy in 1936. Had a dismemberment been performed with the sole aid of a "flashlight" and a knife that he "carried in his jacket pocket," there would have been blood located on more than the sleeves of his jacket. Blood would have been all over everything.

d. The kidnapper would have had to known ahead of time where all of the sewers were located, and he would have had to have the necessary tools to remove the sewer lids in order to deposit the body parts.

e. Suzanne Degnan was kidnapped from 5943 Kenmore Avenue. Five wisps of yellow hair matching Suzanne's were found on a rough stairway board at the rear of 6035-37 Winthrop Avenue near the same spot the wire and handkerchief were located. She was dismembered at 5901-03 Winthrop Avenue.

f. The person was probably an organized killer who carefully planned every detail of his crime.

g. The killer must have had past experience in dissecting humans or animals.

h. By all accounts William Heirens was not an organized killer and he lacked the skills necessary to expertly dissect a human body.

The most logical explanation for the murder of Suzanne Degnan is as follows:

The killer was an "organized killer." He had cased the area ahead of time. If he used the ladder, he knew where the ladder would be well before the early hours of January 7, 1946. He knew that a basement apartment was located nearby the Degnan residence. He knew ahead of time that the little girl would be in her room because he had seen her through the first floor window before this night. He knew ahead of time that he would have access to the basement apartment where the dismemberment took place. He knew ahead of time that the basement apartment contained tubs with running water and working drains that could be used to wash away the blood from a dismembered body. He would know prior to the dismemberment where the individual sewers were located in the dark, cold streets and alleys. He would have been a person who brought with him or had stored in the basement of the apartment the tools necessary to complete a dismemberment of a human body. He would have brought the necessary tools to open the extremely heavy iron storm sewer covers. He would have known that the blood would have to be drained from the corpse in the tubs before the body parts were transported to another location for disposal.

Whoever kidnapped, killed and dismembered Suzanne had experience in this type of crime. The killer, or killers, committed this crime for the thrill of it and to create fear and attention on a national level. Whoever killed her succeeded just as the person or persons who committed the Cleveland Torso Murders had. The murder and dismemberment of this little girl went off like clockwork. Whoever committed this crime was very clever, very diabolical. He managed to kidnap a small child from an occupied residence, take her to an occupied apartment building and dismember her body in a laundry room that just happened to have frosted windows so no one could see in, discard the body parts in several different sewers and catch basins throughout the neighborhood, all without being detected. (There is some evidence that the killer may have taken her to a third apartment building where she was strangled with a wire wrapped with a handkerchief.) This was no ordinary killer. The person, or persons, who killed Suzanne had expert skills. The killer(s) were experts at dismembering a human body. "Dr. William D. McNally, toxicologist, reported to Coroner Brodie that a sharp knife had been used to dissect Suzanne and that the expertise could only have come from a butcher or a hunter accustomed to the dissection of animals." Coroner Brodie concurred, telling the press that: "It was a very clean job with absolutely no signs of hacking as would be evident if a dull tool was used. The bones were all intact, carefully wrenched from their sockets." Dr. Jerry Kearns, the coroner's expert, declared that "the killer had to be an expert in cutting meats because the body was separated at the joints. Not even the average doctor could be so skillful. It had to be a meat cutter." Chief Storms told reporters that the girl's murderer "was either a physician, a medical student, a very good butcher, an embalmer or perhaps a livestock handler" (Note 17, p. 49). Dr. Kearns reported that the killer was "a person with a knowledge of anatomy, either a man whose profession required the study of anatomy or one with a background in dissection."

How in the world seventeen-year-old William Heirens, with no known expertise in any of these fields, could manage, on his first attempt, to skillfully dismember a small child with this amount of precision using a knife he carried in his jacket pocket and with the aid of a flashlight is beyond me. In my opinion, the possibility of William Heirens completing this crime, according to the statements contained in his "confession," and based on the actual facts in this case, on a scale of 1 to 100, is about a 2, and that is being generous. The coroner reported that the death of Suzanne occurred between 12:30 a.m. and 1:00 a.m. The Heirens "confession" reflects that the murder was committed after 2:45 a.m., another "minor" inconsistency.

Consider this: If the body parts were never discovered the killer's grandiose scheme would not be complete. An anonymous tip to authorities suggested that they search the storm sewers. Low and behold, there they find the body parts. Now, you not only have a small, innocent six-year-old-girl kidnapped and butchered, but also her killer dumping her body parts in a sewer. What else in this tragedy could possibly summons more fear, anger and notoriety in the general public? The killer (possibly killers) accomplished exactly what he had set out to accomplish. In addition, he received the satisfaction that the police arrested and the courts sentenced someone else for these crimes.

Ask yourself these questions:

1. Why didn't the killer strangle the victim in her bedroom and leave her there?
2. Why didn't the killer dispose of her body in any number of waste receptacles that were located in the nearby back alleys?
3. Some evidence suggested that the kidnapper did not strangle Suzanne in her bedroom, but, instead, carried her to an apartment house at 6035-37 Winthrop Avenue, where he strangled her with a handkerchief and a wire. If this was the case, then why did the killer have to enter an occupied building at 6035-37 Winthrop to kill Suzanne Degnan? Why didn't he kill her outside the building? Why risk being caught entering an occupied building with a six-year-old girl in the early hours of the morning?
4. If she was strangled to death at 6035-37 Winthrop, why didn't her killer leave her body there and flee the murder scene?
5. After dismembering the body, why didn't her killer hide the body in the basement laundry room or in the coal room?
6. Why didn't the killer dispose of all of the body parts in one sewer? There certainly was enough room, and it had to be very difficult to locate and open four separate sewer covers on that dark, cold evening.

I think that whoever killed Suzanne intended to kidnap, kill, sexually assault, dismember and dispose of her body parts in the sewers long before he exited the Red Line at the Thorndale Station and arrived at the Degnan residence at 5943 North Kenmore Avenue.

Recall the death of Frances Brown. Her killer left a large knife stuck in her throat. By doing this, whoever killed her was sending a message, but no one paid attention. In my estimation there is a very high probability that in the mid-1940's, the Mad Butcher of Kingsbury Run was visiting Chicago, the former home of his old nemesis, Elliot Ness. There certainly seems to be a substantial number of similarities.

Famous mystery writer/researcher Craig Rice pored over the records, interviewed the principals (including State's Attorney Touhy and Heirens himself), and then to the chagrin of the newspaper that hired Rice responded: "Let's think about Billy Heirens. I've seen him. I've talked to him (and) I believe him innocent" (Note 13).

Coroner's Time of Death:

On the bases on undigested food found in Suzanne Degnan's stomach, the experts at the coroner's office fixed the time of death at 12:30 or 1:00 a.m. Monday January 7, 1946 (Note 10). A report to Coroner Brodie by Dr. William D. McNally, Toxicologist, disclosed that the killer had attempted to rape the child. Coroner Brodie indicated, "It appears that a hatchet, ax or *meat cleaver* was used to decapitate the girl" (Emphasis added) (Note 8).

Witness Statements:

12:50 a.m. Miss Ethel Hargrove, a maid in the Flynn apartment, came home from visiting friends. Shortly after she got to bed, she said, she heard the dogs barking and loud voices, men's voices, downstairs (Note 13).

1:00 a.m. "George Subgrunski, a serviceman enjoying furlough on January 6, 1946, had gone to the police shortly after the Degnan murder to report that he had seen a man walking toward the Degnan home at about 1:00 a.m. on the night of the crime, carrying a shopping bag. Subgrunski said he had taken his girlfriend to her apartment at Glenlake and Kenmore Avenues, and had returned to his car when he saw the man walking west on Glenlake Avenue. The man turned south onto Kenmore Avenue, then crossed the street towards the Degnan home. Subgrunski described the man 'as about five feet nine inches tall, weighing 170 pounds, about thirty-five-years-old, and dressed in a light-colored fedora and a dark overcoat with the belt drawn tight'" (Note 17, p. 95-96). Subgrunski's report may have been dismissed by some because of its inconsistency.

1:30 a.m. Cab driver Robert Reisner saw a man and a woman parked in an automobile in Thorndale Avenue just east of the alley behind the Degnans' home. Albert Johnson reported seeing a woman carry a bundle in both arms and that the man opened the door for her. "This woman is described as about 130 pounds, five feet six inches tall, wearing a gray coat with a dark fur collar and a small hat. A man was observed in the front seat of this car. He was bareheaded and had gray hair" (Chief Walter G. Storms).

1:45 a.m. Another witness reported that the dogs in the Flynn apartment above the Degnans' home were barking.

2:30 a.m. A Miss Crawford of 5900 Kenmore Avenue reported that at about 2:30 a.m. that morning she was sitting in a car with a friend on the west side of Kenmore Avenue, just south of Thorndale, when she noticed a gray-colored sedan containing a man and a woman driving up and down the street several times (Note 17, p. 47).

3:00 a.m. "A second witness, Mrs. Marian Klein of 6033 Winthrop Avenue, also saw a stranger in the areaway which separates the building in which she lives from the building at 6035-37 Winthrop. Yesterday Mrs. Klein was questioned by Capt. John L. Sullivan of Summerdale Station. She said that she and a friend, Jake DeRosa, of 742 North Springfield Avenue, were sitting at a window of her apartment about 3 a.m. January 7, when she saw a strange man fumbling at the areaway gate. He seemed in a hurry; he may have been carrying something, she added. Mrs. Klein described him as 35-40, stocky, and wearing a gray hat and tan coat. Detective Storm said the man tried to get into the laundry room but was frightened away." Heirens was 17 years old (Note 10).

3:40 a.m. Mrs. Frieda Meyer, who lived in the first-floor apartment just above the basement laundry room in which the little girl's body was dismembered, said she heard footsteps in the areaway beneath her window. "The man, she said, walked to the laundry room from the alley, and remained there no longer than 10 to 15 minutes. She then said he returned to the alley, stayed there about 10-15 minutes, and returned to the basement. He stayed in the basement only a minute or two, she said, and returned again to the alley, where he stayed for 10 to 15 minutes. He made a third trip to the basement and stayed only a moment. Mrs. Meyer said she heard footsteps of only one person. She said she did not hear the noise of an automobile stopping or starting, although her bedroom window was open about six inches and overlooks the areaway to the alley."

5:20 p. m. January 7, 1946, police found the child's head in a catch basin 16 hours after the kidnapping.

Suzanne's torso was discovered wrapped in a 50-pound *sugar bag* (Note 4). One of the clues in the Cleveland Torso murders was a sugar sack.

The *Cleveland Press* reported on August 17, 1938, "A ragged blue coat, a patchwork quilt, a cracker box, a frozen fish container, and a *sugar sack* apparently stained with blood—These were the clues on which the detectives based their hopes of sifting out the identity of the Cleveland Torso Killer, following the finding today of additional bones of his 12th victim near the scene of yesterday's recovery of the 13th victim."

Pathological Report—Suzanne Degnan

An autopsy was performed on Suzanne Degnan on January 8, 1946. "The head was removed at the level of the 4th cervical vertebra. The trunk was divided at the level of the umbilicus anteriorly and the 2nd lumbar vertebra posteriorly. The left lower extremity has been removed at the level of the hip joint in a direction slightly oblique to the transverse direction medically at the level of the perineum from left to right; the joint cavity contains some black powder and granular material. The upper extremities have been removed at the level of the shoulder joints in a vertical direction; and are absent. The skin and subcutaneous tissues and muscles at the site of the amputation show no tissue retraction." The coroner's opinion as the cause of death was: asphyxiation by strangulation.

Following the murder of Suzanne Degnan, Chicago Chief of Detectives Walter G. Storms received a letter that could have been sent by her killer. It is interesting to note that in the Cleveland Torso Murder case a letter was addressed to Cleveland Chief of Police Matowitz, dated December 23, 1938, from someone who could have been the Mad Butcher of Kingsbury Run. In the case of the Black

Dahlia a pasted note, possibly from her killer, was addressed to Los Angeles Police Captain Donahoe (See chapter 3, page 120, #23). In all three cases, following a murder in which the victim was dismembered, someone, possibly the murderer, wrote a letter to the chief investigator in the city where the murders took place. Could the same person have written all three letters?

Similarities Between the Cleveland Torso Murders and the Murder of Suzanne Degnan (and other possibly related Chicago killings)

Cleveland Torso Murders	Suzanne Degnan and Eunice Rawlings Murders
1.The killer carried body parts in a burlap produce bag.	1. Witnesses saw a woman (or someone dressed as a woman) in the vicinity of the Degnan home carrying a large bundle in both arms at approximately the time when she was murdered. Another witness saw a large, dark man carrying a shopping bag near the Degnan home when she was murdered. Earlier a woman wearing a man's overcoat and a shawl over her head was reported by housewives near the Degnan home to have chased children on the streets. She offered them candy and, one mother said, she scratched her little boy's face with her long bright red fingernails (Note 3).
2. The Cleveland Torso Killer murdered and dismembered several individuals possibly as early as 1935, definitely from 1935-1938, and possibly again from 1938-1942.	2. Suzanne Degnan was murdered and dismembered in Chicago in 1946. The Cleveland Torso Killer may very well have been alive and actively pursuing his trade in Chicago at this time.
3. The Torso Killer may have placed dismembered body parts of victims in Cleveland sewers. On September 10, 1936, Victim No. 6 was found. The lower portion of the trunk, its legs amputated at the hips, was discovered nearby. Both halves had apparently emerged from a sewer near the bridge (Note 19, p. 76-77).	3. Suzanne Degnan's killer discarded her body parts in Chicago storm sewers.
4. The Torso Killer killed in Cleveland from 1934-1938, where Elliot Ness was Director of Public Safety. The killer taunted Ness.	4. Suzanne Degnan was killed and dismembered in Chicago in 1946. Chicago was the former home of the Untouchable Elliot Ness.

5. The Torso Killer could, among other things, have been a "prosector butcher" (Note 18, p. 79).

5. The killer of Suzanne Degnan had "the skill of a butcher." In fact the police arrested a local butcher named George Carraboni, who they suspected might be the Cleveland Torso Killer, but eventually released him. In 1946, the Chicago detectives must have considered the possibility that the Mad Butcher of Kingsbury Run might have been responsible for the murder and dismemberment of Suzanne Degnan. Chicago police even referred to the killer as "the Mad Butcher of Kenmore Ave" (Note 11).

6. The Torso Killer applied oil to the body of a victim.

6. An oily substance was found on the Suzanne Degnan ransom note.

7. Detective Merylo considered the possibility that one or more persons acting together committed all of the Torso murders. If so, then the Torso Killer murdered victims in more than one state.

7. On the night of Suzanne Degnan's abduction a neighbor, Cecelia Flynn, thought she heard voices of the two men on the street. One of the men was heard to say, "This is the best-looking building around."

8. The Torso Killer murdered victims in one location and transported them to another site, where they were dismembered. Some of the victims were then discarded in a third location.

8. Suzanne Degnan was kidnapped from one location and moved to another location, where she was dismembered. She was then discarded in a third location.

9. **The description of Victim No. 3, Flo Polillo, included the following: "Cinders of coal dust were embedded in the skin, and the lower portion of the torso bore the indentations of lump coal** (Note 2, p. 51).

9. There were four laundry tubs in the basement of the building on Winthrop Avenue, just one block south of the Degnan home and in the drain of one of them clung bits of human flesh and matted blond hair. **Further investigation located blood stains in the coal bin underneath a new shipment of coal. They had found the place of the dismemberment** (Note 17, p. 45).

The Degnan Pathological Report contains the following: "the joint cavity contains some black powder and granular material." The *Chicago Daily Tribune* reported on January 20, 1946: "An examination of the windpipe showed no coal dust, indicating that Suzanne was dead when her body was taken to the basement at 5901 Winthrop Avenue."

10. The Torso Killer murdered Flo Polillo, dismembered her corpse in one location, wrapped pieces of her body in newspapers in January, 1936 (winter in Cleveland); deposited some of the body parts at one location (behind Hart Manufacturing Plant) and dumped the additional body parts in another location (in a vacant lot on Orange Avenue.)

Referring to Victim No. 6, Lieutenant Harvey Weitzel stated, "It is my opinion that the missing parts were **not** thrown into the creek when the torso was thrown in" (Emphasis added) (Note 2, p. 82). When Victim No. 7 was found a few feet offshore in Lake Erie, they noted that "a couple of storm sewers emptied into the lake nearby but blockage from snow and ice prevented immediate search" (Note 4, p. 126).

I believe Merylo thought that some of the body parts had been deposited by the Mad Butcher of Kingsbury Run into the city sewers and eventually drained into Lake Erie.

A piece of Victim No 10's leg was found at an opening to a storm drain at the foot of Superior Avenue.

11. The Torso Killer murdered and dismembered several individuals near railroad tracks and Lake Erie in Cleveland. Then he killed an individual in West Cleveland.

12. Detectives in the Torso murders could not determine how the killer moved the heavy bodies without being detected. There was speculation that he used a pushcart. Chicken feathers found in one of the bags containing body parts became a clue.

13. "The killer was large and strong. The bodies of the first two victims—and probably that of the Tattooed Man as well—had been carried, not dragged, some

10. The killer of Suzanne Degnan dismembered her corpse in one location, wrapped pieces of her body with rags, placed the body parts in bags, and deposited the body parts in four separate sewers and a catch basin.

11. Suzanne's killer committed the murder and dismemberment near railroad tracks and Lake Michigan. This murder took place after and west of the Ross and Brown murders. The pattern of murders is similar to the Cleveland Torso murders (from east to west along the lake).

12. Detectives located a metal cart in a boiler room at 5860 Kenmore with blood on it. The blood was later determined to be chicken blood.

13. Her killer may have carried the body from her bedroom, down a ladder, and 150 feet to the place where she was dismembered. The killer also managed to lift four extremely heavy iron storm sewer

distance by the murderer. It was obvious, Director Ness remarked, that the Torso Murderer was 'a big man with the strength of an ox.' Coroner Pearce agreed that all the knife wounds had been executed by an 'exceptionally strong individual.' Since at least three of the victims had been conscious or at least alive when they were beheaded, the suggestion that the killer overpowered his victims reinforced the belief that he was a physically powerful man."

14. Parts of Flo Polillo's body were found in a burlap bags, blood-stained with chicken feathers adhering to them (Note 2, p. 51).

Pieces of victim No. 10 were found in a burlap sack pulled out of the Cuyahoga River May 2, 1938 (Note 2, p. 131). August 16, 1938, the bodies and heads of two victims of the Torso Killer were found in a Cleveland dumpsite at East 9th and Lake Shore. **A piece of striped pillowcase was found with the bodies. A bloodstained sugar sack was discovered nearby** (Note 19, p. 140).

15. The torso of the Lady of the Lakes was found on a Lake Erie beach at the foot of 156th Street.

16. The head of Victim No. 4, the "Tattooed Man," was found wrapped in his pants in Kingsbury Run **June 5, 1936** (Note 2, p. 60-61).

17. The upper torso of Victim No. 9 had been wrapped in three-week old newspapers and packed in a burlap bag. The bag also contained one of the most perplexing clues the police would deal with in the entire series—a cheap woman's silk stocking, in good condition save for a

covers and replace them without being detected.

14. Her right leg was found in a manhole inside a paper shopping bag. **Her torso was discovered wrapped in a 50-pound sugar bag. Also found was a white striped pillow cloth** (Note 5).

15. "The disappearance of a North-side girl (18-year-old Eunice Rawlings) last January 14 was investigated today in connection with the headless, armless body on the beach near Scott" (Note 4). It is interesting to note that Eunice Rawlings lived in an apartment close to where Josephine Ross and Frances Brown lived. Her death was ruled a suicide.

16. The killer of Josephine Ross stabbed her in her throat several times and then wrapped her head in a dress on **June 5, 1945.**

17. The head of Josephine Ross was found wrapped in a dress secured by a tightly bound silk stocking (Note 17, p. 35).

single runner which contained a lone black and white dog hair and several short blond human hairs (Note 19, p. 110 & Note 4, p. 118).

18. "Suddenly, Orley May's words from the previous February took on a prophetic, haunting echo: 'He (the Mad Butcher of Kingsbury Run) gives us one every five months."

18. On June 5, 1945, Josephine Ross was murdered in Chicago. Just over six months later, on December 10, 1945, Frances Brown was murdered in Chicago. Less than one month later on January 7, 1946, Suzanne Degnan was murdered.

19. When dismembering the body of Flo Polillo, the Mad Butcher of Kingsbury Run "cut the skin around the arms and legs and then '**wrenched them from the sockets**'" (Note 2, p. 57-58).

19. Coroner Brodie told the press, "it was a very clean job with absolutely no signs of hacking as would be evident if a dull tool was used. The bones were intact, **carefully wrenched from their sockets**" (Note 17, p. 49).

20. A letter dated December 23, 1938, possibly mailed by the Mad Butcher of Kingsbury Run, was received in Cleveland. The letter was addressed to Cleveland Chief of Police Matowitz. (Both killers may have mailed letters to the Chief of Police in the respective jurisdictions following a murder).

20. Following the dismemberment of Suzanne Degnan in 1946, Los Angeles Chief of Police Storm received a communication, possibly sent by her killer.

The detectives in the Cleveland Torso murders were never able to determine where the killer dismembered the bodies and drained the blood from his victims. The coal dust and indentions of lump coal on the torso of Flo Polillo may indicate that she was placed in a basement furnace/laundry room where coal was stored, just like Suzanne Degnan years later. If this is in fact the case, then it would suggest that the Mad Butcher of Kingsbury Run may have paid a visit to the Windy City in the mid 1940s. Cleveland is not that far from Chicago. The New York Central runs from Cleveland to Chicago.

Chapter 3

GEORGETTE BAUERDORF, ELIZABETH SHORT (THE BLACK DAHLIA), JEANNE AXFORD FRENCH (THE RED LIPSTICK MURDER) AND OTHER LOS ANGELES VICTIMS

Georgette Bauerdorf

A young socialite by the name of Georgette Bauerdorf was found murdered, lying face down in the bathtub in her Los Angeles apartment October 12, 1944. Her killer had removed the lower portion of her pajamas. Dr. Frank R. Webb surmised that she had been strangled with a square of toweling that was thrust deep into her throat. She was then raped, as she lay dying or already dead. Detective A.L. Hutchinson said, "The automatic light over the outside entrance to her apartment had been unscrewed two turns so that the switch wouldn't turn on. Prints lifted off the light bulb . . . and whoever turned the globe must have stood on a chair or used some other physical assistance to reach the electrical outlet which was nearly eight feet from the floor." "Or someone fairly tall," said Sheriff's Captain Gordan Bowers (Note 27, p. 42).

It is interesting to note that in the William Heirens "confession" to the Suzanne Degnan murder, the following dialog took place between the interrogator, Mr. Crowley, and William Heirens: (See page 148)

Mr. Crowley: Did you do anything to that light?
A. No, then I went east, north, I went west then, and I turned that corner in sort of "Z" corner, I went in and looked for a window that was least lighted, I found it and I entered.
Q. Did you use a ladder?
A. Yes.
Q. Before you entered the room did you do anything to the electric light that was lighted outside?
A. No.
Q. Did you hit the bulb with your hand in order to break it?

A. No.

Q. You went into the room with the electric light on?

A. Yes.

Q. Was it pretty well lit up back there?

A. Yes.

I suspect, based on this line of questioning, that the outside yard light at the Degnan home may have been tampered with by her assailant on the night of the kidnapping just as the outdoor light bulb at Georgette Bauerdorf's apartment had been unscrewed prior to her murder. According to June Zeiger, a friend of Georgette, "Georgie dated a very tall soldier." He said he was a first lieutenant in the Air Force. According to Sgt. Gordon R. Aadland, Georgette seemed nervous and excited about a trip the next day to El Paso, Texas. She told him she was rushing home so she wouldn't miss a call from her boyfriend Jerry (private Jerome M. Brown, stationed at Fort Bliss), a soldier she had met six months before at the Hollywood Canteen (Note 32, p. 168). She planned to celebrate his military graduation in Texas and had purchased an airline ticket during the first week in October. "Detective Al Hutchinson responded to the dead body call at Georgette Bauerdorf's apartment. His personal view based on what 'floated' around included the idea of a possible suspect a soldier, about 6'4, who walked with a limp that the victim dated until she thought he was a bad egg. Georgette expressed that she was afraid of him." Sheriff's files identified the soldier as Jack A. Wilson "DOB 8/5/20 other 8/5/24". Hutchinson said, "The guy would've been tall enough to easily unscrew the bulb in the victim's foyer without a ladder or stool, which nobody found." She was murdered before she could use her ticket to Texas. Following her death, Georgette's car was stolen and then abandoned on East 25th Street near San Pedro. Agness Underwood, a top crime reporter for Hearst's *Herald-Express*, received a tip that a tall, thin man with a limp, dressed as a soldier, was seen near her abandoned vehicle.

It is interesting to note that in the December 10, 1945, murder of Frances Brown in Chicago, to which William Heirens pled guilty, her killer removed the bottom portion of her pajamas and draped her over a bathtub. It is also interesting to note that in the Suzanne Degnan case the weather the morning of the kidnapping was above freezing, the ground was moist and soft. Yet no dirt, no mud, no marks were found on the window sill or in the room. Nor was any mark left by the kidnap ladder against the window sill of the child's bedroom, if in fact a ladder was used by the kidnapper. However, Sgt. James Penny of the Sunnydale station said it was possible for the kidnapper to have avoided making mud tracks. A concrete walk extends from the street around the Degnan home to a point under Suzanne's bedroom. But generally the area was soil. (Note 21) Another explanation may have been that a very tall man gained access through her first floor window without the aid of a ladder, possibly the same tall man who killed Georgette Bauerdorf and the victims of the Cleveland Torso murders.

Elizabeth Short (The Black Dahlia)

Elizabeth Short was born July 29, 1924, in Hyde Park, Massachusetts. She lived with her mother, Phoebe Short, in Medford, Massachusetts, until age 16, when she moved to Miami. Eventually Elizabeth ended up in Los Angeles seeking fame and fortune. Her hair was black, and the clothing she wore was black. She, like thousands of other young pretty girls, may have migrated to Los Angeles with hopes of becoming a famous, rich movie star. Servicemen began calling her the "Black Dahlia" because a movie showing at the time was entitled the "Blue Dahlia," starring Alan Ladd and Veronica Lake.

Elizabeth Short (the Black Dahlia) in 1946, age 22, 5' 6", 118 lbs, green eyes, very attractive (photo courtesy of the Delmar Watson Archives, Hollywood, California)

Elizabeth left California in September, 1943, and did not return until April, 1946 (Note 32, p. 95).

It has been verified that Elizabeth traveled by train from Los Angeles to Chicago in 1945 (Note 27, p. 45–47). True crime writer John Gilmore wrote in *Severed* on page 173, "The Dahlia's path was traced back from Massachusetts to Chicago, to St. Louis and Indianapolis, and to Miami through Hollywood and the movie crowd, then to Long Beach again, and San Francisco, Texas, New Orleans, Santa Barbara, and back to Boston—an almost impenetrable, ever-eddying pool of mystery." In 1951, Detective Finnis Brown received a news tip about the Black Dahlia: "It came from Chicago, about a doctor in [Hammond] Indiana who'd examined the girl last spring before her murder." (That would have been in the spring of 1946, shortly after Suzanne Degnan was murdered in Chicago.) Records indicated a woman, who might have been Elizabeth Short, was referred by a Chicago doctor to an Indiana urologist in 1946. All medical records of women with gynecological problems were routinely checked by the Chicago authorities as possible abortions. The handwritten medical report listed the woman as B. Fickle from Lexington, Massachusetts, Age 21, Blood Type: AB. The notations by the Chicago doctor seem to have been:

AB/ND.CO;
F/21/W/AB
HERED.GEN.
Referred to David Stine URO

The name B. Fickle, as written by the doctor, could have been a hastily scrawled B. Fickling. Bette's age, 21, was the same as the patient's. Bette had the same uncommon blood type, AB. The note seemed to indicate that the patient had an inherited problem (HERED) that was either genital (GEN.) or genetic" (Note 32, p. 109-110).

"By the spring of 1946, Bette had re-kindled her war-time romance with Lt. Gordon Flicking. She was on her way to meet Fickling in Long Beach, California, where he was to be mustered out of the service. En route, Bette would have to change trains in Chicago. Extending her layover in order to consult with a specialist was well within the realm of possibilities" (Note 31, p. 110). Detective Finnis Brown indicated that the Hammond, Indiana, doctor, "identified Short as the girl who had visited him at one time." Joseph Gordon Fickling was interviewed by detectives in North Carolina about a letter dated January 8, 1947, six days before Elizabeth Short was murdered in Los Angeles. "Fickling told Charlotte detectives he had received a final letter from Elizabeth dated January 8, 1947, in which she told him not to write to her anymore at her address in San Diego because her plan was to relocate to Chicago." It has been suggested that Elizabeth Short was also in Chicago in early 1946, posing as a newspaper reporter covering the death of Suzanne Degnan. (I do not have verification of this report, but it should be further investigated.) In 1947, a woman by the name of Dorothy French told the *Examiner*, "that Beth's trunk had been shipped from Chicago and held by Railway Express for nonpayment of storage charges. The *Examiner* tracked it to the warehouse in L.A. but called detective Donahoe at the same time to alert the police that they were not interfering or tampering with evidence" (Note 27, p. 137-138). The week after Christmas, 1946, Elizabeth Short wrote a letter to "Duffy" in Chicago (Note 27, p. 110).

Did Elizabeth Short come in contact with her killer on the Chicago to Los Angeles train, or could he have been stalking her as she traveled from California to Massachusetts? There isn't much doubt that the Mad Butcher of Kingsbury Run traveled by train. Is the fact that Elizabeth Short was in Chicago at times during 1945 and 1946 somehow connected to the murders of Josephine Ross, Frances Brown and the murder/dismemberment of Suzanne Degnan?

On January 15, 1947, Elizabeth Short was found murdered and bisected at the corner of 39th and Norton Avenue in Los Angeles. Her nude body had been mutilated and cut in half at the waist. Her arms were positioned above her head. Portions of her skin were missing from her torso. Her mouth had been cut, causing a grotesque smile on her face. There was an unsubstantiated report that her breasts had been burned with what appeared to be cigarettes. Both halves of her body had been drained of blood and washed clean. Grass had been forced into her vaginal cavity. There were rope marks on her ankles, wrist and neck. One of the investigating officers, Detective Lieutenant Jess Haskins, said, "Looks like strangulation, but seems that she was trussed up by ropes or maybe wire from some of the marks, maybe spread eagle or bound upside down the way you would hang a carcass—that nut's probably lining up another one right now." It was determined that she may have been forced to eat feces before being murdered. There were multiple criss-cross lacerations in the suprapubic area which extended through the skin to the soft tissues. At least three of the criss-cross marks in this area appeared to be in the shape of the letter "X." Detective Herman Willis indicated that, "the killer had cut out parts of some basic female organs." (There is some speculation that the organs were not developed and were not there to start with.)

Detective Lieutenant Haskins described the body as, "someone's idea of a dirty postcard that suddenly materialized into real life." It was determined by the authorities that the victim had been killed and mutilated in one location and afterwards transported to the corner of 39th and Norton Avenue.

Elizabeth Short's severed body found on January 15, 1947, near the corner of 39th and Norton Avenues in Los Angeles. Onlookers include Will Fowler (in straw hat), reporter for the *Los Angeles Examiner*. Mr. Fowler closed Elizabeth's eyes at the crime scene. He died at age 81 in 2004 (photo courtesy of the Delmar Watson Archives, Hollywood, California)

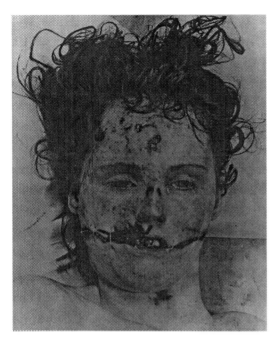

Elizabeth Short (the Black Dahlia) in the Los Angeles Morgue, January 15, 1947, after being tortured, murdered and bisected by Jack Anderson Wilson (photo courtesy of the Delmar Watson Archives, Hollywood, California)

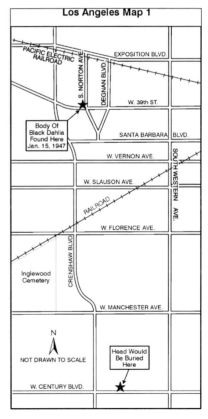

Los Angeles map showing the corner of 39th and Norton Avenues, where the severed body of Elizabeth Short was found January 15, 1947. Also, approximate location where the writer of the December 21, 1938, letter mailed from Los Angeles indicated a severed head would be found on Century Boulevard between Western and Crenshaw Boulevard

Following the murder of the Black Dahlia, her killer began writing and mailing postcards and notes to Los Angeles newspapers. On January 23, 1946, James Richardson, city editor of the *Los Angeles Examiner*, received a telephone call from a man who identified himself as the killer of the Black Dahlia. Richardson described the call in his autobiography, *For the Life of Me: Memoirs of a City Editor*. Richardson described the conversation as follows:

> The story dwindled to a few paragraphs and was about to fade out altogether when one day I answered the phone and the voice I'll never forget. "Is this the city editor?" it asked. "Yes." "What is your name, please?" "Richardson." "Well, Mr. Richardson, I must congratulate you on what the *Examiner* has done in the Black Dahlia case." "Thank you," I said, and there was a slight pause before the voice spoke again. "You seem to have run out of material," it said. "That's right." A soft laugh sounded in the earpiece. "Maybe I can be of some assistance," the voice said. There was something in the way he said it that sent a shiver up my spine. "We need it," I said and there was that soft laugh again. "I'll tell you what I'll do," the voice said. "I'll send you some of the things she had with her when she, shall we say, disappeared?" It was difficult for me to control my voice. I began scribbling on a sheet of paper the words: "Trace this call." "What kind of things?" I asked as I tossed the paper to my assistant on the desk. I could see him read and start jiggling the receiver arm on his phone to get the attention of the switchboard girl. "Oh say, her address book and her birth certificate and a few other things she had in her handbag." "When will I get them?" I asked, and I could hear my assistant telling Mae Northern the switchboard girl to trace my call. "Oh within the next day or so. See how far you can get with them. And now I must say goodbye. You may be trying to trace this call." "Wait a minute," I said but I heard the click and the phone was dead (Note 28, p. 163-164).

A package *wrapped in brown* paper and addressed "To the *Los Angeles Examiner* and Other Papers" was located in a mailbox at the Biltmore Hotel. Elizabeth Short's purse was in the package. The purse contained an address book, business cards, Elizabeth Short's birth certificate and Social Security card, several photographs of her with different servicemen, and claim checks or stubs for suitcases she'd checked at the Greyhound depot. According to Detective Herman Willis, "Everything had been soaked in gasoline to remove any trace of latent prints" (Note 27, p. 147-148). Detective Brown stated that the package was the killer's genuine work because, "It was the same kind of psychopathic cleanliness he'd used in handling the corpse."

Another note received by a Los Angeles newspaper read, "A certain girl is going to get the same as E.S. got if she squeals on us. We're going to Mexico City-catch us if you can. (signed) 2 k's." This note indicates that two individuals may have been involved, one way or another, in the death of Elizabeth Short.

Elizabeth Short did become famous as a result of the terrible death she suffered at the hands of a mad butcher. If the person who killed Elizabeth Short was also responsible for the Cleveland Torso Murders and if Elizabeth Short was in Chicago at different times during 1945-1946, when Josephine Ross, Frances Brown and Suzanne Degnan were murdered, then there is a possibility that the same person who killed Elizabeth Short may be responsible for all of the murders of Ross, Brown and Degnan in Chicago. The clues and evidence seem to indicate that the same person might have committed the murders in Cleveland, Chicago and Los Angeles.

Cleveland Detective Peter Merylo, "suggested that the Black Dahlia murder and some other similar Los Angeles homicides that followed might have been the work of the Torso murderer. His theory was not taken seriously by the California authorities or by anyone else" (Note 31, p. 190). Had his theory been vigorously pursued by the Los Angeles detectives at that time, the case against William Heirens might have had a completely different outcome.

Hundreds of investigators tried to solve the Black Dahlia murder. Included among them was Los Angeles Detective John St. John, a/k/a "Jigsaw John." It is interesting to note that Detective St. John's assessment of the December 23, 1938, letter mentioned in Chapter 1 is as follows: "There was no connection," St. John said. "That had been checked out thoroughly. The Cleveland killer had a particular signature. All the Cleveland victims were killed quickly and decapitated. Those were two elements which never deviated"(Note 32, p. 133). St. John explained: "Signature is different from MO," he said. "Signature is the extra things a predator does, the obsessive things he needs to do that aren't necessary if his objective is to kill someone. Killing quickly was the Cleveland killer's MO; the decapitation was his signature. Torture and posing the body was not involved, like in the Elizabeth Short murder" (Note 32, p. 133). In her book *Childhood Shadows: The Hidden Story of the Black*

Dahlia Murder, author Mary Pacios wrote about her interview with Detective St. John: "St. John said the murder of Elizabeth Short was unique. 'There was never one like it before, and there hasn't been one like it since. The perpetrator combined a number of elements that have never been seen together—a unique signature.' St. John was adamant. He believed the killer struck only once. St. John said that Finnis Brown and Harry Hansen were the only two people who watched the autopsy being performed—no reporters or other policemen were present. St. John hedged when I asked him if the killer had any medical training or had used medical equipment. 'I can't go into that,' he said and then laughed. 'Our job is to get information, not give it . . . The perpetrator may have had some knowledge of anatomy, but he wasn't necessarily in the medical profession'" (Note 32, p. 132-133). John St. John was in my opinion an excellent detective, but he made a mistake here, the same mistake detectives continue to make when searching for highly intelligent serial killers: they fail to accept the fact that the killers intentionally change locations to cross jurisdictional lines and alter their methods of killing, intending to throw their pursuers off course.

Several years after the murder of Elizabeth Short the Los Angeles Police Department received a tip that a certain individual had information regarding her murder. The individual was being paid by an informant to supply information to the police department about someone who might have had information about the murder of the Black Dahlia. The whole affair was orchestrated so that the entire conversation amounted to hearsay and was not admissible against anyone named. The individual brought a tape recording and other information to Los Angeles Detective Marvin Enquist. "Enquist, in turn, called upon St. John and his partner, Kirk Mellecker to hear the informant repeat his story." The informant related facts on tape to Detective Enquist, including how the body was severed, that the body had been severed on 31st Street near San Pedro and that the person, "who had told the informant these facts was using the name Arnold Smith." The informant described Smith as, "very tall, over 6', very thin, with one leg shorter than the other. Smith blamed the murder and bisection of the Black Dahlia on a female impersonator he called "Al Morrison." St. John determined that there was no Al Morrison and that Al Morrison was a made-up person who was in reality a 6'4" sodomist by the name of Arnold Smith (Jack Anderson Wilson). "What Smith is doing," St. John said," is airing what he possibly knows of the murder first hand, while putting the words in someone else's mouth, an as-told-to story, if you get my drift" (Note 29, p. 95).

According to the information given, the informant had met "Smith" quite a few years earlier at an apartment in the Silver Lake area occupied by a man named "Eddie" and a girl. According to the informant, "Smith said that wasn't where the cops had been looking, Eddie told us that Smith had known the Black Dahlia and he'd seen a photograph of them together . . . I asked him about it, but mostly Smith talked to me about some other guy, a female impersonator from Indianapolis" (Note 27, p. 180-181).

"Eddie" was a fence for burglarized electronics. He was suspected by the F.B.I. of being involved in an earlier kidnapping" (Note 27, p. 227).

"Of the time the informant met with Smith, he said the man never referred to Elizabeth Short by name, He did not call her Elizabeth, or the Short girl, or Beth. He would say 'her, who we're talking about,' if I didn't follow what he was saying and asked me what I meant" (Note 27, p. 181).

Keep in mind the Cleveland Torso victim No. 2, Edward Andrassy, had a friend by the name of "Eddie" (Note 30, p. 60). Author John Bartlow Martin wrote on pages 59-60 in his article about the Torso Murders in the book *Butcher's Dozen*:

Now, the murderer had emasculated the bodies of both Andrassy and the unidentified man (the genitalia were found near the bodies). The police believed this indicated that the murderer was a sexual pervert and they wondered if Andrassy was one himself. The evidence was contradictory. During the summer Andrassy visited a nightclub several times, each time with a different woman, including a Chinese. On the other hand, a woman recalled that her son said Andrassy had picked up another boy in a park and had taken him to a speakeasy. A married couple told the queerest story of all. The man, who had known Andrassy most of his life, said that early in the summer Andrassy had remarked "how bad" the man's wife looked. "She had female trouble," the police reported, and then Andrassy spoke up and told them that he was a "female" doctor and that he would like to examine her. In doing so Andrassy committed sodomy upon her (it isn't clear whether her husband did not protest because he didn't understand or because Andrassy was bigger than he). "He then told Mr. and Mrs.____ that if he would go home and get his instruments he could fix her within a month, so that she could have children." But they "told Andrassy not to bother." Searching Andrassy's room later, detectives reported finding "two doctor books and five physical magazines." A while later the couple moved, and one night the man found Andrassy and a stranger standing in the dark outside the door of his new home. Andrassy said they were considering sleeping in the adjoining apartment, which was empty. Andrassy introduced his friend as "Eddie," a chauffer for a wealthy woman in suburban Lakewood whom Andrassy "was doctoring . . . for the same trouble," The host invited them in for coffee, but "Eddie" seemed very nervous and they left in a large new touring car, a Lincoln or a Buick. "Eddie" was described as "28-30, 5-6, 150 good looking very good set of teeth, appeared to have had a broken nose and wore a dark trousers blue shirt, checkered gray cap, and dark brown hair." The detectives never could find "Eddie." The couple said he was not the unidentified man found dead a month later with Andrassy. But oddly, they said a cap found near the bodies was his.

A person by the name of Eddie was also described in the Cleveland Torso murder of Flo Polillo: "About six weeks after the death of Edward Andrassy, Flo Polillo returned to her hotel, this time with 'an unknown Italian,' described as twenty-seven-years old, five feet eight or nine, 135 pounds, dark complexioned, wearing a dark suit and dark cap, a description that nearly matched the description of Andrassy's friend, 'Eddie'" (Note 30, p. 65).

A transcript at the Los Angeles County Sheriff's files includes the following statement from Arnold Smith (Jack Anderson Wilson): Smith is talking about his fictitious character "Al Morrison." The transcript was developed from the tape recordings of Smith provided by the informant to Los Angeles Sheriff's Detective Marvin Enquist:

> She'd told Morrison she slept on the couch downstairs in Hassau's after he spotted her walking to the corner of Hollywood across the street from the Roosevelt Hotel. So he says, "Hey, what the hell are you doing?" She got in the car and sat with him for awhile, and then she got out and was walking away from the car.
>
> She gets sad and gets back into the car, and he heads south on La Brea. She wanted to know where he was going and he headed down to Washington and then east as far as Flower. Then he drove down that way, going south from there to San Pedro Street. They drove further south, to another hotel near 29th

Street, also called the Roosevelt Hotel, but not connected to Hollywood's Roosevelt Hotel.

He got the key there, that guy that knew the blond—this is the one that shacks up with the Chinaman, and she had the key. Then he drove her to the Chinaman's house on 31st, but he couldn't get into the place.

There was something wrong with the key, as I remember the situation, as it had been described to me. Morrison had to drive to a small factory on the corner, around on 33rd Street and Trinity, to straighten out the problem with the key. She was complaining about having to get back because of Henry's wife. Later on, I asked him, "You think she was trying to get back to see me?" He turned red when I said that. You see, the first thing is you couldn't fuck her at all. He said he'd screwed her and I said he was a liar. See, she made my dick hard every time I looked at her mouth. But I swear to God, I never put it in her, and I knew he was a lying sonofabitch.

There was a red bottle, had a glass stopper you use for putting fancy perfume in. And he could've taken her eyes out with that. But you understand, that's what he said. Because his mind has gone. You know, half those hoods had their mind eaten away because of syphilis. I know his mind has gone to have done what he did to her, and knowing he did it all along, but knowing it was just that he had to do it, you see what I am saying, so there was an excuse in part of this.

I remember being told something about pulling the car into the dirt driveway and to the back by the incinerator. The car was parked there so that it was close to the building. There was just so much room, so you get out and go around front to the building, since the back door's locked.

This is the Chinaman's house in the 200 block on East 31st Street by San Pedro Street and Trinity . . . . This is an older two-story brown wood-framed building that rented rooms and units.

You go up to the place by these steps right in front that're wood and you go in the hall. Right there is the stairs going up. So what we're talking about, he goes up behind her to the second floor. This place smells so bad like it's been closed up for a long time. Right away he opened the beer and sat on the couch, but he didn't pull that goddamn drape back. That's the problem, there, because she says she can't breathe because it is so dusty, but he doesn't say anything—he is just waiting there.

He has to tell her to be quiet, again. But she says she has to make a call and when she starts to use the phone there he says, "You can't." He put it back down. She said something like she is a prisoner and he says, "That's right. You're a prisoner." She says she is going to make a call from the market ... She means the market where they just were. She gets her handbag up, and he says, "No, you're not going." But she was starting out, just starts out of the room. He came out of the hall up there and goes to the head of the stairs where she is standing, and he says, "You better come back inside of here. You better not go outside now."

She didn't say anything and he said okay. And he went to her and grabbed her arm like this, and started to pull her back and she hauled off and let him have it with the purse. Just swing it out and caught him across the side of the face. He slugged her once and her knees got weak. He pulls her back into the room, and he leans her against the door while he locks the door with the key. She just stayed there as though she was unsure exactly what would follow or admit it. He said he then grabbed her and pushed her and she fell down like it was against or on the couch. Then off that and is on the floor with her dress on her body. He said he stood over her and said something about he was going to screw her ass.

She started to yell so he bent down and slugged her again. He said he put his hand on her neck and holds her head still for a couple of times. She didn't move. Now he didn't know what he was going to do, except he went out of the room, through the door he had locked and went downstairs to the rear of the first floor to the kitchen . . . . He knew what was going to happen.

When he got outside he heard the funniest sounds he'd heard. He couldn't tell whether it was the people making noises inside the joint or whether hearing people over the fences in those crummy houses. He wasn't sure. He could almost hear voices like they were talking, you understand? Anyway, he checked the gas in the car and checked under the seat in the car. He had to get north. He went back upstairs and through the back door, through the back part, there was this concrete. They were cementing a walk for the back part there, and he had to step over it or sink his shoe in the dirt, the mud there. He remembered a hose that was going. It was leaking and the water was running down the back, just leaking and going back by the incinerator.

It was on his mind all the time. Everything that was going to happen. He said he didn't have to think about anything, because it was laid out in front of him.

He got a small knife or he got the knife on the back of the porch, like a paring knife, and on the back of the porch was a rope, this clothesline hunk of a rope. This is what he had in mind for the waitress. Then he said there was a larger knife, like a long butcher knife that was two inches, the width of the blade near the handle. He said he thought that such a knife could be used to dismember the body. He said he didn't know what he was going to do with the knife, except to scare her or keep her back up in the room. He went upstairs but she hadn't gotten up off the floor, but up on an elbow or an arm and was looking around.

She was on the edge of the couch, I think maybe he had her arm—up here at this part of the arm—and had brought her to the couch, but this wasn't a couch like you think; it was a studio bed on a metal frame, only it was littler than a regular bed you'd consider for that, and he said, "You had enough trouble?" She said she had so he opened this bottle . . . . This is what he said, oh, and had this opened from the sink place downstairs, the washtub just before you went to the back door. She kept saying, "What are you going to do?"

Drinking that, and she said her mouth hurt. She was scared of the knife and got up and was moving but he ran to her and hit her again, but it didn't put her out and didn't seem to stop her. So it was necessary at this point to indicate that he was going to hurt her with the knife.

He tore at the clothes, not tearing but cutting at the clothing. I don't know what . . . , I didn't know he said something and I can remember him scared or his face was white and his eyes didn't even look anywhere near like it was real eyes. Like they were glass and they were shining and he was cold but he was sweating and he turned the light away . . . . This light, like a desk light, and it was bright as this is. It was like when you see flashes of light when you get hit in the head. But he put a rag in her mouth. He used her underpants and he knocked her out a few times. She was all tied up to that couch and she'd been stripped of all the clothes and cut up bad.

I couldn't tell you how bad it was. I mean, this is the information I have that I know about. I knew it had to be some other Chinese. They'd cut her mouth across it and there was blood on the couch. He knew he'd stuck her with it and had to get rid of it.

She was naked, only he'd tied her hands and these were up over her head like this, and he stabbed her with a knife a lot, not deep, not enough that would kill you, but jabbing and sticking her a lot and slitting around one tit, and then he cut her face across it. Across the mouth. After that she was dead.

Her legs weren't tied at this particular point, but it was plain that they had been tied by the rope—this hunk that had been tied was cut, but it was still anchored at the frame, and there was the piece of it that was still there.

The knife was on the floor next to where the rope pieces were, a small knife, a paring knife that had been used to stick her with. I think it was seeing the rope down in the back, and the wire stuff, like a gauge heavier. I don't mean the wire part of the hanger but like you got on the other kind of hanger, that's the hook on the top part of it, going over the clothes pole, but it wasn't like that, it was soft and around the frame part. That's what stands out in one's mind.

There was the matter of getting rid of her, and what probably was the first thing was the incinerator out back. Burn the clothes and things and the knife. He got the knife idea from the situation that someone had put the rope around her neck, and held her down on the couch. Now these underpants or these ladies pants, they were all clotted with her blood, like a wad of some blood that was hard to see right off since the material was black, but blood does show on black, and there were these other particles of material that probably didn't belong to her and the problem that these had to be burned as well. So, it is easier to try to think what he told me about all this situation, though you look at a movie, you see what I am saying?

There is a larger knife that can be used, but he had to go back and outside and get these boards they were using for forms. Maybe there were three of these boards, or maybe there were four of them back upstairs, and went through the room she was in and into the bathroom which was off this one room, but there was a short hall. It's not a hall in that sort of sense except with—well, this window and you can see the roof of the car and the trunk of the car if you look out. And on the other side is the alcove, not a closet because there is no door, but it is arranged with a clothes pole going across, and some curtain material that is a bathtub shower curtain, there is one of these in front of where the clothes pole is across. But in the bathroom these boards are put across the tub, straight across it—set out that way. She was brought into the bathroom first, if I recall exactly what the information is. So, partly brought into the bathroom. I think dragged the rest of the way, and looking down at her, is the way I understand it. He had fooled around with her stomach, too, using the knife on her, the decorations in that manner. He had done a few other things to the body, figured she'd still been alive, and seeing how she could take it.

As much as possible, you understand, well . . . . There was a purpose to this in such a way though a person undergoes so much and it's possible that this person has to be, what you would call—anesthesia. It's a word in a crossword puzzle . . . .

There was this other muscle portion or the part of the jaw, during the time she was dying. But this had been taken care of, and she had to be laid across the tub, on top of the boards. Then he tied the arms and tied the hands to the faucet handles and the shower, the pipe. And then put a leg, the one that was nearest hanging over the side of the tub. Her leg was put on the tub, on the boards, the board that was arranged for that part of the leg, she was laying across one board just underneath the back part, and the other was underneath the hips here, under the ass—see, a rope around each leg and pulled them downwards, pulling them so that you then tied these ropes around the bottom of the can—the toilet bowl, but there is the pipe. There is not the wall section of the water storage, the tank. It is the vacuum housing part there and the water pipe, so he had her drawn and fixed down, because there wasn't a particular way of getting into the tub with that kind of knife. That particular knife.

The idea was first cutting off the legs at the top of her thighs but then this would have to be done twice, so the decision to separate, to cut this in half, that way to move the two parts easily, and get her there was the way to transport . . . .

Burning of the body in the incinerator was not the actual plan, but that the body could be separated for disposal purposes so there was this commencing with a different approach. The body was on the planks over the bathtub. Her middle was over the tub and the boards were width-wise so she was open, at the waist and back, and so the cut was across the middle, pulled tight like she was, as it could go clean through and have her body opened.

The knife was a larger knife. I would say it was approximately ten inches long, the length of the blade and there were two inches at the handle part, not the handle of it but just at the end of the blade. It went in further than figured with this knife and went all the way across and down through her body. The drain was into the tub below. But blood did not come out and onto the boards and some even jumped out of her, came out and upwards in such a way, but it was clean through, and then there was some trouble with going through her backbone of the bone's part there. The important thing is that the starting of it has to be finished. If one would intend to make the separation as to what we're talking about.

When the board was removed from underneath the rear part, that low section went down into the tub, but hanging on an angle, and drained in this manner. The same with the top half which hung down into the tub and there were marks that were made on the body's back, the upper part. Both sections of the body drained in this way, leaning, you could say laying down at an incline into the bathtub, but the bottom half, the hips and these parts of the leg was leaning against the slope of that part of the tub, but the upper part was straight down, not straight as the back of a chair, but straight more down than the lower section. She stayed in the tub and the boards were taken down and out back. The boards and stuff went into the incinerator.

The broom was where the mop was and the mop and the rags were used, and then these things went down and were put in the incinerator and lighted on fire.

The covers and the mattress padding—it wasn't a padding, but it was like thick as felt, like a heavy material. It was covered with shit. It was messed so bad, and these were bundled, put into a bundle. They were not put on top of her, but the water was in the tub. It had run before, the tub had been filled with the water. So it was put up around where the hands were, up around where the faucets were and this way not in the tub. The blood was thinned out by the water. It was on the chain, a stopper, down in the drain, but it was plugged-in first and then the water made the body rise, and it came up as the water filled the tub.

There was some worry about the rope areas, and these were then cut. He said he was sitting on the toilet and he cut the rope, the part that went around the base of the bowl and these then were taken off of the places of the body where they were tied around. It was in the water but was drained and it was filled again and the body was in the water at this time. The body tended to stay higher with the surface as it came up. There was movement in the bathtub with the body when the tub was filled with water. And whatever skin contact there was, this was removed when there was the draining. And it was removed by cleaning it off. There was this idea that she was not dead because her eyes were open and they had a look in them that she was not dead. This, I think, what it was, that he was scared and getting more scared and knowing that they had to be gotten rid of. I think it was that the water drained and ran in and around the open parts of the body . . . . It was not excitement or that sort of feeling, but because of the jaw that I said earlier, it made it so it was necessary to take care of the rest of it.

The skin contact had been taken care of, and then back downstairs was the oilskin tablecloth off the kitchen table. But this wasn't enough, so there were these curtains and shower curtain from the hall there by the pipe. She was wrapped over in the curtains, both parts in the two curtains, and what was it . . . . It was used to pull on the tablecloth or I think it was the shower curtain to take the sections downstairs. The bag was on the floor of the truck. This was the cement bag from the rear of the house.

She was put into the trunk of the car, and then drove until the place was reached that he could put the body—put her out of the car. The top section was carried by the arms held up and put down on the ground and the bottom section was on the bag and put down that way. The body was put down in the manner that the bottom was put down and moved this way. Moved by one leg this way, more away from the sidewalk, and then the top part was picked up again and put in order.

The cement sack was left where it was when he took hold of the ankle and put away from the sidewalk. The shower curtain and the tablecloth were in the trunk of the car. There was nothing of the clothes that was not cut, except the shoes and purse. The pocketbook was on the floorboard. It was put into a storm drain. All of this was put into a storm drain (Note 27, p. 185-193).

Los Angeles County Sheriff's Detective Joel Lesnick determined that Smith, as Grover Loving, Jr., first appeared in Los Angeles in the late 1930's, then did not reappear there until 1942, as Jack Anderson Wilson. The Cleveland Torso murders "officially" ended in 1938, at or about the same time Cleveland Chief of Police George Matowitz received the letter from someone purporting to be the Mad Butcher of Kingsbury Run. Additional Torso murders were reported in Pennsylvania from 1938-1942. Most of Wilson's early years were spent growing up in Ohio (Note 27, p. 199). Lesnick was able to obtain documentation that Wilson (a/k/a Smith) while incarcerated during the fall of 1958, in Oakland City Prison, California, told an inmate a story about a queer's head he'd seen in a glass box in Cleveland. He'd said this was at the time he saw Johnny Weissmuller as Tarzan. "It would seem to me to tie in," Lesnick says, "with Wilson saying Elliot Ness had been outsmarted by a Cleveland killer that was never caught" (Note 27, p. 199). Forensic Psychologist Paul Cassenelli pointed out what Wilson had said about Sally Rand, the striptease artist, that he had "jacked off" in his pants while watching her dance in Cleveland. Sally Rand was featured at the 1936 Great Lakes Expo held in Cleveland. Ester Williams appeared in the aquacade with Johnny Weissmuller, and the city of Cleveland had a police exhibit dealing with the Cleveland Butcher, which included a replica of one of the victim's heads contained in a glass box. Although Wilson talked about the decapitated head as that of a homosexual, and spoke derogatorily about homosexuals in general, his rap sheet showed arrests for crimes against nature—sodomy and he seemed to prefer the skid row homosexual bars and juke joints. (Recall the 1937 letter referred to in Chapter 1 sent to the Cleveland Police Department from someone in North Hollywood. In that letter a suspect in the Cleveland Torso Murders was identified as a person with the last name "Wilson." This suspect was identified as being 17 years old in 1937. Jack Anderson Wilson's birth certificate shows that he was born in 1920. He would have been 17 years old in 1937. Also recall that the suspect's father was identified as "Walter *F.* Wilson." Jack Anderson Wilson's birth certificate shows his father as "Alex *F.* Wilson.") "Wilson seemed to prefer the company of low-lifes," Lesnick says, "the moochers, and apparently second-rate female impersonators. He referred to one being connected with a murder in Indianapolis, and he mentions this person working in a bar called the Pair of Jacks, and another joint, Jud Logan's Bar in the same area. He alludes to that room in the 7000 block of West 10th Street, downtown, and all of this having some peculiar skid-row feeling of activity to it, and these talks about rape and murder that are in the transcripts-the methods mentioned by Wilson coming peculiarly close to the actual conditions to do with the bathtub murder of Georgette Bauerdorf. Of course this became of great interest to the unsolved homicide division of the sheriff's department" (Note 27, p. 199-200).

The following is a list of the aliases of Jack Anderson Wilson (Note 27, p. 202):

	Initials
Jack Anderson Wilson	J.A.W.
Jack Olsen	J.O.
Hanns Anderson Von Cannon	H.A.V.C.
Jack A. Taylor	J.A.T.
John D. Ryan	J.D.R
Eugene Deavilen	E.D.
Jack McCurry	J. M.
Jack H. Wilson	J.H.W.
Grover Loving Jr.	G.L.
Grover Loving Wilson	G.L.W.
Jack Anderson McGray	J.A.M.
Jack Smith	J.S.
Arnold Smith	A.S.

It is also interesting to note that Federal agents in St. Louis seized twenty-five-year-old Grover Casey of Troy, Alabama, for making telephone calls to the Degnans saying their child was safe and demanding $500. He was charged with making a threat over interstate communications. On February 15, 1946 Grover Casey was sentenced to five (5) years in a federal penitentiary.

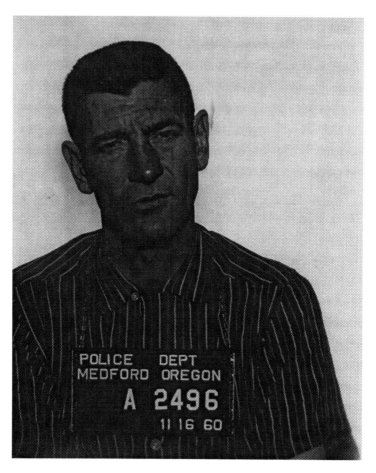

Medford, Oregon Police Department arrest photograph of Jack Anderson Wilson,
a/k/a Jack Wilson, November 16, 1960
(photo courtesy of the Museum of Death, Hollywood, California)

Wilson had a five-page rap sheet with a number of aliases and three Social Security numbers. In Tennessee, Wilson was caught having sex with another man in a park. His rap sheet listed Los Angeles as his place of birth and included two separate dates of birth. In Tennessee, Wilson's arrest record listed his birthplace as *Canton, Ohio*, not Los Angeles. Detective Lesnick stated: "It appeared that the mother of either Alex Wilson or Minnie Buchanan came to Canton from the Newland region in North Carolina and lived in that house when Wilson and Minnie relocated to southern California, leaving the boy behind. Apparently he remained in Canton with the relative from Newland. Though it appears he was shuttled back and forth between Canton and North Carolina, most of his early years were spent growing up in Ohio" (Note 27, p. 199). The first Torso murder in Cleveland occurred in 1935. If Wilson was born in 1920, he would have been 15 years old in 1935. Canton, Ohio is located not far from Youngstown, New Castle and West Pittsburgh, Pennsylvania, and Cleveland, Ohio. The New York Central runs through Minerva, Ohio, twelve miles from Canton.

In her research on the Black Dahlia, the author of *Childhood Shadows*, Mary Pacios tracked down the information on Jack Anderson Wilson. Pacios called author John Gilmore. "Gilmore had relatives in Canton who could obtain Wilson's birth certificate. A few days later a hand-corrected document arrived in the mail. The name on the certificate was Grover Loving, Jr., with a birthdate of August 5, 1920. The name of the father, Grover Loving, was crossed out and the name Alex F. Wilson written in. The mother was listed as Minnie Buchanan. Both mother and father gave North Carolina as their place of birth. An attached affidavit signed by Minnie Buchanan and dated November 10, 1942, listed Jack Anderson Wilson as the correct name of the child with Alex F. Wilson as the correct name of the biological father." Mary Pacios writes:

> Upon my return to San Francisco I visited a library that specializes in genealogy—the Sutro Library. Looking through old census tracts, telephone books, and city directories, I traced the whereabouts of Jack Anderson Wilson and his mother, Minnie Buchanan Wilson. I found a trail of listings that placed Minnie Wilson in the city of Wilmar, a suburb of Los Angeles, between 1939 and 1942. Her name disappeared from the telephone books and city directories in 1943. The 1940 Los Angeles City Directory listed a Jack A. Wilson living on Hill Street in Los Angeles. The 1941 and 1942 city directories had a Jack A. Wilson working at Cogar Brothers Sign Company in Los Angeles with a residence in Wilmar. All the information, with exact dates and addresses, I passed on to John Gilmore.

> John obtained Wilson's military file. Wilson had been in the army from January 12, 1944, to March 15, 1945. I created a chronology combining Wilson's arrest record with the new information, but a major gap appeared—no paper trail existed for Wilson's whereabouts between his

entry into the army and his arrest in 1948 for vagrancy and lewd behavior. There was nothing to indicate whether or not Wilson was in the Los Angeles area when Elizabeth Short was murdered (Note 32, p. 166). See information concerning Georgette Bauderdorf's murder on page 72.

It is interesting to note that Jack Anderson Wilson's rap sheet reflects an arrest on 3/22/43, for violation of the Selective Service Act. The related murders in Los Angeles appear to have begun with the death of Georgette Bauerdorf on October 12, 1944. Ross, Brown and Degnan were killed in Chicago during 1945-1946. The Black Dahlia, Jeanne French and other Los Angeles victims were killed from 1947-1949. No arrests appear on Wilson's rap sheet from March 22, 1943-July 26, 1948, after which time he was arrested and incarcerated on a fairly regular basis.

John St. John wanted some tangible evidence that would connect Smith with the Black Dahlia. He wanted to meet with Smith and discuss the details of the Black Dahlia murder.

Eddie introduced true-crime writer John Gilmore to Jack Arnold (Arnold Smith) in the late 60's. They met at "Eddie's" flophouse in Silver Lake where, after a few drinks, Smith would eventually begin to reveal to Gilmore information he knew about the Black Dahlia murder. More than a dozen years later Smith called Gilmore and said, "It's probably time we got together and talked about the murder." "What murder?" Gilmore asked. Smith replied, "Her murder. You know who I mean . . ." (Note 27, p. 228-229). Gilmore met with Arnold Smith at Harold's 555 Club in Los Angeles in early 1980. Smith showed Gilmore a photograph of Elizabeth Short and a handkerchief that he said was in her purse on the day she was killed. Smith related details of the murder to Gilmore that only the killer would have known. Gilmore relayed the information he obtained from Smith to Detective St. John. After meeting with Gilmore, St. John said, "This is the guy that I have got to talk to." He was nearly certain Arnold Smith was the murderer of Elizabeth Short. "He's blaming somebody else for the homicide, but he's got details only the killer could know-or details only the killer could have told him. He either takes us to this other joker or takes the rap for it himself . . . this is the break I've waited for. All I need to make a connection between Smith and Short—linking them together at the same time . . . the perfect piece of evidence is the photograph you saw. With that, we'll bring him in, and I'll close the book on this case. I'll retire after fifty years of working this shit by closing the door on this one." St. John contacted the informant to arrange a meeting with Smith and to find out certain information about the Dahlia murder. "When the informant talked to Smith about getting together at the 555 Club the last of January, he also asked him about a couple of little things that St. John had been interested in—some articles of clothing and a washcloth. Did Smith have any recollection of items like that? Yes, some things were stuffed in a storm drain a couple of miles south of San Pedro. There was blood on the clothes—his clothes, Smith said. He'd wiped all the makeup off her face with a washcloth. He threw that away with the clothes." (Note 27, p. 202).

Unfortunately, just days before his arrest, Jack Anderson Wilson (Smith) died on February 4, 1982, as a result of a fire in the Holland Hotel near downtown Los Angeles. St. John was unable to obtain the corroborative evidence that would establish beyond a reasonable doubt who murdered the Black Dahlia, although Jack Anderson Wilson certainly appeared to be the killer.

As you will see this case has more twists and turns than a bent corkscrew. St. John was close–really close, but according to author John Gilmore, "John St. John's dream of being the cop to 'officially' break the Dahlia case had gone up in smoke with the death of Arnold Smith, a/k/a Jack Anderson Wilson." Contrary to popular belief, this case can be solved even though Arnold Smith has gone up in smoke. When Smith met with John Gilmore in the early 80's Smith made a statement that is of significance. Smith, speaking of the Black Dahlia said, "One time she was giving a blowjob to a sailor in a back booth and nobody was paying fucking attention, well . . . almost nobody. Someone saw it as a betrayal. Going against what someone's got in their thinking. That's why she wasn't living any longer than she did." Smith was also quoted earlier as saying that the killing of the Black Dahlia was "justified." In my estimation Smith may very well been exhibiting jealousy towards the Black Dahlia. If this was in fact the case, then there is a possibility that he stalked her and may have followed her to Chicago in 1945 and 1946. It would be interesting to find out if Illinois State Police records reflect an arrest record on Jack Anderson Wilson during that time. To reinforce the jealousy theory, consider this: Following the murder of the Black Dahlia, Los Angeles policewoman Myrl McBride reported that on the afternoon of January 14, 1947, Elizabeth Short approached her "sobbing in terror." Short told McBride, "Someone wants to kill me." Officer McBride said that Short told her she "lives in terror" of a former serviceman whom she had just met in a bar up the street. McBride added, "She told me the suitor had threatened to kill her if he found her with another man" (Note 28, p. 237). If the former boyfriend was Jack Anderson Wilson, then it would appear that he may have been jealous and if he was a jealous suitor, he may very well have been stalking her. It may then logically follow that Jack Anderson Wilson might have been stalking Elizabeth Short during 1945-1946 when she was in Chicago, at the same time Ross, Brown and Degnan were murdered in that city.

I discovered the corroborating evidence that John St. John needed to connect Arnold Smith with the murder of the Black Dahlia, in the history of a Cleveland Torso murders that occurred twelve years before the murder of Elizabeth Short. According to the Cleveland Police records in 1937, Cleveland Detective Orley May reported on a tip that was typical of thousands of tips the police department were given regarding the Cleveland Torso murders. Orley is quoted as having said:

> Detective Musil and I received information from a person who does not want her identity revealed and who stated that while she was in the workhouse, a woman by the name of Helen O'Leary, who was the former wife of a man who was shot and killed several years ago—since got married to Gas House O'Malley, a stage hand, told her that she knew the man that killed Florence Polillo. She asked him who it was and she said "You know, his name is Jack Wilson." We learned from the informer that Jack Wilson was a former butcher and worked for Sam who operated a grocery store and meat market on St. Clair Avenue, and that he was known to carry a large butcher knife. Informant also stated that this Wilson was a sodomist, and that he committed sodomy on a number of persons known by the informant and is committing these decapitated (sic) murders in Kingsbury Run and may be killing them for the purpose of committing Sodomy on the victims, and would be a good suspect in the above murder (Note 26 & Note 20, p. 58).

Unless there were two sodomists by the name of Jack Wilson during this time period who were butchering people, then it is a reasonable assumption that Jack Anderson Wilson of Los Angeles and Jack Wilson of Cleveland, fingered by the woman from the workhouse as the killer of Flo Polillo and other victims in Kingsbury Run, was one and the same person. That being the case, then Jack Anderson Wilson, a/k/a Arnold Smith, a/k/a Jack Wilson was, more than likely, the Mad Butcher of

Kingsbury Run and, as John St. John suspected, but was unable to definitively prove, the murderer of the Black Dahlia.

On July 18, 1990, Dr. Money, a forensic sexologist associated with Johns Hopkins University, commented on the Arnold Smith (Jack Anderson Wilson) interview: "Despite the incoherency of parts of the interview, the overall content is consistent with the possibility that Ms. Short met her death as the victim of a lust murderer. Lust murder is one of the 40 different paraphilias. Its Greek name is erotophonophilia . . . . I think it is very likely that Arnold Smith himself was the murderer of Ms. Short." Keep in mind that in the case of Suzanne Degnan, Dr. Jerry Kearns of the coroner's office indicated that her killer was "motivated by a powerful sex obsession" (Note 24).

There has always been a question surrounding the Cleveland Torso Murders regarding the reason for lack of resistance that was exhibited by the Butcher's victims. It was reported that a few of his victims may have been decapitated while still alive, which is highly unusual. Typically a person is killed by some other means and then the body is dismembered. For example, acting detective Charles O. Nevel theorized that the Tattooed Man had arrived in Cleveland by rail and had fallen asleep in Kingsbury Run. Nevel said, "While he was sleeping the maniac attacked him. First he cut his throat. Then he hacked away at the neck. Then he undressed the victim" (Note 20, p. 65). Torso witness Helen O'Leary thought that Jack Wilson "was committing sodomy on his victims." Keep in mind that there were reports of sexual perversion and promiscuity associated with several of the Torso Murders victims. Now consider what Arnold Smith (Jack Anderson Wilson) stated in his taped recordings when speaking about the Black Dahlia murder in Los Angeles: "See, she made my dick hard every time I looked at her mouth." Remember also that Jack Anderson Wilson had been arrested on May 9, 1948, for having sex with another man in a park. Wilson hung out with female impersonators and in 1958 while incarcerated in the Oakland City Prison he spoke about a queer's head he had seen at the 1936 Great Lakes Exposition in Cleveland. I suspect that a reasonable explanation for the lack of resistance exhibited by the victims of the Torso Killer may have been the result of immediate decapitation by the killer following a sexual act performed on the executioner by his victims. This may also account for the heads that were never found in several of the Torso Murders.

Jeanne Axford French (The Red Lipstick Murder)

Jeanne Axford French lived an interesting life in Los Angeles, albeit a short one. To her credit she had been an actress, registered nurse who traveled with famous people, and one of America's first female pilots. She became known as "the Flying Nurse." Like the Black Dahlia, Jeanne French became famous not in life but as a result of her untimely death at the hands of a deranged killer. On February 9, 1947, Jeanne French's life went into a tailspin. At 7:30 p.m. Sunday, February 9, she was seen with two men at the Plantation Café 10984 Washington Boulevard in Los Angeles. One of the men had "dark hair and a small mustache." French had been drinking heavily and appeared intoxicated. After she finished her meal at the Plantation she left the restaurant possibly with both men. At 10:00 p. m. that evening witnesses reported seeing French at the Turkey Bowl restaurant 11925 Santa Monica Boulevard. Half an hour later she was seen at a bar at 10421 Venice Boulevard. Fifteen minutes later she was at her estranged husband's home at Sanford and Colorado Boulevards. The two argued and she eventually drove off in her 1928 Ford Roadster. Just after midnight she showed up at the Picadilly drive-in restaurant at 3932 Sepulveda Boulevard. Again witnesses reported seeing her with "a dark-haired man with a small mustache." Detectives speculated that she latter left the Picidilly and drove off with the dark-haired man. A little after 8:00 a.m. in the morning of February 10, 1947, exactly twenty-seven days after the murder of the Black Dahlia, construction worker Hugh Shelby discovered the nude body of Jeanne French in the 3200 Block of Grandview Avenue. According to Captain Jack Donahoe, she had been beaten with "a heavy weapon, probably a tire iron or a wrench, as she crouched naked on the highway" (Note 28, p. 189-195).

On November 15, 1950, Lt. Frank Jamison gave the following report on the Jeanne French murder:

> The body of Jeanne French was discovered at 8:15 A.M. on February 10, 1947, at a spot in the weeds, lying face up with her feet sixteen feet from Grand View Avenue, at a point 303 feet north of Indianapolis Street in West Los Angeles. Her body was nude and her clothes were piled on top of her body. Her shoes were found some fifty or sixty feet in two different directions, apparently thrown by the murderer into the field. Her pocketbook

was lying some ten feet from her body. A piece of lipstick was found just under the body, and written on the body in lipstick was the writing, "Fuck you, B.D." and "Tex." These writings were on the lower abdomen of the body. Her face was completely covered with bruises, blood and mud. The face had been apparently beaten into a pulp. There were no knife cuts on the body. The tissues of the anus were bruised about one-eighth of an inch. There was no death weapon found. There were several wounds in head, apparently administered by a steel blunt instrument, and which could have been, according to Autopsy Surgeon Newbarr, a socket wrench. These blows on the head did not cause death. The cause of death was due to hemorrhage and shock from fractured ribs and multiple injuries caused by stomping no doubt with feet, as heel prints were visible on the chest of the victim and a small heel print appeared in the mud right near the victim's face which appears to be smaller in size (six or seven shoe in men's sizes). There were other footprints further away from the body which were prints of larger sizes; however, the Crime Laboratory Chief, Lee Jones, believes they could have been caused by the newspaper reporters coming up later. According to Dr. Newbarr, the victim no doubt took some period of time to die after the administration of the stomping and the crushing of the ribs, which had penetrated her lung and liver causing hemorrhage, and which caused the victim to slowly bleed to death, as she was no doubt knocked unconscious by the blow on the head in the first instance. The physical evidence establishes the victim was murdered at the scene where the body was found, but apparently she had been knocked unconscious, possibly by the suspect's car, and dragged from the car into the field where he administered the stomping. See the enlarged photographs attached and also the crime Lab. Plaster cast of the killer's heel. Dr. Newbarr stated that it was possible that this victim was administered this beating and stomped as early as 2:30 A.M. or 3:00 A.M., February 10, 1947.

This crime became known as "the Lipstick Murder." The Los Angeles detectives thought that the murder of Jeanne French might have been linked to the murder of Elizabeth Short. Short had been killed on January 14, 1947. After the murder of Elizabeth Short a Corporal Joseph Dumais had supposedly signed a bogus confession to the crime. Detectives theorized that the Black Dahlia Avenger may have killed French in order to establish that Dumais was not the killer. There also has been as much speculation that the murder of Jeanne French was a completely separate murder and in no way connected to the murder of Elizabeth Short. There are clues that point towards the same killer that should be considered:

1. There may have been two individuals involved in the murder of Jeanne French, one of which may have worn size 6-7 men's shoe size. Keep in mind that two men may have been involved in the kidnapping/murder/dismemberment of Suzanne Degnan in Chicago on January 7, 1946.

2. The Los Angeles detectives found a man's white handkerchief at the scene of the French murder. A man's "balled-up handkerchief" was associated with the murder of Suzanne Degnan in Chicago and a man's "balled-up handkerchief" was found at the murder scene of Gladys Eugenia Kerns, February 14, 1948, in Los Angeles, exactly one year after the murder of Elizabeth Short. Some Los Angeles detectives thought the Kerns murder may have been related to the murder of The Black Dahlia.

3. The killer of Jeanne French had draped her coat, trimmed with red fox fur-cuffs, and her red dress over the body before leaving the scene. The Mad Butcher of Kingsbury Run wrapped the severed head of the Tattooed Man in his pants and the killer of Josephine Ross and Frances Brown wrapped a dress and pajamas around the heads of his Chicago victims.

4. The killer of Jeanne French wrote in red lipstick on her abdomen, "Fuck you, B.D." The killer of Frances Brown left a message on her wall written in red lipstick. The Mad Butcher of Kingsbury Run wrote the word "NAZI" on the abdomen of one of his victims.

5. The murder of Jeanne French occurred exactly 27 days after the murder of the Black Dahlia. The murder of Suzanne Degnan occurred exactly 27 days after the murder of Frances Brown in Chicago.

6. The body of Jeanne French was deposited in a vacant lot in Los Angeles. The body of Elizabeth Short was deposited in a vacant lot in Los Angeles.

7. On Tuesday, February 11, 1947, Los Angeles cab driver Charles Schneider discovered a note in his cab possibly written by the killer of the Black Dahlia. The note read: "Take it to examiner at once, I've got the number of your cab. $20,000 and I'll give B.D. up. Is it a go? B.D." Following the murder of Suzanne Degnan, her killer left a ransom note in her bedroom demanding $20,000.

In 1946, Captain Donahoe "told the public that in his opinion the Black Dahlia and the Lipstick Murders were likely connected" (Note 28, p. 195).

Is it possible that the same person or persons who killed Ross, Brown and Degnan also killed the Black Dahlia and Jeanne French the following year? Could the killer or killers have traveled from one state to another and committed similar crimes? If it could be established that whoever killed the Black Dahlia and Jeanne French in 1947, also killed Ross, Brown and Degnan in Chicago, then obviously it would be physically impossible for William Heirens to have committed the offences he was charged with because he was in custody in Chicago at the time the Black Dahlia and Jeanne French were killed in Los Angeles in 1947. From a statistical standpoint it is unlikely that a sadistic psychopathic killer would be dismembering a child in Chicago in January, 1946, and a different individual would commit a similar crime in Los Angeles one year later. From a probability standpoint it may be more plausible that the same individual was involved in both series of murders. For Mr. Heirens' benefit both the Los Angeles and the Chicago murders should be reevaluated to see if there is any connection.

Here is an odd coincidence: according to A. L. Brodie's Coroner's Report dated January 8, 1946, Suzanne Degnan was born in Worchester, Massachusetts, in 1940. Before moving to Miami Beach in 1942, Elizabeth Short lived with her mother in Medford, Massachusetts, approximately 35 miles from Worchester. Could there be some connection here that went unnoticed? Was Elizabeth an acquaintance of the Degnan family? According to published reports, she may have been in Chicago in 1946 when Suzanne Degnan was murdered. There is also some speculation that Elizabeth Short had a great deal of interest in the Degnan murder. Jim and Helen Degnan (parents of Suzanne Degnan) had grown up on the East Coast and had moved only recently from Baltimore, Maryland, where they resided while Jim Degnan traveled to Washington, D.C., to his position with the Office of Price Administration, popularly known as the OPA. The OPA had been created during the war in order to issue ration cards and keep prices under control. Degnan had been instrumental in its formation, but already the organization was meeting resistance from areas under control, particularly the meat and dairy industry, where black market meat was continuing to thrive in the oppressed market. Degnan had been transferred to Chicago to assist in the administration of the troubled Midwest contingency. It is interesting to note that according to his rap sheet, one of Jack Anderson Wilson's many social security numbers may have been obtained while in the State of Maryland.

OTHER LOS ANGELES VICTIMS

Ica Mable M'Grew

On Wednesday, February 12, 1947, two days after the murder of Jeanne French, twenty-seven-year-old Ica Mable M'Grew reported that she was kidnapped and forcibly raped in Los Angeles. She reported that two men forced her into their car and drove her to an isolated location on East Road in Los Angeles where they both raped her. One of her attackers warned her, "Don't tell the police, or I'll do to you the same as I did to the Black Dahlia." A news article described the two rapists as "two swarthy men."

Evelyn Winters

On March 12, 1947, the nude body of Evelyn Winters was found on a vacant lot at 830 Ducommun Street, near railroad tracks. She had been severely bludgeoned. The cause of death was due to "blunt force trauma causing a concussion and hemorrhage to the brain" (Note 28, p. 402). The killer had wrapped the victim's dress around her neck. (Recall the case of Josephine Ross in Chicago, June 5, 1945, in which her killer wrapped her head in a dress.) Evelyn Winters was an alcoholic who frequently visited downtown bars on Hill Street in Los Angeles. The police believed her murder was related to the deaths of Elizabeth Short and Jeanne French. The LAPD listed the following similarities in the murders of Elizabeth Short, Jeanne Axford French and Evelyn Winters:

1. All three girls frequented cocktail bars and sometimes picked up men in them.
2. All three were slugged on the head (although Mrs. French was trampled to death and Miss Short tortured and cut in two).
3. All three were killed elsewhere and taken in cars to the spots where the bodies were found.

4. All three were displayed nude or nearly so.
5. In no case was an attempt made to conceal the body. On the contrary bodies were left where they were sure to be found.
6. Each had been dragged a short distance.
7. Each killing was a pathological case, apparently motivated by psychological lust.
8. In each case the killer appears to have taken care not to be seen in company with the victim.
9. All three women had good family backgrounds.
10. Each was identified by her fingerprints, other evidence of identity having been removed.
11. Miss Short and Miss Winters were last seen in the same Hill Street area. For whatever it is worth, I am adding another similarity:
12. Evelyn Winters was an alcoholic. On the night she was abducted and murdered, Jeanne French had a blood alcohol content of .30, twice what was then considered legally drunk. By all accounts Elizabeth Short was well liked and a very good person. There has been, however, some speculation, although unproven, that she may have prostituted herself and was down on her luck. All of the women seemed to fit the type of person this predator looked for.

Laura Elizabeth Trelstad

On May 11, 1947, Laura Elizabeth Trelstad's body was found in the 3400 block of Locust Avenue in Long Beach, California. The cause of death was strangulation with "a piece of flowered cotton cloth, believed torn from a man's pajamas or shorts." She had been raped and the autopsy confirmed the presence of semen. If still available, there may be a possibility of DNA analysis.

Rosenda Josephine Mondragon

On July 8, 1947, the body of Rosenda Josephine Mondragon was located at 129 East Elmyra Street in Los Angeles near railroad tracks. She was drunk the night of her murder. A silk stocking was found wrapped around her neck. Her right breast had been slashed. (Recall that the right breast of Elizabeth Short had been severed.)

Los Angeles Map 2

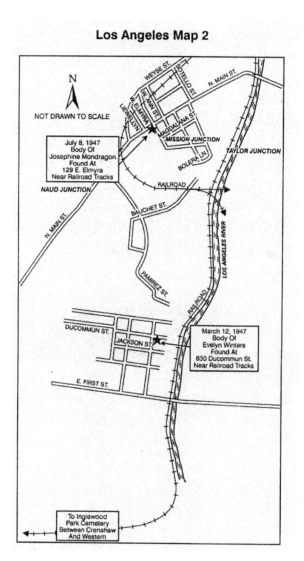

Los Angeles map showing the location of the bodies of Josephine Mondragon and Evelyn Winters. Note the close proximity to railroad tracks

Viola Norton

On February 14, 1948, Viola Norton was savagely attacked near the location where the Black Dahlia had been killed. "Two men both appearing to be approximately 40 years of age approached her in a car and asked her to get in." She was walking home from a cocktail lounge in Alhambra near Los Angeles. She was forced into the car and severely beaten on her face and head with a tire iron. Her assailant left her for dead four blocks from where the Black Dahlia had been found a little more than one year earlier on January 15, 1947.

Louise Margaret Springer

On June 13, 1949, Louise Margaret Springer was kidnapped and murdered in Los Angeles. She was strangled with a thin white clothesline cord. She worked at a beauty parlor in a department store at Santa Barbara and Crenshaw just two blocks from where Elizabeth Short's body had been found two and a half years earlier (Note 30, p. 411). Her assailant inserted a 14-inch length of finger-thick tree branch into her vagina. Witnesses reported the assailant of Louise Margaret Springer as a "white man with curly hair."

Similarities Between Jack Anderson Wilson, the Cleveland Torso Killer and the killer of Josephine Ross, Frances Brown and Suzanne Degnan

If Jack Anderson Wilson did in fact commit the Torso Murders between 1935-1938, in Cleveland and the murder of the Black Dahlia on January 14, 1947, it is a fairly safe bet that he committed other murders somewhere else between those time periods. Josephine Ross, Frances Brown and Suzanne Degnan were all killed during the years 1945-1946. Los Angeles County Detective Joel Lesnick stated: "With his 'rightful name' documented, Wilson now shows up in L.A., working as a sign hanger for Coger Brothers on Bixel Street. He gets picked up by the police for a Selective Service violation, then leaves the sign hanging job and drifts back to Indianapolis. He seems to hang out again with a female impersonator and turns twenty-four in August, 1943. He is bumbling around the city until a young female, a WAC, is murdered in a downtown hotel. And it seems that immediately Wilson leaves Indianapolis and turns up back in Los Angeles." Keep in mind that Josephine Ross was murdered on June 5, 1945, in Chicago. Indianapolis is located approximately 185 miles from Chicago. The New York Central runs from Indianapolis to Chicago.

1. Jack Anderson Wilson spent his early years in Ohio, and he admitted attending the Great Lakes Exposition in Cleveland in 1936.
2. The Cleveland Torso Murders began in 1934, and "officially" ended in 1938.
3. Jack Anderson Wilson "appeared in Los Angeles in the late 1930's."
4. Additional Torso murders took place from 1938-1942, in Pennsylvania.
5. Wilson reappeared in Los Angeles in 1942.
6. Wilson was regarded as a probable suspect in the murders of Georgette Bauerdorf and Elizabeth Short.
7. The killer of Elizabeth Short used a large knife to bisect her.
8. Wilson may have discarded clothing and other evidence down storm drains. The Cleveland Torso Killer and the killer of Suzanne Degnan discarded body parts and other evidence down storm sewers.
9. The New York Central runs from Indianapolis to Chicago and from Indianapolis to Cleveland. Jack Anderson Wilson was in Indianapolis when he turned 24. "He is bumbling around the city until a young female, a WAC, is murdered in a downtown hotel. And it seems that immediately Wilson leaves Indianapolis and turns up back in Los Angeles" (Note 27, p. 200-201). One of the victims William Heirens pled guilty to killing, Frances Brown, was a WAVE.
10. Cuyahoga County Coroner Samuel Gerber speculated that the Butcher was probably right-handed and dismembered his victims with a large heavy butcher's knife. As Arnold Smith's (Jack Anderson Wilson's) transcript provided, "Then he said there was a larger knife like a long butcher knife that was two inches, the width of the blade near the handle" (Note 27, p. 188).
11. Victim No. 6 was found in Kingsbury Run September 10, 1936. At the scene the police found a twelve-by-sixteen-inch piece of faded green underwear bearing the laundry mark "J.W." on the waistband. Could the initials have stood for "Jack Wilson"?
12. The bloody underwear found with the remains of Victim No. 4 (the "Tattooed Man") had the following laundry marks: "J.D.A." or J.D.X." One of Jack Anderson Wilson's alias's was "Jack Deavilen." Could the initials have possibly stood for "Jack Deavilen Anderson or Jack Deavilen?" The "X" was usually included as

a laundry mark if two laundry customers have the same last name.

13. Torso witness Helen O'Leary indicated that the person who killed Flo Polillo in 1935, was "Jack Wilson." She also indicated that Jack Wilson was a former butcher who worked in a Cleveland butcher shop, carried a large butcher knife and was a sodomist.

14. Jack Anderson Wilson was a convicted sodomist.

15. The Cleveland Torso killer was a necrophiliac.

16. The person who killed Elizabeth Short was a suspected necrophiliac.

Similarities Between the Cleveland Torso Murders and the Murder of the Black Dahlia

Cleveland Torso Murders	Black Dahlia
1. Torso victim Edward Andrassy had rope burns on his wrist.	1. She had rope burns on her wrists.
2. Torso Victim No. 2 may have been immersed in some sort of fluid before being dumped at the base of Jackass Hill in Cleveland.	2. She may have been immersed in water before being dumped in a vacant lot. Detective Finnis Brown stated, "maybe she's been in water" (Note 27, p. 13).
3. The body of Edward Andrassy had been drained of all its blood by his killer before being dumped.	3. Her body was drained of all blood before being dumped in the vacant lot.
4. The Torso Killer transported some body parts in burlap sacks and baskets.	4. Her lower torso was carried from the killer's vehicle on a cement bag.
5. Authorities thought the Torso Killer had either medical training or was a butcher. If Jack Wilson of Cleveland and Jack Anderson Wilson of Los Angeles were the same person and if he was in fact born in 1920, then Wilson would have been just over 15 years old on January 23, 1936, when Flo Polillo was murdered and dismembered in Cleveland.	5. Her killer had the "finesse of a surgeon."

6. When disposing of his victims, the Torso Killer "manifested an odd combination of obsessive neatness and casual sloppiness." The killer of Victim No. 4 (the "Tattooed Man") placed his shoes about twenty feet from the head, their laces tied together and stuffed with a pair of dark striped socks with orange tops. The head of the fourth victim had been carefully rolled up in his pants and deliberately deposited under a willow tree, just as pieces of Flo Polillo's body had been neatly wrapped in newspapers, placed in burlap bags, packed in baskets and deposited behind Hart Manufacturing Plant 2340 East 22nd in Cleveland six months before (Note 20, p. 63).

6. Her killer carefully "arranged her shoes on either side of her head an equal distance of approximately ten feet.

"The upper torso appears to have been placed asymmetrically approximately twelve inches above the lower portion and offset to the left approximately six inches. Both of the victim's arms are raised above the head, the right arm at a forty-five-degree angle away from the body, then bent at the elbow to form a ninety-degree angle. The left arm extends at a similar angle away from the body, and then bends again to form a second ninety-degree angle that parallels the body. This was no normal 'dumping' of a victim to get rid of a corpse quickly. In fact, the body had been carefully posed, just six inches from the sidewalk at a location where the victim was certain to be discovered, to create a shocking scene" (Note 28, p. 13).

7. Torso Killer inserted a pants pocket into a female victim's rectum.

8. The Torso Killer left deep gashes in the thighs of Victim No. 10.

9. The Torso Killer left his victims' bodies naked.

10. Some of the Torso Killer's victims were killed in one location and transported to another.

11. The Torso Killer used a large, sharp knife.

12. The Torso Killer drenched a victim's body in oil.

13. The Torso Killer taunted the police with their inability to catch him.

14. The Torso Killer was an "organized killer."

15. On December 23, 1938, someone sent a letter to the Chief of Police in Cleveland suggesting that he might be the Torso Killer, that he had gone to Los Angeles for the winter, and that he buried a head "without the features" on Century Boulevard between Crenshaw and Western in Los Angeles.

7. Her killer cut flesh from her leg and pushed it up her rectum.

8. Her killer cut a chunk of flesh from her thigh.

9. Her killer left her body naked.

10. She was killed elsewhere and dumped in a vacant Los Angeles lot.

11. Her killer used a large, sharp knife.

12. Her personal belongings were drenched in gasoline.

13. Her killer taunted the police with their inability to catch him.

14. Her killer was an "organized killer."

15. On or about January 14, 1947, the severed body of the Black Dahlia was found on the corner of 39th and Norton between Crenshaw and South Western in Los Angeles.

16. The Torso Killer may have refrigerated a body of one of his victims.

17. According to the Cleveland police, the Torso Killer was probably a necrophiliac.

18. The Torso Killer bisected the bodies of six of his victims.

19. One of the Torso Killer's victims' palms was burned. He may have been tortured.

20. The skull of Victim No. 8, tentatively identified as belonging to Rose Wallace, was found under the Loraine-Carnegie Bridge in Cleveland in 1936. "On the afternoon of her disappearance Merylo learned Wallace had been doing her laundry when a friend arrived and informed her that an unidentified man wanted to see her at an East 19th and Scoville bar close to her home. She left her laundry in the tub and headed for the sleazy establishment. According to witnesses, she later left with a dark-skinned white man named **Bob** for a party on the west side. Later still, a woman identified only as Mrs. Carter of Hazen Court reported seeing her in a car with three white men, but after that Rose Wallace simply vanished" (Emphasis added)(Note 20, p. 115).

21.**Flo Polillo, Victim No. 3, was bisected at the second lumbar vertebra* and**

16. Detectives thought her body may have been frozen before being severed.

17. Her body "was lacerated in an area below the naval down to the pubic area. The attacker may have had some usage of this area of the body." In other words he may have been a necrophiliac if sexual activity was after the victim was dead.

18. Her body was bisected.

19. She was tortured by her killer. She may have been burned on her breasts, possibly with cigarettes, although this was never confirmed, and possibly forced to eat human feces. I reviewed this issue with a highly respected Michigan coroner because similar granular material was found in Suzanne Degnan after she was dismembered. The coroner indicated that force applied to the body could push the person's own feces into the upper areas of the body.

20.On February 3, 1947, the *Los Angeles Herald-Express* ran an article about a forcible rape that occurred "near the Dahlia murder spot. A 30-year-old woman named Sylvia Horan had gone to Los Angeles alone to watch a movie. Afterwards she was standing on the corner of 7th Street and Broadway when a 'suave stranger', driving a black coupe, offered to drive her home. 'I accepted the ride,' she said, 'due to the late hour.' The stranger, who identified himself as '**Bob**,' drove her to a lonely spot on Stocker Boulevard between Crenshaw and LaBrea Avenues, only eight blocks from where the body of Elizabeth Short had been found, and forcibly raped her. Sylvia Horan might have been an important living witness to detectives in the Black Dahlia investigation had they linked the Horan crime to the Short case." (Emphasis added) (Note 28, p. 184).

21. **"The incision was performed through the abdomen above the naval**

a longitudinal incision ran the length of the lower half* (Dr. Reuben Straus, County Pathologist).

and then through the second and third lumbar vertebrae.*There is a gaping laceration of four-and-one-half inches which extends longitudinally to the superficial lacerations*(Dr. Frederic Newbarr, Chief Autopsy Surgeon for the County of Los Angeles). The incision may have been used as an artificial vagina postmortem. To quote Vincent Bugliosi in his book *And The Sea Will Tell*, "Aloha evidence."

22. It was speculated that the Torso Killer was a "large powerful man" (Note 20, p. 39).

22. The killer may have been "abnormally strong."

23. The Mad Butcher of Kingsbury Run "flaunted his crimes and horrified society with his atrocities." "The urge to show off his butchery was evident in the Torso Murder's decision to leave his final pair of Cleveland victims on the busy lakefront in full view of city hall and the Office of Safety Director Ness (Note 31, p. 216).

23. The Black Dahlia Avenger was an egomaniac who planned the murder to show the world he was a superman, someone who could, "outwit and outthink the whole world." The killer had placed the body where it would be quickly found and mutilated it so horribly to attract the greatest attention on the part of the police and public (Note 28, p. 164-165).
The killer of Suzanne Degnan fits the same mold.

24. Three murder victims were found at McKees Rocks, Pennsylvania, on May 3, 1940. One of the victims had the word "NAZI" carved in his chest. The pattern of dismemberment strongly resembled that practiced by the Torso murderer. Dr. P. R. Heimfold, a coroner's physician in Pittsburgh indicated that the killer tried to burn the bodies. He also indicated that the bodies had been cut "by an expert who had some knowledge of anatomy **or was a butcher**" (Emphasis added) (Note 22, p. 153).

24. The killer of Jeanne French wrote the words, "Fuck You B.D." on the midsection of her body in red lipstick.

25. The body of Victim No. 9, unlike any other, had been dismembered. The entire abdomen had been split open and its contents gutted. The heart had also been removed; the killer had cut through the

25. Detective Herman Willis indicated that, "the killer had cut out parts of some basic female organs." There was an apparent cavity where it appeared that organs had been removed from the body (Note 27, p. 5).

chest with a single decisive stroke and ripped out the organ with his hand. None of the internal organs were ever located (Note 20, p. 120).

26. Victim No. 11 was found at the East 9th Lake Shore dumpsite in Cleveland. The human torso was wrapped in **heavy brown paper** used by butchers (Note 20, p. 134).

26. Following the murder of the Black Dahlia, a mysterious package was located at the Biltmore Hotel. The package was **wrapped in brown paper.**

27. Deputy Coroner Chamberlain reported that Edward Andrassy had a mysterious, small pock-mark like scar on his forehead.

27. The killer of the Black Dahlia carved a scar on her forehead.

28. The sex organs were mutilated on No.'s 1,2,3 & 7. Detective Merylo believed the murderer committed crimes "solely for the sexual satisfaction he secured."

28. The Black Dahlia's killer performed a postmortem hysterectomy on her.

29. The thighs of Victim No. 11 were held together with rubber bands.

29. Arnold Smith brought a See's Candy box held together with rubber bands.

30. Cuyahoga County Coroner Samuel R. Gerber indicated "He may have been a doctor or medical student sometime in the past, a butcher, osteopath, chiropractor, orderly, nurse or hunter in order to accomplish the dissection with such finesse" (Note 22, p. 168).

30. The Black Dahlia was bisected by someone "with the finesse of a surgeon."

31. The torso of Victim No. 9 was found in 1937 packed in a burlap bag that was labeled "One Hundred Pounds of Purina Chicken Feed." The bag also contained a "perplexing clue": a cheap woman's silk stocking, in good condition, which contained a lone black and white dog hair and several short blond human hairs (Note 20, p. 118). Victim No. 9 was a forty-year-old man. Was the victim or his killer wearing silk stockings?

31. Several subsequent victims associated with the Black Dahlia murder were found strangled with silk or nylon stockings.

*Pathological Report on Suzanne Degnan dated January 8, 1946: "The trunk has been divided *at the level of the umbilicus* anteriorly and the *2nd lumbar vertebra* posteriorly," (Emphasis added) What you have here are two bisections at exactly the same location at the second lumbar vertebra, followed by a longitudinal laceration on the lower portion of the torso. This, coupled with the facts that the victim is nude, the blood has been completely drained from the body, and the bisection was done by someone with a great deal of skill, may cause the accusing finger to be pointed in one direction and one direction only. That there were two sadistic psychopathic killers in this same approximate time period, performing nearly identical incisions and mutilations on the bodies of their victims is not very likely. In the 1930's and 1940's the authorities determined that several different torso killers had mysteriously begun to appear in various locations in the United States. The torso killers manifested several of the same behaviors: In New Castle and in Cleveland they buried the head of a victim near the body in such a manner so that the police were sure to find it. They did not bury the body. In Cleveland, New Castle, West Pittsburgh, Haverstraw and Youngstown they all deposited torsos along or near railroad tracks; the bodies were nude, in several of the different locations the head was not with the torso, the blood was drained from the bodies, the dismemberments were completed by someone with a great deal of skill, and so on.

Similarities Between the Murder of the Black Dahlia and the Murder of Suzanne Degnan

The Black Dahlia

1. The Black Dahlia's body was bisected on or about January 14, 1947.

2. In the Jeanne French case, which was thought to be related to the Black Dahlia murder, the killer left a ransom note demanding $20,000.

3. The Black Dahlia Avenger wrote a note following the murder of the Black Dahlia: "Here is the photo of the Werewolf's killer's I saw him kill her." (California newspapers also described the killer of the Black Dahlia as the "werewolf," so the

Suzanne Degnan

1. Just over a year earlier on January 7, 1946, the dismembered body of Suzanne Degnan was found in Chicago.

2. The killer of Suzanne Degnan left a ransom note at the scene of the crime demanding $20,000.

3. Following the arrest of William Heirens in 1946, a Chicago daily newspaper wrote "The Werewolf was in Chains."

fact that the Chicago newspapers made reference to a werewolf may or may not mean anything.)

4. *Degnan* Boulevard is located approximately 370 feet from the corner of 39th and Norton in Los Angeles where the Black Dahlia was killed.

5. The killer of the Black Dahlia is suspected of using a tub and a knife in his murder.

6. Jack Anderson Wilson indicated that he discarded evidence in storm drains.

7. Jack Anderson Wilson burned evidence after the Black Dahlia was bisected.

8. The cut went straight through the narrowest part between the bottom of her ribs and navel.

9. Gladys Eugenia Kerns was killed in Los Angeles February 14, 1948. The man had dark curly hair. The murder weapon was an eight-inch jungle knife wrapped in a man's handkerchief. A balled-up handkerchief was found in the kitchen sink near the body.
In the Jeanne French homicide a man's white handkerchief was found near her body. Author Steve Hodel wrote on page 317 in *Black Dahlia Avenger:* "In my experience—which included the investigation of more than three hundred homicides—I have never encountered a case in which a suspect left a handkerchief at the scene of his crime. It is as if this was a 'calling card,' like dropping an ace of spades on the body."

10. Black Dahlia's killer soaked her purse and belongings in gasoline to destroy trace evidence.

11. "She was trussed up by ropes or maybe *wire* from some of the marks . . ." (Emphasis added) (Captain Jack Donahoe

4. Suzanne *Degnan* was killed in January, 1946.

5. The killer of Suzanne Degnan used a tub and knife in his murder.

6. The killer of Suzanne Degnan deposited body parts and other evidence in sewers (storm drains).

7. The "confession" of William Heirens in the Suzanne Degnan case indicates that evidence may have been burned following dismemberment.

8. Pathological Report on Suzanne Degnan: The trunk has been divided at the level of the umbilicus anteriorily and the 2nd lumbar vertebra posteriorly."

9. Two men's handkerchiefs were found at the Degnan murder scene. One found close to a loop of wire and the other rolled into a ball that may have been used as a gag (Note 22).

10. Her killer poured oil on the ransom note to destroy trace evidence.

11. A loop of *wire* may have been used to strangle her.

at Central Homicide). Marian Davidson Newton had been strangled in Los Angeles July 16, 1947, with a thin *wire* or cord." Arnold Smith talked about using wire on the Black Dahlia: "I don't mean the wire part of the hanger but like you got on the other kind of hanger, that's the hook on the top part of it, going over the clothes pole, but it wasn't like that, it was soft and around the frame part" (Transcript of Arnold Smith a/k/a Jack Anderson Wilson at the Los Angeles County Sheriff's Department).

12. Henry Silver, a document expert hired by the *Los Angeles Examiner* in 1947, said, "The sender is an egomaniac and **possibly a musician.** The fluctuating base line of the writing reveals the writer to be affected by extreme fluctuations of mood, dropping to melancholy" (Emphasis added) (Note 28, p. 173-174).

12. Arthur C. Becker, noted musical scholar, pointed out that resemblances of the ransom note to the letters in musical signs **indicated that the slayer of Suzanne Degnan was a musician** (Emphasis added).

"Investigators speculated yesterday on whether the slayer could have been a musician. The speculation arose after it was noted that some of the letters were similar to notes and symbols used in writing music. Musical scholars said an accomplished musician might unconsciously form letters to resemble the symbols (Note 25). In the murder investigation of Frances Brown, several of her musician friends were questioned since a few of the letters in the "red lipstick" message resembled musical notes.

13. On January 23, 1947, James Robinson, editor of the *Los Angeles Examiner,* received a telephone call from someone claiming to be the killer of the Black Dahlia. The caller indicated that he had certain items that belonged to the Black Dahlia, including "her address book and her birth certificate and a few other things she had in her handbag."

13. "Earlier today it was reported a mysterious man telephoned the Degnan home, demanded the ransom and asserted that he had a lock of Suzanne's blond hair and a piece of her blue pajamas."

14. The Black Dahlia's body was bisected on or about January 14, 1947.

14. Just under one year earlier, on January 7, 1946, the dismembered body of Suzanne Degnan was found in Chicago. One year earlier on January 14, 1945, Eunice Rawlings disappeared in Chicago.

15. The Black Dahlia was killed and bisected at one location and discarded in another.
16. The Black Dahlia was bisected by someone "with the finesse of a surgeon."
17. Georgette Bauerdorf was murdered in her Los Angeles apartment. The bottom portion of her pajamas was removed and she was found draped over her bathtub. The outside light to her apartment had been tampered with prior to her murder. She had been raped as she lay dying or was already dead.

18. Mimi Broomhower disappeared on August 24, 1949, in Bel Air. An unidentified witness found her white purse at 9331 Wilshire Blvd. in Beverly Hills, with a note written directly onto the purse. The note read, "POLICE DEPT,—WE FOUND THIS AT BEACH THURSDAY NIGHT" (Note 28, p. 322).

19. On June 13, 1949, Louise Margaret Springer was strangled to death in Los Angeles with a white sash cord. On July 16, 1947, Marion Newton was strangled to death in Los Angeles with a thin wire or cord (Note 28, p. 407).

15. The killer of Suzanne Degnan dismembered her at one location and discarded her body in another.
16. Suzanne Degnan was dismembered by someone with the "skill of a butcher."
17. Frances Brown was murdered in her Chicago apartment. Her killer had removed the bottom portion of her pajamas. She was found draped over the bathtub. Questioning in the William Heirens "confession" in the Suzanne Degnan murder case indicated that an outside light may have been tampered with by her assailant prior to the abduction. She may have been sexually assaulted.
18. Eighteen-year-old Eunice Rawling's torso was found on a Lake Michigan beach in Chicago on August 12, 1946. She had been missing since January 14, 1945. Her head and arms were missing and at the time the police determined the case to be a suicide. On January 17, 1945, a purse containing the girl's name on a slip of paper was found on the lake shore rocks near Addison. Eunice Rawlings lived in an apartment on Roscoe near Josephine Ross and Frances Brown. Does it make any sense that she would end her life by voluntarily jumping into the frigid waters of Lake Michigan in the middle of the winter? This is not a typical method for a young woman to commit suicide. Two days before she disappeared, Eunice was out looking for employment. It sounds a little odd for someone contemplating suicide to be out looking for a job. Could she have been forced to write the suicide note that indicated she could be found in Lake Michigan?
19. Two sash cords, apparently blood-stained were found in the alley near the Suzanne Degnan crime scene. "A loop of wire with a handkerchief was found north of the Degnan home" (Note 29, p. 49).

20. The killer of Jeanne French wrote on her body in **red lipstick**, February 11, 1947, in Los Angeles.

21. Los Angeles County Coroner Chief Surgeon, Fredrick Newbarr, noted that Elizabeth Short's stomach "was filled with greenish **brown granular material**, mostly fecal matter and other particles" (Emphasis added).

22. Following the murder of the Black Dahlia, the *Los Angeles Herald Express* received the following in pasted letters, "To Los Angeles Herald Express **I will Give up** in Dahlia Killing **If I Get 10 years.** Don't try to find me" (Emphasis added).

20. The killer of Frances Brown wrote on her living room wall in **red lipstick**, December 10, 1945 in Chicago.

21. The Pathological Report on Suzanne Degnan dated January 8, 1946, indicated that "the mucosa of the posterior pharynx, the aryepiglottic fold epiglottis and larynx were swollen and wrinkled pinkish red in color and covered with a **brownish granular viscid material**" (Emphasis added).

22. Shortly after the murder of Suzanne Degnan, Chicago Police Chief Walter G. Storm received the following communication: "Why don't you catch me. If you don't ketch me soon, I will cummit suicide. There is a reward out for me. **How much do I get if I give myself up.** When do I get that 20,000 dollars they wanted from the Degnan girl at 5901 Kenmore Avenue. You may find me at the Club Tavern at 738 E. 63rd St. known as Charlie the Greek's or at Conway's Tavern at 6247 Cottage Grove Av. Please hurry now" (Emphasis added). Jack Anderson Wilson was an alcoholic. In each series of murders bars become a meeting place.

Consider this:

Cleveland Torso Murders: Victim # 8, Rose Wallace. On the afternoon of her disappearance, Merylo learned Wallace had been doing her laundry when a friend arrived and informed her that an unidentified man wanted to see her at an East 19th and Scoville bar close to her home.

William Heirens Case: The killer wrote "you may find me at the Club Tavern at 738 East 63rd St. known as Charlie the Greeks or at Conway's Tavern at 6247 Cottage Grove Avenue.

Black Dahlia Murder: Jack Anderson Wilson met John Gilmore at Harold's 555 Club in Los Angeles. "In Indianapolis he (Wilson) mentions this person working in a bar called the Pair of Jacks and another joint Jud Logan's Bar in the same area."

Both individuals wrote a letter shortly after committing a murder. Both wrote the same content in their letters:

1. One wrote: "If I get ten years." The other one wrote: "How much do I get"
2. The other one wrote: "If I give up." The other one wrote: "I will give up."

Keep in mind that both killers murdered and bisected a human shortly before writing the letter (if in fact the letters were written by the killers). Both killers wrote a limited number of short communications, so with this in mind the similarities are striking.

Take notice the sequence of events in the Black Dahlia case that are followed by a message written by her killer:

1. On January 14, 1947, Elizabeth Short is murdered and professionally bisected in one location and then secretly transported to another location where her body is deposited.
2. Soon after her murder the killer writes a note to the *Los Angeles Herald-Express*.
3. The note reads:

> To Los Angeles Herald-Express
> I will give up in
> Dahlia killing if I *Get*
> 10 years
> *Don't* try to find me (Emphasis added)

Now compare this to the sequence of events in the Suzanne Degnan case:

1. On January 7, 1946, Suzanne is taken secretly from one location to another where she is professionally dismembered and then taken to other locations where her body parts are discarded.
2. Soon after her murder her killer writes a note (ransom note) that reads:

> *Get* $20,000
> Reddy &

Waite
For Word
Do not notify
FBI or
Police
Bills in 5's &
10's (Emphasis added)

Both messages start out with a statement that includes the word "get" and end with a command that included either the word "don't" or the words "do not."

Here is another interesting comparison:

A fifth note sent by the Black Dahlia Avenger on January 29, 1947, provided;

A certain girl is going to get same as E.S.
got if she squeals on us.
We're going to Mexico City-*catch* us if
You *can* (Emphasis added)

Now compare this to the red lipstick message written on the wall of Frances Brown's apartment following her murder on December 10, 1945:

For heavens
sake *catch* me
before I kill more
I **can**not control myself (Emphasis added)

Note # 4 from the Black Dahlia Avenger to the *Los Angeles Herald-Express* reads as follows:

To Los Angeles Herald Express
I will give up in
Dahlia killing *if I get*
10 years
Don't try to find me (Emphasis added)

Following the murder of Suzanne Degnan, Chicago Police Chief Walter G. Storms received the following communication:

> Why *don't* you catch me. *If* you
> don't ketch me soon *I will*
> cummit suicide. There is a
> reward out for me. How much
> do *I get if I* give
> myself up. When do *I get*
> that 20,000 dollars they
> wanted from that Degnan girl at
> 5901 Kenmore Avenue.
> You may find me at the Club
> Tavern at 738 E. 63rd St
> Known as Charlie the Greeks. Or
> At Conway's tavern
> At 6247 Cottage Grove
> Av
> Please hurry now.

(It is interesting to note that the Degnan home was located:

5943 Kenmore Avenue.

The place of dismemberment:

5901 Winthrop Avenue.)

23. On January 30, 1947, The Black Dahlia Avenger wrote a pasted note to Captain Donahoe: "Have changed my mind, **you** would not give me a square deal. Dahlia Killing justified" (Emphasis added).

24. The nude body of Rosenda Josephine Mondragon (Los Angeles, July 8, 1947) was found with a silk stocking wrapped around her neck.

The body of Geneva Hilliker Ellroy was found June 22, 1958, in El Monte, California, with a nylon stocking wrapped around her neck (Note 28, p. 418). Elspeth Long was found January 22, 1959, in La Puente, California strangled to death. The suspect used Long's nylon as a ligature (Note 28, p. 420).

25 On January 14, 1947, the Black Dahlia is murdered in Los Angeles. Twenty-seven days later on February 10, French is brutally murdered and her killer writes on her body in red lipstick.

26. At 7:30 p. m. Sunday, February 9, 1947, the day before she was killed, Jeanne French was seen in the company of two men. Waitress Christine Studnicka described one of them as having, "dark hair and a small moustache." Studnicka observed that the two men appeared, "to be arguing over which one was going to accompany the victim.

On February 14, 1948, Viola Norton was approached near the east-southeast city limits of Los Angeles by two men in a car. The two men, both appearing to be approximately 40 years of age, approached her in a car and asked her to get in. "Viola was kidnapped by the two men, beaten savagely about the face and head. Her skull was fractured with a tire iron, and the two men left her for dead in an isolated area just four blocks from where the body of Elizabeth Short had been found thirteen months earlier."

Twelve hours later, Gladys Eugenia Kern

23. In the letter to Chief Storm, following the murder of Suzanne Degnan, the killer wrote, "**You** may find me at the club Tavern . . ." (Emphasis added)

24. Josephine Ross had a dress wrapped around her head securely tied with a silk stocking.

25. On December 10, 1946, Frances Brown is brutally murdered in Chicago. Her killer left a message on her living room wall in red lipstick. Twenty-seven days later Suzanne Degnan is murdered and dismembered.

26. On the night Suzanne was murdered, Cecelia Flynn heard the sound of two men arguing on the street below.

Several months earlier two men had driven up to the Degnan house and attempted to force Suzanne into the car with them as she was returning home for lunch. Her screams had brought neighbors to the window and the men had fled, but it seemed more than coincidental.

was found at 4217 Cromwell Avenue. She had been stabbed with an eight-inch jungle knife that was found in the kitchen sink wrapped in a man's bloody handkerchief. Two witnesses, Japanese gardeners working across the street from the murder scene at the hillside mansion, were located by the police and told of seeing "two men coming out of the mansion, and down the steps on Saturday afternoon, the day of the murder."

27. "The broom was where the mop was and the mop and the rags were used and then these things went down and were put in the incinerator and lighted on fire" (Transcript of Jack Anderson Wilson on file at the Los Angeles County Sheriff's Department).

28. Following the murder of the Black Dahlia, her killer washed her body in a tub.

29. Jack Anderson Wilson was employed in Los Angeles as a sign hanger for Cogar Brothers on Bixtel Street.

30. Los Angeles County Sheriff's Detective Joel Lesnick indicated that "Wilson (Jack Anderson Wilson) seemed to prefer the company of low-lifes, the moochers and apparently second-rate female impersonators. He referred to one being connected with a murder in Indianapolis and he mentions this person working in a bar called the Pair of Jacks and another joint, Jud Logan's Bar in the same area."

31. Cleveland's director of Public Safety, Elliot Ness's assistant, was John R. Flynn.

32. A pasted note, possibly mailed by the killer of the Black Dahlia, was addressed to Los Angeles Captain Donahoe, following her murder.

27. "Charles Wilson, head of the police crime laboratory, disclosed that bits of cotton fabric saturated with blood found in the laundry room drain of the apartment house at 5901 Winthrop Avenue indicated that the basement room in which police believe the girl's body was dismembered subsequently had been mopped."

28. Following the murder of Frances Brown, her killer washed her body in a tub.

29. A length of picture wire drawn into a noose was associated with the murder of Suzanne Degnan.

30. In the communication received by Chicago Chief of Police Walter G. Storm the individual stated: "You may find me at the Club Tavern at 738 E. 63rd Street known as Charlie the Greeks or at Conway's Tavern At 6247 Cottage Grove Av."

31. Louis and Cecelia Flynn occupied the second floor of the building at 5943 Kenmore in Chicago where the Degnan family lived. Cecelia Flynn was also involved with the OPA.

32. Chicago Police Chief Storm received a note in 1946, following the murder of Suzanne Degnan, possibly mailed by her killer.

33. "Of the times the informant met with Smith, he said the man never referred to Elizabeth Short by name. 'He did not call her Elizabeth, or the Short girl, or Beth. He would say **her**, or like he would say **her**, who we're talking about'" (Emphasis added) (Note 27, p. 181).

33. Suzanne Degnan's killer wrote on the reverse side of the ransom note, "BuRN This FoR **heR** SAfeTY" (Note 28, photo following p. 200).

34. Wrote large letter before small letter in same word of a note: "To HeralD-EXPess
        BUiLDiNG1234
        TReNton.St.
        Zone is LoS ANGele"
    (Note 20, p. 178)

34. Wrote large letter before small letter in the same word in the ransom note (See No. 33 above).

35. Letter "P" in word "EXPRESS" on the Black Dahlia Avenger's envelope to *Los Angeles Herald Express,* postmarked Jan. 28, 1947, is similar to letter "P" in the Suzanne Degnan ransom note. (Note 28, p. 175)

35. Letter "P" in the Suzanne Degnan ransom note is similar to letter "P" on the Black Dahlia Avenger's envelope postmarked January 28, 1946 (Note 29, photo following p. 200).

36. While in Indianapolis Jack Anderson Wilson associated with female impersonators.

Twenty-one-year-old Dorothy French had befriended Elizabeth in Los Angeles. Elizabeth stayed with her for a while. After the murder, Dorothy recalled an incident that took place shortly after Elizabeth was killed: "A couple of days later some people came to our door and knocked. There was a man and a woman, and another man was waiting in a car parked on the street in front of the house. Beth became very frightened—she seemed to get panicky and didn't want to see the people or answer the door. They finally went back to the car and drove away. Even our neighbors thought all of this was very suspicious" (Note 29, p. 110).

36. On the night of her abduction a witness saw a woman carrying a large bundle in both arms in the vicinity of the Degnan home. "She got into what seemed to be a waiting automobile where a balding man sat behind the wheel."

37. The FBI suspected that Jack Anderson Wilson's friend "Eddie," was involved in an earlier kidnapping."

37. Suzanne Degnan was kidnapped. At first the detectives suspected that two men might have been involved in the kidnapping.

38. Captain Jack Donahoe was of the opinion that a woman may have been the murderer based on the nature of the injuries and the spite with which

38. In the murder of Frances Brown detectives speculated that a woman was involved because of wording in the lipstick message: "For Heavens Sake." Frances

they were inflicted. (Possibly a female impersonator?)

39. On the afternoon of January 14, 1947, Elizabeth Short was identified by Los Angeles police officer Myrl McBride as the woman who ran up to her "sobbing in terror" and told her that "someone wants to kill me." Short said that she had come from a bar up the street and had just run into an ex-boyfriend. Officer McBride said that Short told her she "lives in terror" of a former serviceman whom she had just met in a bar up the street. McBride added, "She told me the suitor had threatened to kill her if he found her with another man." McBride said she walked the victim back into the Main Street Bar, where she recovered her purse. A short time later, McBride again observed the victim "reenter the bar, and then emerge with two men and a woman" (Note 28, p. 236-237).

40. Jeanne French's killer draped her blue coat and her red dress over her body before leaving the scene (Note 28, p. 190). Evelyn Winters was found with her dress wrapped around her neck (Note 28, p. 403). Louise Springer's body was found draped and covered with a white cape-type material which belonged to the victim (Note 28, p. 411). Geneva Ellroy's killer placed her dark blue coat over the lower portion of her body (Note 28, p. 418).

41. The cause of Evelyn Winter's death was listed as "blunt force trauma causing a concussion and hemorrhage to the brain (Note 28, p. 402). Viola Norton's skull was fractured with a tire iron (Note 28, p. 410).

42. Following the murder of the Black Dahlia a witness by the name of John Jiroudek told detectives he saw Elizabeth Short at the corner of Hollywood Boulevard and Highland Avenue. She was a passenger in a 1937 Ford Sedan. A blond female was driving the car (Note 28, p. 236).

Brown and Josephine Ross were both viciously attacked.

39. On the night of Suzanne's abduction and murder Cecelia Flynn recalled hearing two men talking in the street near the Degnan home.

40. Josephine Ross' head was wrapped in her daughter's red dress (Note 29, p. 35). Frances Brown was found draped over her tub, half covered with a housecoat and her pajamas looped around her neck.

41. Josephine Ross was hit repeatedly in the head with a heavy object. Her killer stuck a knife four times in her throat (Note 29, p. 35).

42. On January 7, 1946, on the morning of the kidnapping, a witness by the name of Robert Reisner saw a man and a woman in a "1940 or 1941 Ford four door sedan, and the first two numbers of the 1945 Illinois license were 11 (Note 29, p. 47-48). The design of a 1937 Ford sedan, and a 1940 Ford sedan, although slightly modified, were very similar. Keep in mind that the witness reports were made over six years after the date of the crimes in 1946, and 1947, respectfully and one of the vehicles was sited after dark at 2:00 a.m.

In Appendix D to the book *Childhood Shadows: The Hidden Story of the Black Dahlia Murder*, author Mary Pacios included a list of major suspects in the Black Dahlia case.

The Cleveland Butcher is listed on page 249 and Jack Anderson Wilson is listed on page 250. Unknown at the time her book was written, these two suspects, identified on back-to-back pages, might have been the same person. Jack Anderson Wilson might have been the Mad Butcher of Kingsbury Run, the killer of the Black Dahlia and more than likely the killer of Jeanne French, Georgette Bauerdorf, Josephine Ross, Frances Brown, Suzanne Degnan and several other individuals during the 1930's and 1940's.

Chapter 4

THE PHANTOM KILLER OF TEXARKANA

This is the true story about one of the most feared and elusive serial killers of all time. It begins on a cold night in February, 1946, in Texarkana one hundred seventy five miles northeast of Dallas, Texas. Texarkana is now located on Interstate 30 between Dallas, Texas, and Conway, Arkansas, directly across the eastern Texas State line. In 1946, together with its twin city, Texarkana, Texas, its population was about forty thousand. On February 22, 1946, 19-year-old Mary Jeanne Larey attended a local Texarkana movie theater with her friend, 24-year-old Jimmy Hollis. After the movie was over the couple drove down and parked off Richmond Road. Mary Jeane's report of what happened next appeared the next day in the *Texarkana Gazette:*

Jimmy and I parked about 11:45 P.M. just off Richmond Road about a mile north of Beverly. We had been there about ten minutes when a man walked up. He wore a white mask over his head with cutout places for his eyes and mouth. He was pointing a flashlight and pistol at us. He came up on the driver's side of the car, shined his flashlight into our faces and told Jimmy something like this 'I don't want to kill you fellow, so do what I say.' We both got out of the car on Jimmy's side and stood by the man. The man then told Jimmy to 'take off your (expletive deleted) britches.' I told Jimmy to please take them off because I thought if he did, we wouldn't be hurt. After Jimmy had taken off his corduroy trousers, the man hit Jimmy twice on the head. The noise was so loud I thought Jimmy had been shot. I learned later that the sound was his skull cracking. I picked up Jimmy's pants and took the billfold out of his pocket. I said 'Look, he doesn't have any money.' The man told me I was lying. He said that I had a purse but that I told him I had not. Then he hit me. I thought with a piece of iron pipe. He knocked me to the ground but I managed to get up.

The man told her to run. She went towards the ditch, but he told her to go down the road. She passed an old car parked along the road. Mary Jeanne recalled: "Just after I got past the car the man overtook me and asked me why I was running. I told him because he told me to run. He called me a liar again and then I knew he was going to kill me." The man struck her again and she fell to the ground (Note 46). He sat on top of her then coughed, then wheezed, then snorted like a bull (Note 45). He did not rape her but she said he "abused her terribly." News reports later indicated that he used the barrel of his gun to sexually assault her. Both Mary Jeanne Larey and Jimmy Hollis survived the attack. Hollis later gave the police a statement. There was one key difference in Mary Jeanne's and Jimmy's account. She thought he was a light-skinned black man. Mary Jeanne "believed he was a Negro because of the way he pronounced the curse words he growled at her" (Note 47, Sunday, June 2, 1946). Jimmy thought he was a dark-tanned white man. Mary Jeanne described her attacker as a six-foot tall male.

A little over one month later on March 24, 1946, local war veteran, 29-year-old Richard Griffin and 17-year-old Polly Ann Moore, an employee of the Red River Arsenal, were found murdered in a car near Highway 67 on South Robinson Road one mile out of the Texarkana city limits. Their car and bodies were found not far from the Highway 67 nightspot called Club Dallas. Did someone stalk them from Club Dallas? Griffin and Moore were both shot in the back of the head. Their bodies were found in the rear seat of Griffin's car on the outskirts of Texarkana (*Washington Times-Herald*, April 15, 1946). According to Arkansas State Trooper Max Tackett, Moore had been killed in front of the car on a blanket and placed in the vehicle after she had been murdered. The couple was last seen around 10:00 P.M. the previous Saturday night in a West Seventh Street café where they ate dinner with Griffin's sister, Eleanor Griffin (*Texarkana Gazette*). Bullets found at the scene of the murders matched those fired from a .32 caliber pistol believed to be a Colt that was used in other of the Phantom killings.

One month later on April 13, 1946, Betty Jo Booker, a pretty 15-year-old brunette, was playing her saxophone with a band in a high school orchestra called the Rhthmaires at a local VFW dance hall at Fourth and Oak Streets in Texarkana. The dance was for "young people" (FBI Report on Phantom Killings). At about 1:30 A.M. 16-year-old James Paul Martin picked up Betty Jo after the dance and drove her to Spring Lake Park in Texarkana. The next day Martin's lifeless body was found on the side of Cork Lane north of Interstate 30. Betty Jo Booker's body was later located in a wooded area about a mile and a half away north of Interstate 30. Both victims had been shot dead with a .32 caliber Colt revolver (*Texarkana Gazette*). Bette Jo's saxophone was missing but was located four months later in a marshy area in the vicinity where her body was discovered. According to Jerry Akins, a member of the Rhythmaires Band, someone knew it was there and told authorities where to look for it. Did some other young person in the 15-16 age bracket, who attended the young people's dance, stalk and kill Booker and Griffin, or was someone waiting to stalk them as they left the dance?

In May, 1946, in Texarkana, Mrs. Aleene Peavy, age 30, was shot dead and Mrs. J. C. Johnson, age 42, was in critical condition from gunshot wounds. Mrs. Peavy had been shot in the head and died instantly. According to Bowie County Sheriff, W.H. Presley, "Mrs. Johnston was shot in the head, the bullet entering on the right side near the ear and leaving through the top of her skull." A revolver "of small caliber" was found beside Mrs. Johnston's body. Officers did not believe the attacks were the work of the Phantom Killer.

The Phantom Murders occurred on weekends. Each murder was approximately one month apart. On May 3, 1946, the Phantom Killer struck again, this time nine and one-tenth miles north of Texarkana on U.S. Highway 67. A 36-year-old farmer by the name of Virgil Starks sat quietly reading his newspaper when someone fired two shots from a .22 caliber semiautomatic from three feet through a closed front porch window of his farm house. Stark was struck in the back of his head and died instantly. His wife, Katy Starks was also shot by the same assailant through her right cheek and jaw but managed to escape and fled to a neighboring farmhouse owned by A. V. Prater. Three twenty-two long rifle Super X cartridge casings were found at the scene, together with a questionable footprint impression made with a left shoe, the size of which was approximately 9 ½ to 10 ½. The Texas Rangers investigated the string of unsolved Phantom Murders. Captain Manuel (Lone Wolf) Gonzaullas was the lead investigator. The Rangers were joined by at least forty-seven police officers, including Bowie County Sheriff W.H. "Bill" Presley, the Federal Bureau of Investigation and Sheriff W.E. Davis of Arkansas' Taylor County.

At the time detectives had very few clues to work with.

The Dallas Morning News reported on February 24, 1946, that "a woman clad in a nightgown, a housecoat and a street coat was found shot to death on the sidewalk in the 3600 block of Wendelkin shortly after midnight Monday." The lady's name was Beatrice Graham Thraser. "A .32 revolver with one shot fired was found lying at her feet." "The woman's crumpled body lay approximately in the middle of the block on the east side of the street. A single bullet hole was behind her right ear."

Texas Rangers had arrested a suspect in the Phantom Murders by the name of Youell Swinney. Swinney had a long arrest record. He was eventually convicted of car theft and was sentenced. Authorities questioned whether Swinney was the Phantom Killer because when he was in jail two murders, similar to the Phantom Murders, took place at Dania Beach in Fort Lauderdale, Florida. Edythe Elaine Eldridge, age 24, from South Chatham, Massachusetts, and Lawrence Overman Hogan, age 23, of Miami, Florida, formerly of Roanoke, Virginia, were found shot to death near Hogan's parked car on a lonely, secluded area on Dania Beach near the ocean. The weapon used was a .32 caliber.

In February, 2006, I received the complete FBI Report on the Phantom Murders under the Freedom of Information Act. Based on the information I have researched regarding the Phantom Murders, it is my understanding that most of the information contained in the FBI Report was never made public and, unless released in federal court at a later date, I doubt that anyone at a later date copied the non-disclosed information. According to the FBI Report on the Phantom Murders, a Mr. Clark Brown of 1417 Locust Street, Texarkana, the stepfather of Betty Jo Booker, received a letter and envelope after the murder of his stepdaughter. The letter was dated December 19, 1946, and was postmarked at Texarkana, Arkansas, on December 12, 1946, at 4:30 PM.

found on the morning of April 14, 1946, at approximately 6:30 AM near Spring
Lake Park north of Texarkana, Texas. The victim's car was found approximately
1½ miles southeast of his body. The body of BETTY JOE BOOKER was discovered
at approximately 11:30 AM on the same date in a wooded area southwest of the
body of JAMES PAUL MARTIN. BETTY JOE BOOKER had been shot twice; once through
the left side of the nose and the other through the left fifth rib. PAUL
MARTIN had been shot four times; once through the nose to the left of the
nasal arch, another bullet through the left level of the fourth rib, a third
bullet wound in the right hand, and the fourth bullet in the right part of his
head to the right of the middle line level of the upper portion of the ear.
A .32 automatic was again used, and the gun is identical with the gun used in
the first double murder. BETTY JOE BOOKER had definitely been assaulted.
These cases remain unsolved.

b6
b7C

At approximately 9:15 PM on May 3, 1946, VIRGIL STARKS, a
farmer and special deputy sheriff of Miller County, Arkansas, residing approximately 9½ miles north of Texarkana, Arkansas, was killed instantly while
sitting in his home. [   ]

[   ] The gun used
was a .22 caliber similar to a Colt Woodsman pistol. This case is also unsolved.

The stepfather of BETTY JOE BOOKER is CLARK BROWN, an employee
of the Gifford-Hill Company, Texarkana, Texas, and who formerly resided in the
Sussex Downs Addition of Texarkana, Texas, until approximately October of 1946,
at which time he moved to 1417 Locust Street, Texarkana, Arkansas. Since
December, 1946, BROWN has received the following letters:

  1st Letter — Postmarked: Texarkana, Arkansas-Texas
             December 17, 1946
             At 4:30 PM

      Addressed to: Mr. Clark Brown
             1417 Locust St
             City

"MR. BROWN:

   THIS IS ADDRESSED TO YOU PERSONALLY AND IS ONLY TO HELP
YOU AND MRS. BROWN. THE FOLLOWING INFORMATION IS CONFIDENTIAL
AND IF YOU DO NOT CARE FOR IT BURN IT UP IMMEDIATELY. CANNOT
COME TO EITHER OF YOU PERSONALLY. THIS CAR NUMBER AND PARTIES
WAS SEEN BY YOUNG GIRL WHO DOES NOT AND WILL NOT COME TO YOU

— 2 —

"ON ACCOUNT OF FEAR AND FOR HER SAKE IF NOT USED PLEASE BURN.
INFORMATION WAS GIVEN TO BOTH LAWS HERE AND ANOTHER AUTHORITY
SO BE CAREFUL AND FOR YOUR BENEFIT AND SUCCESS IN THIS USE
HIGHER AUTHORITIES. ▢▢▢▢▢▢▢▢▢▢▢▢▢▢▢▢▢▢▢▢▢▢▢▢▢▢▢▢▢

▢▢▢▢▢▢▢▢▢▢▢▢▢▢▢▢▢▢▢▢AND THAT IS WHY PROTECTED. KEEP
THIS INFORMATION CLOSE AND SORRY CANNOT SIGN AND SEE YOU
PLEASE BURN IF OF NO VALUE BUT IT IS IF YOU ONLY KNEW IT.
BE CAREFUL AND IF USED TRY HIGHER AUTHORITIES AND PLEASE DO
NOT QUESTION THIS AT ALL. THIS IS ONLY GIVEN FOR YOUR SAKES
AND NOTHING WANTED OR ASKED ONLY SUCCESS IF USED. MANY
KIND THOUGHTS FOR BOTH OF YOU AND USE CONFIDENTIAL"

* * * *

2nd Letter — Postmarked: Texarkana, Arkansas-Texas   b6
                             January 3, 1947
                             At 6:00 PM   b7C

              Addressed to: Mr. Clark Brown
                             1417 Locust Street
                             City

"AS A FOLLOW UP OF LETTER WRITTEN TO YOU SOME FEW DAYS AGO.
THE CAR LICENSE NUMBER GIVEN YOU WAS RIGHT AND THIS CAR HAS
RECENTLY BEEN SOLD. ALSO ASK HOW COME FBI TO CHECK BLOCK AT
▢▢▢▢▢▢▢▢SOME TIME AGO AND WHO WITHIN THIS WAS RELATED
IN A MANNER TO THESE PEOPLE AT FARM. ALSO HOW WAS GUN
TRANSFERRED TO NOT BE IN JUST ONE HAND AND IS STILL KEPT
GOING FROM ▢▢▢▢▢▢▢▢▢▢▢▢▢▢▢▢▢▢▢▢▢▢▢▢▢▢▢▢▢▢▢▢▢▢

WITH VIRGIL STARKS JUST ONE OR TWO HOURS BEFORE HIS DEATH.
ALSO HIGHER AUTHORITIES THAN THESE HERE WOULD BE THE ONES
FOR YOU TO GO FOR HELP. ALSO BOTH LETTERS HAVE BEEN WRITTEN
BECAUSE WAS TOLD YOU HAD INFLUENCE WITH RIGHT AUTHORITIES
AND PLEASE IF NOT USED WOULD YOU BE KIND ENOUGH TO BURN WHEN
READ ▢▢▢▢▢▢▢▢▢▢▢▢▢▢▢▢▢▢▢▢▢▢▢▢▢▢▢▢▢▢▢▢▢▢▢

* * * *

3rd Letter — Postmarked: Texarkana, Arkansas-Texas
                             March 21, 1947
                             At 5:30 PM

- 3 -

130

Typed in upper CASE

Addressed to: Mr. Clark Brown
1417 Locust Street
Texarkana, Arkansas

"SORRY YOU DID NOT BELIEVE IN LETTERS SENT YOU LAST YEAR AS
YOU EITHER DID NOT OR ELSE LONG TIME USING SAME. SEEMS IT
WOULD BE SO EASY BY GIVEN GOOD INFORMATION AS GIVEN. THESE
SAME PARTIES ARE STILL MOLESTING AND IF YOU HAD OF THOUGHT
INFORMATION GIVEN YOU AS BENEFICIAL YOU WOULD HAVE CAUSED
OTHER GIRLS LESS SUFFERING. BUT CANNOT BLAME YOU AND ONLY
WISHED YOU HAD. OF COURSE IT IS BETTER TO GO FACE TO FACE,
BUT IN THIS CASE THAT COULD NOT BE DONE AND SORRY HEARTACHE
AS WELL AS YOURS CANNOT BE EASED. RIGHT PARTIES COULD OF
RUN THIS DOWN. MONEY WAS NOT AND IS NOT NOW THE INTENTION
OF THIS AND REMEMBER

b6
b7C

THIS IS NOT MADE UP.
WHY IS THIS WRITTEN? WELL IF YOU ONLY COULD OF HAD RIGHT
PARTIES TO LOOKED INTO THIS A BODY OF A YOUNG GRIL WHO IS
STILL LIVING BARELY THOUGH WOULD CEASE CRYING AND HURTING.
NOT FOR A MINUTE WOULD I APPEAL TO YOUR SYMPATHY ONLY SORRY
YOU CANNOT USE THE INFORMATION GIVEN. PLEASE DO IF YOU CAN."

* * * *

4th Letter — Postmarked: Texarkana, Arkansas-Texas
May 2, 1947
At 5:30 PM

Addressed to: Mr. Clark Brown
1419 Locust St
City   Personal

"SOMETIME AGO YOU WERE WRITTEN AND GIVEN VALUABLE INFORMATION
AND NOTHING SEEMS TO COME OF IT. THE NAMES GIVEN YOU AND
ALL WAS CONFIDENTIAL AND DO NOT MEAN TO SORRY OR REMIND YOU.
MUST BE IF YOU TRIED TO FIND OUT THEY PLAYED INNOCENT. JUST
A LITTLE WHILE BACK THERE WAS A DEATH OF A GIRL AND YOU NO
DOUBT READ ABOUT IT THERE POSSIBLY WILL BE ANOTHER IF YOU
HAVE ANY INFLUENCE WOULD BE SO GLAD YOU USE IT. MAYBE YOU

- 4 -

131

"DID NOT RECEIVE LETTER WILL REPEAT NAMES GO TO HIGHER OFFICIALS AS THESE PEOPLE ARE HELPED BY THE LAW.

DO NOT BE MISLEAD ABOUT ANY OF THIS. ALL OF THIS WAS HEARD NEAR STARKS ALSO BLOOD NEAR MARTINDALE FARM THE NIGHT YOUR STEP FATHER KILLED THEY MET THERE LATER. NOT ALL THIS AT MURDERS BUT PLAYED THEIR PARTS AND ACCORDING TO ANY LAW WILL BE GUILTY DO NOT BE MISLEAD. KEEP THIS CONFIDENTIAL. BURN THIS JOT NAMES DOWN.

b6
b7C

PLEASE IF YOU HAVE ANY INFLUENCE CARRY THIS TO HIGHER AUTHORITIES. DO NOT GIVE TO THESE HERE FOR THEY WILL TELL YOU NOTHING TO IT. YOU CAN SEE WHY CAN'T YOU. HURRY. MAYBE YOU DID NOT GET FORMER LETTERS THIS WILL BE LAST WRITTEN. WISH YOU COULD DO SOMETHING AS THAT WILL BE MORE. SYMPATHY WITH YOU AND YOURS BY MANY BE ASSURED OF THAT AND ONLY TOO GLAD TO HELP TO BRING JUSTICE DON'T THINK FOR ANY OTHER PURPOSE. KEEP THIS CONFIDENTIAL AND MANY THANKS IF YOU CAN DO ANYTHING ABOUT THIS."

All of the above four letters have been typewritten in upper case and all except the letter postmarked March 21, 1947, have been submitted to the FBI Laboratory for examination.

Reference is made to the report of Special Agent [   ] dated May 12, 1947, at Dallas, Texas, which sets out the details of the two extortion letters received by victim FEAGINS, one postmarked April 29, 1947, at 7:30 PM, and the other postmarked May 5, 1947, at 2:30 PM, both at Texarkana, Arkansas-Texas. These letters were also submitted to the FBI Laboratory for examination.

By letter dated June 2, 1947, the FBI Laboratory advised that the two letters addressed to victim FEAGINS were prepared on the same machine as the typewriting appearing on the first letter and envelope addressed to Mr. CLARK BROWN. This is the letter postmarked December 17, 1946. The Laboratory also advised that they had concluded that the typewriting appearing on the letters addressed to Mr. BROWN bearing the postmarks of January 3, 1947 and May 2, 1947, were also prepared on the same machine. This typewriting corresponds with the Laboratory standards of Underwood elite type, spaced 12 letters to the inch. Type similar to this may be found on both Underwood

b6
b7C

- 5 -

FBI Report in case DL #9-616 in the Phantom Murders; letters to Clark Brown, stepfather of Betty Jo Booker.

It is interesting to note the following with regard to the Clark Brown letter:

1. The letter was written by an unknown sender to the stepfather of a young girl who had been brutally murdered.
2. The letter was mailed to the stepfather almost exactly eight months after Betty Jo Booker was killed.
3. The letter was neatly typewritten.
4. The letter was typed entirely in upper case.
5. The first line of the letter begins with the words: "This is . . .".
6. The content of the letter is written as an offer to assist.
7. Nearly all of the Phantom attacks and murders occurred on weekends.

The FBI determined that an Underwood typewriter was used by the author of the Clark Brown letter in 1947. No latent fingerprints were found on the envelope or the letter.

Elmer Feagins lived close to Clark Brown at 3119 Locust Street, Texarkana, Arkansas. He received a letter mailed April 29, 1947, demanding three thousand dollars in cash to be delivered to Spring Lake Park, Texas. Later additional letters were mailed by the same suspect in the Booker/Martin murders to Elmer Feagins.

The following are excerpts from the FBI Report regarding the Brown and Feagin letters:

The three bullets referred to above as specimens Q11, Q12 and Q13 were found to be most similar to caliber .22 long rifle Western lubaloy bullets. These specimens were too mutilated to ascertain definitely the type of weapon from which they were fired. There is some indication, however, that they may have been fired from a weapon with a barrel having six lands and grooves with a left hand twist. This would indicate that they were fired from a caliber .22 Colt automatic pistol or caliber .22 Colt revolver. There are no individual microscopic markings present on these bullet specimens suitable for comparison purposes in the event a suspect weapon is recovered.

The three cartridge cases referred to above as specimens Q14 and Q15 are Western Super-X caliber .22 long or long rifle cartridge cases. These were compared microscopically with each other and it was possible to identify them as having been fired in the same weapon and that they have been loaded into and extracted from an auto loading weapon similar to the caliber .22 Colt Woodsman pistol.

As a result of grouping tests conducted on the human blood appearing on the pieces of linoleum, specimen Q1, it was ascertained that this blood was derived from an individual belonging to International Blood Group "O". The human blood contained in the two vials, specimens Q5 and Q6, was determined to have been derived from an individual belonging to International Blood Group "O". Two small spots of human blood were also found on the brown wrapping paper, specimen Q2; however, the amount of blood on this paper was too limited for a grouping determination. Preliminary chemical tests for blood were obtained on the right kitchen window curtain, specimen Q3, but the amount of stain thereon was too limited to confirm the presence of blood or to determine its origin. No blood was found on specimen Q4.

Traces of soil were found on the pieces of linoleum numbered 1, 2, and 3 and also on specimen Q3. The soil on the number 1 and 3 pieces of linoleum was different in color from K1 but was contaminated with blood which may have affected the color. The amounts were too small to analyze and compare. The soil removed from the number 2 piece of linoleum was different in color and other characteristics from K1 and did not come from the same source. The trace of soil on the curtain, Q3, was too small to compare with K1.

Specimen Q4 contained a trace of cobwebs and insect material and a small sliver of wood, the significance of which is not known. The pieces of linoleum numbered 4 and 5 contained no soil of value. No further material of significance was found on the curtains.

No hair was found in the folded paper, specimen Q7; however, one dark purple wool fiber was found in the cellophane wrapper in which the paper was contained. The source of this fiber is not known.

The questioned footprint impression listed above as Q10 was made with a left shoe, the size of which is approximately 9½ to 10½. From the submitted

134

DL #9-616

portable and standard typewriters. On special request type similar to this may be found on other makes of typewriters. The letter also advised that the typewriting on the letter to Mr. BROWN postmarked December 17, 1946, and the two letters to Mr. FEAGINS corresponds with the Laboratory standards of Underwood Pica type, spaced 10 letters to the inch. This style of type is usually found on various types of Underwood typewriters. On special request type similar to this may be found on other makes of typewriters.

No latent prints of value were developed on the letters and envelopes addressed to Mr. E. E. FEAGINS. However, the Laboratory advised by letter dated May 28, 1947, in the case entitled "UNKNOWN SUBJECT; BETTY JOE BOOKER; JAMES PAUL MARTIN – VICTIMS; MURDER, April 14, 1946, TEXARKANA, TEXAS; POLICE COOPERATION", that one latent palm print had been developed on the typewritten message beginning "Sometime ago you were written and given valuable..." which was received by Mr. CLARK BROWN with the letter postmarked Texarkana, Arkansas-Texas, May 2, 1947.

All of the envelopes used in the six letters are large size stamped envelopes that can be purchased at the Post Office, with the exception of the letter postmarked December 17, 1946, to Mr. CLARK BROWN. This envelope appears to be a personal envelope. The paper used in writing the messages appears to be regular typewriting paper 8½ inches wide, but in each instance a portion of the paper has been torn and only part of the sheet sent each time. The only exception to this is the letter to FEAGINS postmarked April 29, 1947, which appears to have been written on a scratch pad of some type, and the bottom of the sheet has also been torn as the other sheets. The only paper bearing any watermark is the message contained in the envelope addressed to BROWN postmarked March 21, 1947, and this paper bears the watermark "Atlantic Bond". This letter and this envelope have been secured from the Sheriff's Office, Texarkana, Texas, and are being forwarded to the FBI Laboratory for examination.

It should be noted that none of the individuals mentioned in the letters to Mr. BROWN have previously been considered suspects in the murder cases by the local officers. It should also be noted that Mr. BROWN moved to the Locust Street address in October of 1946 and received his first letter postmarked December 17, 1946. Mr. FEAGINS moved to 3119 Locust Street on April 2, 1947, and received his first letter postmarked April 29, 1947. It should also be pointed out that the first letter to FEAGINS instructed him to ▮▮▮▮▮▮▮▮▮▮▮▮▮▮▮ the proposed "pay-off spot". It should be noted that this location is only approximately 200 yards from where the car being used by victim BOOKER and MARTIN was abandoned near Spring Lake Park, and that it is the opinion of the investigating officers from the evidence secured that the subject of the murder cases first approached victims

b6
b7C

– 6 –

135

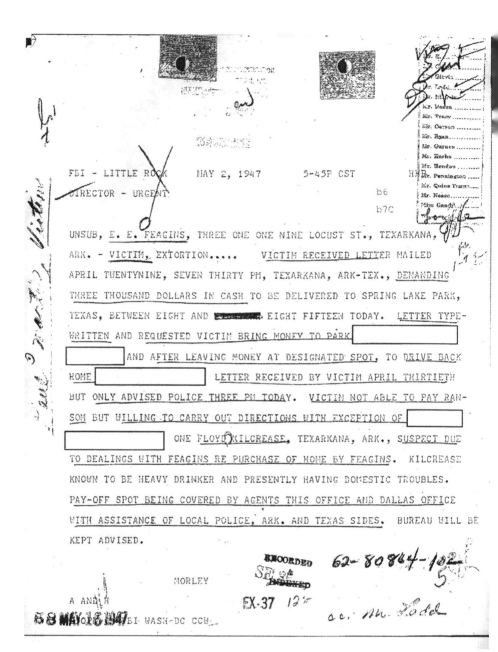

FBI - LITTLE ROCK   MAY 2, 1947   5-45P CST

DIRECTOR - URGENT

b6
b7C

UNSUB, E. E. FEAGINS, THREE ONE ONE NINE LOCUST ST., TEXARKANA,
ARK. - VICTIM, EXTORTION..... VICTIM RECEIVED LETTER MAILED
APRIL TWENTYNINE, SEVEN THIRTY PM, TEXARKANA, ARK-TEX., DEMANDING
THREE THOUSAND DOLLARS IN CASH TO BE DELIVERED TO SPRING LAKE PARK,
TEXAS, BETWEEN EIGHT AND ████████ EIGHT FIFTEEN TODAY. LETTER TYPE-
WRITTEN AND REQUESTED VICTIM BRING MONEY TO PARK ████████████
████████ AND AFTER LEAVING MONEY AT DESIGNATED SPOT, TO DRIVE BACK
HOME ████████████ LETTER RECEIVED BY VICTIM APRIL THIRTIETH
BUT ONLY ADVISED POLICE THREE PM TODAY. VICTIM NOT ABLE TO PAY RAN-
SOM BUT WILLING TO CARRY OUT DIRECTIONS WITH EXCEPTION OF ████████
████████ ONE FLOYD KILCREASE, TEXARKANA, ARK., SUSPECT DUE
TO DEALINGS WITH FEAGINS RE PURCHASE OF HOME BY FEAGINS. KILCREASE
KNOWN TO BE HEAVY DRINKER AND PRESENTLY HAVING DOMESTIC TROUBLES.
PAY-OFF SPOT BEING COVERED BY AGENTS THIS OFFICE AND DALLAS OFFICE
WITH ASSISTANCE OF LOCAL POLICE, ARK. AND TEXAS SIDES. BUREAU WILL BE
KEPT ADVISED.

MORLEY

A AND H

58 MAY 15 1947   FBI WASH-DC CCW

RECORDED
INDEXED

EX-37 12

62-80864-102

cc. Mr. Todd

FEDERAL BUREAU OF INVESTIGATION

Form No. 1
THIS CASE ORIGINATED AT LITTLE ROCK, ARKANSAS   FILE NO. 9-616 MJH

REPORT MADE AT	DATE WHEN MADE	PERIOD FOR WHICH MADE	REPORT MADE BY	b6
DALLAS, TEXAS	5-12-47	5-2 & 6-47		b7C

TITLE	CHARACTER OF CASE
UNKNOWN SUBJECT; ELMER EDWARD FEAGINS - VICTIM	EXTORTION

SYNOPSIS OF FACTS: Victim, a resident of Texarkana, Arkansas, received note 4-30-47 instructing him to leave $3,000 in Spring Lake Park, Texarkana, Texas, on Friday, 5-2-47, at 8:15__. Surveillance of pay-off negative. Victim then received second note on 5-6-47, advising him that his accusations were wrong. No additional instructions as to pay-off received. Notes forwarded to FBI Laboratory.

- RUC -

DETAILS:

Mr. ELMER EDWARD FEAGINS, 3119 Locust Street, Texarkana, Arkansas, contacted the writer at the Resident Agency, Texarkana, Texas, at approximately 3:00 PM, on May 2, 1947. He furnished the writer with a stamped envelope addressed to E. E. FEAGINS, 3119 Locust Street, City, bearing the postmark "Texarkana, Ark-Tex, 7:30 PM, April 29, 1947". Mr. FEAGINS advised that he received the envelope and the enclosed note on the morning of April 30, 1947, at his residence in Texarkana, Arkansas. He did not decide to report the matter until May 2, 1947. Enclosed in the envelope was the following typewritten note:

"WHEN YOU HAVE BEEN A RAIL ROADER YOUR SELF YOU NO DOUBT UNDERSTAND RAILROADING. SINCE YOU HAVE DONE THIS THEN YOU UNDERSTAND THE GAME. SINCE THIS IS THE CASE YOU DID IT IN THE PAST WILL ASK FOR RET URN WITH INTEREST. AT THE SPRING LAKE PARK VAULT AFTER ENTERING GATE AT HEAD OF SPRING AT VAULT ON EAST SIDE PUT THIS SPONDULUX. IN AN OILCLOTH OF DARK COLOR AND THEN TIED WITH DARK STRING CAN'T FIND PAINT OILCLOTH THIS AMOUNT OF MONEY IN AS SMALL BUNDLE

APPROVED AND FORWARDED:	SPECIAL AGENT IN CHARGE	DO NOT WRITE IN THESE SPACES	RECORDED & INDEXED
COPIES DESTROYED		62-80864-105	133
11 NOV 18 1964 COPIES OF THIS REPORT			
5 - Bureau			
3 - Little Rock (Enc.)		31 MAY 16 1947	EX-27
2 - Dallas			
62 MAY 20 1947			

U. S. GOVERNMENT PRINTING OFFICE   7-2034

"AS POSSIBLE IN AS LARGE AMOUNT OF MONEY AS POSSIBLE.
LARGE BUNDLE SO AS TO NOT MAKE POSSIBLE. PUT THIS ON
FRIDAY OF THIS WEEK BETWEEN EIGHT AND EIGHT FIFTEEN ▮▮▮▮▮
▮▮▮▮▮▮▮▮▮▮ THEN LEAVE GO HOME STAY
QUIET. WITHOUT ALLOWING ANYONE TO KNOW ABOUT THIS IN ANY
WAY YOU KNOW WHAT I MEAN. THE AMOUNT IS THREE THOUSAND
DOLLARS THIS IS ONLY FIRST REQUEST TO GET BACK YOUR REQUEST
OR RAILROADING? REMEMBER??? YES YOU DO. DON'T HAVE ANY
WATCH DOG OR PROWLERS. KEEP QUIET ABOUT THIS OR ELSE.
YOUR RAILROADING OTHER PEOPLE IS OVER. REMEMBER YOUR FAMILY
AND KEEP RULES AND MUM OR??????"

It should be particularly noted in the note that the victim
was instructed to put the bundle on Friday of this week (which was May 2,
1947) between 8:00 and 8:15. The note does not state whether A.M. or P.M.
However, since the victim did not report the matter until after 8:15 A.M.,
arrangements were made to surveil the pay-off spot in Spring Lake Park,
Texarkana. The victim stated that he did not have $3,000 but agreed to place
a package at the point designated in the note. He did not desire to have
▮▮▮▮▮▮▮▮▮▮▮▮▮▮▮▮▮▮▮▮▮▮▮▮▮▮▮▮▮▮ and re-
quested that an officer be left at his residence while he was making the
trip from his residence to the park, and that an officer accompany him concealed in his automobile. A surveillance of the pay-off spot was maintained
by the writer and Special Agent ▮▮▮▮▮▮▮▮▮ of the Little Rock Division, and
Bowie County Deputy Sheriff ▮▮▮▮▮▮▮▮▮▮▮▮▮▮ A surveillance
was maintained at the entrance of the park by Special Agent ▮▮▮▮▮▮▮▮▮
of the Little Rock Division and Miller County, Arkansas, Deputy Sheriff ▮▮▮▮▮
▮▮▮▮▮ Arkansas State Policeman ▮▮▮▮▮▮▮▮ remained at the victim's
residence, and Arkansas State Policeman ▮▮▮▮▮▮▮ accompanied the victim
from his residence to Spring Lake Park. The victim placed the package at the
appointed place at approximately 8:10 PM. A surveillance was maintained at the
various places from approximately 7:15 until 11:00 P.M. Nothing of value was
noted at any of the above-mentioned points.

At the time the victim reported the receipt of the letter, he
stated that he suspected only one individual. This individual was FLOYD
KILCREASE, a former owner of a welding shop and garage at Dudley and Jackson
Streets, Texarkana, Arkansas. The victim had purchased the residence at
3119 Locust Street from KILCREASE approximately one month prior to the receipt
of the letter. He furnished the following information which caused him to
suspect KILCREASE. KILCREASE was in California at the time he negotiated through
▮▮▮▮▮▮▮▮▮▮ real estate dealer with ▮▮▮▮▮▮▮▮▮ for the purchase

- 2 -

DL #9-616

"MANY A SLIP HAS BEEN MADE BETWEEN THE CUP AND THE LIP.
YOUR LIP DID IT TOGETHER WITH YOUR FAMILY. YOU ASKED FOR
IT. YOUR VERSION WRONG ACCUSATION WRONG LIP TOO BIG YOU
ASKED FOR IT TOGETHER WITH OTHERS LIP. YOU WERE TOLD TO
DO SOMETHING. IT IS WHAT YOU HAVE DONE IN PAST NOT OTHERS.
YOU AND YOUR LIPPERS WILL FIND THIS OUT IN TIME. YOU ASKED
FOR IT."

Again FEAGINS advised that the only individual he could
suspect would be FLOYD KILCREASE. He stated that this note was not handled,
and it was immediately placed in a cellophane envelope. He described
KILCREASE as being approximately 5' 10½" tall, weight 135 to 140, age
approximately 45, slightly gray hair, brown eyes, and slender build. He
did not know KILCREASE until he transacted the real estate deal [   ]
[   ] KILCREASE through the Jennings Real Estate Company.

The extortion notes and envelopes are being forwarded to
the FBI Laboratory.

ENCLOSURES TO LITTLE ROCK — Photostatic copies of the two extortion notes.

REFERRED UPON COMPLETION TO THE OFFICE OF ORIGIN

- 4 -

139

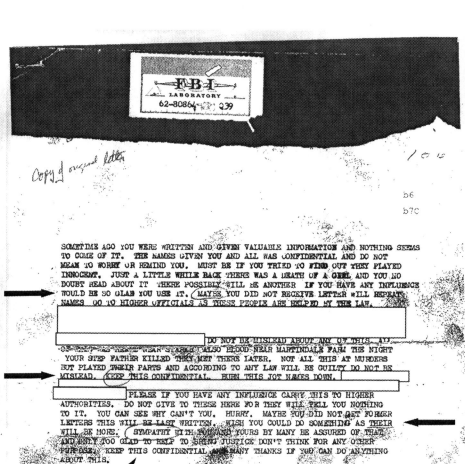

Copy of original letter

b6
b7C

SOMETIME AGO YOU WERE WRITTEN AND GIVEN VALUABLE INFORMATION AND NOTHING SEEMS
TO COME OF IT. THE NAMES GIVEN YOU AND ALL WAS CONFIDENTIAL AND DO NOT
MEAN TO WORRY OR REMIND YOU. MUST BE IF YOU TRIED TO FIND OUT THEY PLAYED
INNOCENT. JUST A LITTLE WHILE BACK THERE WAS A DEATH OF A GIRL AND YOU NO
DOUBT READ ABOUT IT THERE POSSIBLY WILL BE ANOTHER IF YOU HAVE ANY INFLUENCE
WOULD BE SO GLAD YOU USE IT. MAYBE YOU DID NOT RECEIVE LETTER WILL REPEAT
NAMES GO TO HIGHER OFFICIALS AS THESE PEOPLE ARE HELPED BY THE LAW.

DO NOT BE MISLEAD ABOUT ANY OF THIS. AT
OR NEAR STARKE ALSO BLOOD NEAR MARTINDALE FARM THE NIGHT
YOUR STEP FATHER KILLED THEY MET THERE LATER. NOT ALL THIS AT MURDERS
BUT PLAYED THEIR PARTS AND ACCORDING TO ANY LAW WILL BE GUILTY DO NOT BE
MISLEAD. KEEP THIS CONFIDENTIAL. BURN THIS JOT NAMES DOWN.

PLEASE IF YOU HAVE ANY INFLUENCE CARRY THIS TO HIGHER
AUTHORITIES. DO NOT GIVE TO THESE HERE FOR THEY WILL TELL YOU NOTHING
TO IT. YOU CAN SEE WHY CAN'T YOU. HURRY. MAYBE YOU DID NOT GET FORMER
LETTERS THIS WILL BE LAST WRITTEN. WISH YOU COULD DO SOMETHING AS THEIR
WILL BE MORE. SYMPATHY WITH YOU AND YOURS BY MANY BE ASSURED OF THAT
AND ONLY TOO GLAD TO HELP TO BRING JUSTICE DON'T THINK FOR ANY OTHER
PURPOSE. KEEP THIS CONFIDENTIAL MANY THANKS IF YOU CAN DO ANYTHING
ABOUT THIS.

140

BOOKER and MARTIN in Spring Lake Park at a point only approximately 200 yards from the spring mentioned in the first extortion letter to FEAGINS. According to Sheriff W. H. PRESLEY, [redacted] description as victims BOOKER and MOORE. Sheriff PRESLEY stated that from his personal observation, he felt that [redacted] for either victim BOOKER or victim MOORE. It should also be noted that the individuals mentioned in the letters to BROWN reside in the same general neighborhood as FEAGINS.

Sheriff PRESLEY has determined that there is an individual by the name of [redacted]

It should be noted that the word "spondulux" has been used in the first letter to Mr. FEAGINS, and that the writer of the letter also speaks of the "head of the spring". These expressions are not frequently used.

[redacted]

company was the sole wholesale distributor for Atlantic Bond paper in the Texarkana, Texas-Arkansas territory. The paper is manufactured by the Eastern Manufacturing Company of Bangor, Maine. [redacted] examined the paper used in the four letters to Mr. BROWN. He stated that the letter postmarked March 21, 1947, was written on Atlantic Bond paper, while the other letters are written on what he described as a Number 4 bond paper which contains no watermark and is produced by practically all of the paper companies. The first letter to Mr. FEAGINS is written on what he described as a cheap memo pad paper with a gum label at the top. The second letter to Mr. FEAGINS which bore the postmark May 5, 1947, is written also on the Number 4 bond paper and bears no watermark. According to [redacted] the majority of all firms in Texarkana, Texas, would use Atlantic Bond paper and also have available for use a Number 4 bond paper. Both are used for letterheads. This should be particularly noted since a portion of each sheet has been torn off. The memo pad paper used in the first letter to FEAGINS, according to [redacted] is made from pure wood pulp and has no rag content. [redacted] stated that it would nearly be impossible to identify the business firms using the paper in question inasmuch as it is a common grade of paper used by all places of business.

[redacted]

the Ragland Office Equipment Company, 218 Main Street, Texarkana, Texas, and

- 7 -

FBI Report in the Phantom Murders covering letters to E.E. Feagins.

It is interesting to note the following:

1. All of the suspect letters were neatly typed in upper case.
2. In the letter marked DL #9-116, the fourth sentence from the bottom begins with the word "Maybe" and the last sentence begins with the word "Keep."
3. The follow-up Feagin letters are fairly lengthy and by the tone of the letters the writer seems to be getting perturbed because of lack of attention.
4. One of the letters mentions "the game."
5. The first Feagin letter was mailed April 29, 1947.
6. One of the Phantom letters mentions the word "sympathy" followed in the same letter with the word "justice" (see page____).
7. One of the Phantom letters indicates that if some action is taken "you would have caused other girls less suffering."
8. One of the letters written to Mr. Feagin identified as Q39 includes the following sentence: "wish you could do something as their will be more."
9. One of the letters to Mr. Feagin included the word "lip."
10. The letters written in the Phantom case contained odd words including: "head of the stream" and "spondulux."

Floyd Kilcrease, operator of a welding and repair shop in Texarkana, Arkansas, received a *hand printed* letter, postmarked 1-29-47, at Texarkana, Arkansas-Texas. (The Zodiac letters were hand printed. See Chapter 5.)

It should be noted that as a result of an examination by the Federal Bureau of Investigation Laboratory, the FBI determined that the anonymous letters to Mr. Brown and the extortion letter to Mr. Feagins were prepared on two typewriters found in the office of W.C. Kuhl, 108 East Third Street, Texarkana, Arkansas. The FBI further identified a forty-year-old woman by the name of Madeline Mary James as the suspect- author of the extortion communications directed to Victim Feagins. James had been employed at the office of W.C. Kuhl and resided at 3112 Locust Street, Texarkana, Arkansas, which address is directly across the street from the home of Mr. Feagins.

The subject James was interviewed by the Little Rock Office of the FBI in

1947, and denied writing the Feagins letters or any other letters involved in these related cases. The August 15, 1947, FBI Report states: "As the subject has continually denied authorship of any of these communications, it is observed that the evidence in connection with the letters addressed to Victim Feagin is only circumstantial inasmuch as Feagin's letters were prepared on the typewriter located in the W.C. Kuhl Realty Office."

The United States Attorney at Fort Smith, Arkansas, authorized the filing of a complaint against James. On August 26, 1947, a Federal Grand Jury returned a two count indictment against James. On September 24, 1947, she entered a "not guilty plea" to each count of the indictment before Judge Harry J. Lemley at Texarkana, Arkansas. A trial date was set for November 10, 1947. On November 11, 1947, when the trial of James opened, defense attorneys Ned Stewart and Ben Shaver "vigorously contested the admissibility of these specimens." Judge Lemley denied the defense motion to suppress and the evidence was deemed admissible. James' trial was postponed from November 10, 1947, to November 11, 1947. On Wednesday, November 12, 1947, a psychiatrist found the defendant, James, "mentally ill and not in possession of sufficient mental competency to understand the nature of the proceedings against her and rationally unable to advise with counsel as to her defense." On Thursday, November 13, 1947, due to the facts in the psychiatrist's report, United States Attorney R.S. Wilson made a motion that the proceedings against James be dismissed. The motion was granted by Judge Lemley and the case against Madeline Mary James was dismissed.

Now let's move the clock ahead twenty years and track the killer to Riverside, California.

Chapter 5

THE ZODIAC KILLER
OCTOBER 30, 1966

CHERI JO BATES

On Sunday, October 30, 1966, Cheri Jo Bates went to church with her father, Joseph Bates, at St. Catherine's Catholic Church in Riverside, California. On Halloween her lifeless mutilated body was found by a college groundskeeper. She was a very pretty, blond-haired, blue-eyed, five-feet-three, 110-pound, eighteen-year-old freshman cheerleader at the Riverside City College. Cheri was studying at the college library on that fateful Halloween night. Unknown to her, at the same time, someone lingered in the darkness near her lime-green Volkswagen Beetle in the college library annex parking lot. Had the same person seen her earlier at St. Catherine's Church? Whoever it was knew the car was driven by Cheri Jo Bates. Detectives determined that her killer had tampered with her vehicle's engine by pulling out the electrical distributor coil and disconnecting a wire to the distributor. Cheri eventually left the library and went to her car. She tried to start her Volkswagen but to no avail. At that moment a man approached Cheri and probably offered assistance or a ride home. The stranger persuaded Cheri to go with him down an unlit gravel path leading out of the parking lot, a walk that would end in tragedy. The stranger assaulted Cheri with a small knife, slamming her to the ground. A neighbor would later recall that he heard two screams between 10:15 and 10:45 P. M. . . . . Her assailant kicked her in the head then slashed her face and throat, cutting her jugular vein and voice box, almost severing her head from her body. Her purse was found next to her body, and nothing appeared to have been taken. She was not sexually assaulted. Detectives were puzzled by the motive of this vicious murder. As her lifeless body lay on the cold gravel, the mysterious killer disappeared into the darkness.

The case did eventually take a strange turn. Within thirty days after the death of Cheri Jo Bates, the Riverside Police and the *Riverside Press-Enterprise* received identical typewritten letters entitled: "The Confession"

By_____

The author of this letter typed the document all in upper case through approximately twelve carbon papers. The copy mailed was taken from the last copy, rendering a typewriter trace nearly impossible. The killer wrote:

"The Confession" letter written in the Zodiac case
(courtesy of Tom Voigt, *zodiackiller.com*)

May 1, 1967

On May 1, 1967, the Riverside Police Department and the *Riverside Press-Enterprise* received hand-addressed envelopes, each postmarked locally and mailed with double postage. Inside each envelope was the following message:

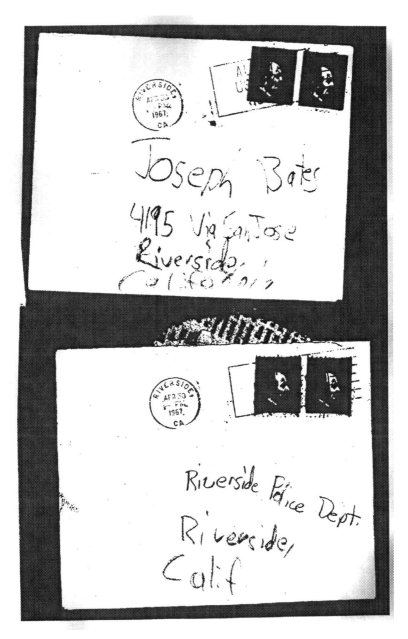

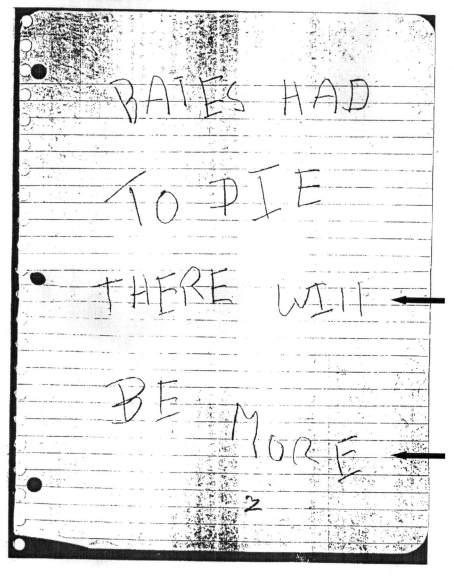

"Bates Had To Die" letter writt en in the Zodiac case
(courtesy of Tom Voigt, *zodiackiller.com*)

This time the notes were signed with either a "2" or a "Z." An identical letter was mailed to Joseph Bates, father of Cheri Jo Bates. This murder case grew cold with no promising leads. Four years later and several hundred miles to the north in San Francisco, detectives there learned that the death of Cheri Jo might be related to a series of random murders and attacks in their jurisdiction.

The following clues and facts can be ascertained from the information associated with the death of Cheri Jo Bates:

1. Her assailant wanted publicity and his name in the newspaper.
2. He wrote the police and a newspaper following a murder he committed.
3. The letter he wrote was lengthy, typewritten in capital letters, and single spaced.
4. Her assailant was interested in poetry and quoted poetry.
5. She was slashed in the face and her head was almost severed from her body.
6. Following the murder, her assailant wrote a letter to Cheri Jo Bates's father. The letter was written in block letters like those a child would write.
7. In his letter to the *Riverside Press-Enterprise* the killer threatened to cut off female parts and deposit them for the whole city to see.

No one was ever arrested and charged with the murder of Cheri Jo Bates. All that now remains is cold file #352-481 at the Riverside Police Department. It is interesting to note that:

1. The "Confession" letter was entirely typed in upper case
2. The "Confession" letter mentions "**the game**."
3. The "Confession" letter includes a sentence that starts with the word "**Maybe**" followed shortly thereafter by a sentence that starts with the word "**Keep**."
4. The "Bates Had To Die" letter was mailed to Joseph Bates, father of Cheri Jo Bates after Cheri Jo had been brutally murdered.
5. The "Bates Had To Die" letter was mailed to Joseph Bates on April 30, 1967, exactly six months after Cheri Jo Bates was murdered.

6. The poet John Keats (1795-1817) wrote in *Hyperion: Book II* "And just as thou wast *not he first* of powers so art thou *not the last*." If the phrase "not the first and not the last" was borrowed from the works of John Keats, then one could deduce that the writer of "The Confession" letter may have a keen interest in the poetry and writings of Keats. It is well known that Keats wrote volumes of material, so it may not be surprising that several of the words used by the Zodiac are also found Keats's work including but not limited to: Zodiac (*Lines On the Mermaid Tavern*), whence, I am here, leave me alone, wandering, spray, blast, paradise, delicious, slaves, dripping, collecting, rile, wipe, cheer, clean, mask, Phantom, sensible, inflict, twitched (*The Eve of St. Agnes*) happy, and so on.

7. Detectives suspected that the Zodiac used a portable Royal Typewriter to type the "Confession" letter.

8. The Zodiac indicated in this letter that if some action is taken "It just might save that girl in the alley."

9. "The Confession" letter written by the Zodiac included the word "lip."

10. The Zodiac's "Bates Had To Die" letter included the following words:" There will be more."

11. The Zodiac wrote odd words in his letters including "unflappable," "Mask the sound," and "positively ventalate."

12. The Zodiac signed his "Count Marco" letter: "The Red Phantom (red with rage)"

13. Zodiac began most of his letters with the words: "This is . . ."

14. The 1977, movie entitled *The Town That Dreaded Sundown* may provide additional clues. Although based on a true story, several of the factual accounts concerning the Phantom Murders depicted in the movie are not completely accurate. For example, the cloth-hood worn by the Phantom Killer in the movie had holes for the eyes but not the mouth (The Phantom Killer and the Zodiac both wore cloth-hoods with cutout holes for the eyes and the mouth). There are a few scenes from the movie that I mention here for whatever value they may be worth:

   a. In the movie, the Phantom Killer is seen opening the hood of the automobile driven by a character depicting Phantom Victim, Jimmy Hollis, and removing several wires before attacking the couple.

In the case of Cheri Jo Bates, the Zodiac Killer opened the hood of her Volkswagen and "pulled out the distributor coil and the condenser and disconnected the middle wire of the distributor" (Note 48, page 165).

b. In the movie, the character depicting Betty Jo Booker is tied up and then stabbed with a knife several times in her back by a man with a cloth-hood over his head.

Zodiac Victim, Cecelia Shepard, was stabbed with a knife five times each in the front and back by a man with a cloth-hood over his head.

c. In the movie, the Phantom Killer uses a gun with some sort of silencer attached to it.

Zodiac Victim, Mike Mageau, "got the impression the gun had some sort of silencer on it" (Note 48, page 27).

Confidential

Editor —
Put Marco back in the hell-hole from whence it came — he has a serious psychological disorder — always needs to feel superior. I suggest you refer him to a shrink. Meanwhile, cancel the Count Marco column. Since the Count can write anonymously, so can I —
the Red Phantom
(red with rage)

"Count Marco" letter written in the Zodiac case
(courtesy of Tom Voigt, www.zodiackiller.com)

151

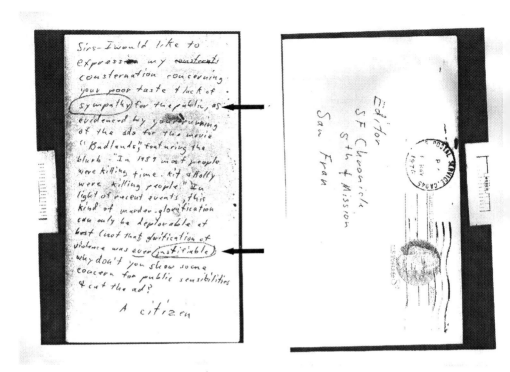

"Citizen" letter written in the Zodiac case
(courtesy of Tom Voigt, zodiackiller.com)

BETTY LOU JENSEN AND DAVID ARTHUR FARADAY
December 20, 1968

The Zodiac had migrated from the Los Angeles area to San Francisco by late 1968. At that time no one knew he might have been responsible for the savage murder of Cheri Jo Bates two years earlier in Riverside, California. The Zodiac was smart. He didn't continue to commit his deadly crimes in the same location for a very long period of time. This would have increased the chance of being identified and eventually apprehended. One small mistake could lead to the evidence that would end his career as a serial killer. He was too clever to allow the authorities time enough to set a trap that would snare him. Over the course of a couple of years the Zodiac would do exactly what he eventually wrote: "I shall change the way the collecting of slaves. I shall no longer announce to anyone. When I commit my murders, they shall look like routine robberies, killings of anger, and a few fake accidents, etc. The police shall never catch me because I have been too clever for them" (Zodiac's letter to the *San Francisco Chronicle*, November 9, 1969). I believe the Zodiac may have read and studied true crime, detective magazines, the history of Jack the Ripper and other famous serial killers to educate himself so that he would not get caught after committing his murders. He knew that if he continued to kill in the same location for an extended period of time he stood a better chance of being caught, tripped up by some act of indiscretion.

It is also interesting to note that on Sunday, April 19, 1970, "a man in a late-model hardtop at the corner of Bay Street and Embarcadero seemed to have an obsession about the crime rate in San Francisco. He went on in great detail to list all thirty-five of the city's murders so far that year. 'It's not safe to walk alone,' he told Christopher Edwards, a ship's steward, 'with all the muggings, murders, rapes, and crime.' Edwards had stopped to ask directions while walking to Fisherman's Wharf and he was getting 'bad vibrations' from the stranger. The man identified himself as a British engineer who had lived in San Francisco for ten years; he offered the steward a lift. Edwards declined, but listened while the stranger went on with great knowledge about all of the murders in the city, save those that were on the minds of most people-the Zodiac killings.

The stranger's reluctance to talk about Zodiac impressed Edwards, and he could not shake the incident from his mind. As soon as he got to the wharf, he called

153

the police. Later at Central Station, he identified the man from a composite drawing of Zodiac" (Note 48, page 142).

On Friday, December 20, 1968, the Zodiac had set his deadly web in Vallejo, 25 miles north of San Francisco. Two young people, sixteen-year-old Betty Lou Jensen and seventeen-year-old David Arthur Faraday went on a date. They were typical California teenagers out for a good time, enjoying life. David drove his mother's 1961 Rambler station wagon to Betty Lou Jensen's home in Vallejo. The couple drove to Mr. Ed's, a drive-in, and after drinking a Coke drove to a lover's lane off Lake Herman Road. Not long after they had parked a car pulled up alongside of the Rambler. The authorities later reconstructed the events of that fateful evening: They thought a stranger exited his car and walked up to the side of the Faraday vehicle, where he probably ordered David and Betty Lou out of their car. At first the couple might have ignored his order so he drew a gun and fired two shots, one of which went through the side of the rear window of the Rambler. Both Jensen and Faraday started to flee from the vehicle. Davis was met by the stranger as he attempted to exit the vehicle. He was shot behind the left ear and the bullet lodged in his brain. David Faraday was mortally wounded. The gunman then turned his rage on Betty Lou Jensen who had dashed from the car screaming in terror. The gunman raised his weapon and fired five shots at the fleeing victim striking her five times in the back. Betty Lou Jensen's life ended where she fell.

Mrs. Stella Borges lived on Lake Herman Road a little over two miles from where David Arthur Faraday and Betty Lou Jensen had been murdered. At 11:10 p.m. that evening Mrs. Borges went for a ride with her mother-in-law and daughter to Benicia. They came upon the gruesome scene and summoned the police. When the police arrived they had no clue who had committed these crimes. There were no fingerprints or other physical evidence except the expended shell casings and slugs recovered at the crime scene. The bullets were made by Winchester and appeared to be a .22 caliber that may have been fired from a J.C. Higgins Model 80 or a Hi Standard Model 101. The killer used Winchester Super X copper-coated long rifle bullets. The bullets recovered had a right hand twist with six land groves, a "six and six" (for definition see page 10, *Zodiac*).

On August 1, 1969, the *Vallejo Times-Herald*, the *San Francisco Chronicle,* and the *San Francisco Examiner* all received variations of the following letter from the Zodiac killer:

Dear Editor

This is the murderer of the
2 teenagers last Christmass
at Lake Herman & the girl
on the 4th of July near
the golf course in Vallejo
To prove I killed them I
shall state some facts which
only I & the police know.

Christmass

1 Brand name of ammo
   (Super X)

2 10 shots were fired

3 the boy was on his back
   with his feet to the car

4 the girl was on her right
   side feet to the west

4th July

1 girl was wearing patterned
   slacks

2 The boy was also shot in
   the knee.

3 Brand name of ammo was
   Western

Over

Here is part of a cipher the
other 2 parts of this cipher are
being mailed to the editors of
the Vallejo times   + SF Exam
iner.

I want you to print this cipher
on the front page of your
paper. In this cipher is my
identity.

If you do not print this cipher
by the afternoon of Fry. 1st of
Aug 69, I will go on a kill rampage Fry. night. I will cruse
around all weekend killing lone
people in the night then move
on to kill again, untill I end
up with a dozen people over
the weekend.

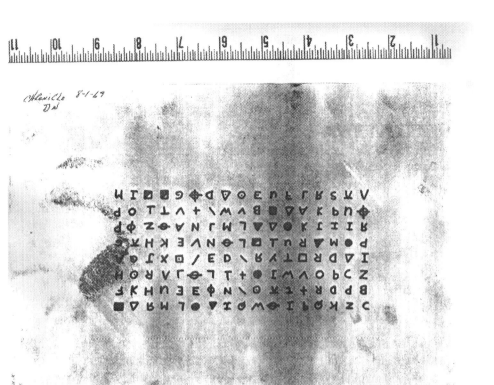

Dear Editor

I am the killer of the 2 teenagers
last christmass at Lake Herman &
the girl last 4th of July. To prove
this I shall state some facts which
only I + the police know.

Christmass
1 brand name of ammo — Super X
2 10 shots fired
3 Boy was on his back with feet to
   car
4 Girl was lyeing on right side
   feet to west

4th of July
1 girl was wearing patterned pants
2 boy was also shot in knee
3 ammo was made by Western

Here is a cipher or that is part
of one. The other 2 parts are
being mailed to the Vallejo Times +
S.F. Chronicle

I want you to print this cipher on the front page by
Fry afternoon Aug 1-69 . If you

158

do not print this cipher, I
will go on a kill rampage
Fry night. This will last the
whole, weekend, I will cruse
around killing people who are
alone at night untill Sun Night
or untill I kill a dozen
People.

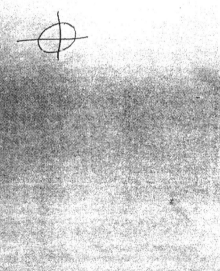

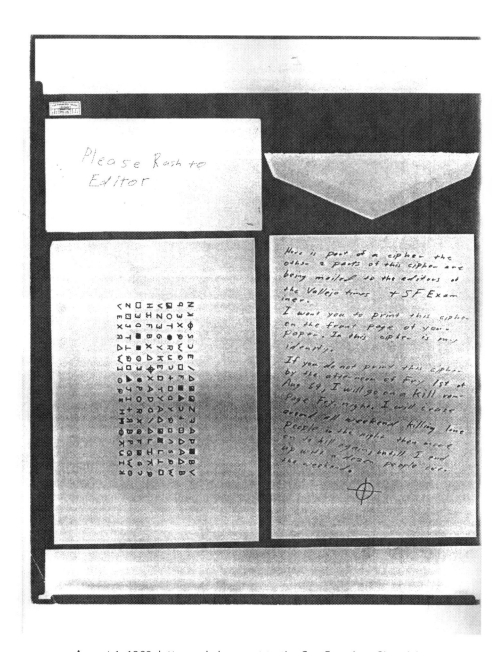

August 1, 1969, letter and ciper sent to the *San Francisco Chronicle*
and August 1, 1969, letter sent to the *San Francisco Examiner*,
in the Zodiac case. (courtesy of Tom Voigt, www.zodiackiller.com)

The letter was completed by a symbol, a circle with two lines through it.

From July 5, 1969, through August 10, 1969, the front page articles of the *San Francisco Chronicle* and the *San Francisco Examiner* were devoted to the murders committed in Michigan by John Norman Collins and the murders of Sharon Tate, Jay Sebring and Abigail Folger by the Manson Family. The Zodiac had not been receiving the front page press that he craved.

DARLENE FERRIN AND MICHAEL MAGEAU
July 4, 1969

In 1962, sixteen-year-old Darlene Ferrin traveled to Texas with her Mother and sisters, Pam, Linda and Christina. At that time Darlene was a shapely, blue-eyed brunette. She changed her hair color a couple of years later from brunette to blond. They visited relatives in the Dallas/Fort Worth area where they met a couple of men who appeared to be in the Navy and another man who I will refer to as the "stranger." At the time, Darlene's sister, Pam, had very long hair that was quite attractive. In a bowling alley the stranger paid special attention to Pam's long hair and commented on how pretty her eyes were. To Pam's displeasure the stranger would try to run his hand through her hair. The incident caused such concern with Pam that she elected to have her hair cut upon returning to Vallejo. In the bowling alley the stranger tried to "come on to" Darlene but she refused his advances and "told him to get lost" in no uncertain words. Pam could remember that one or more of the individuals they had met in Texas obtained their Vallejo telephone number and address. When Darlene Ferrin and her family returned to Vallejo they received several unwanted telephone calls that might have been placed by the men they had met in Texas. Their mother got so upset with the calls she had her telephone number unlisted.

In January, 1969, a stranger was seen hanging around Darlene Ferrin's home in Vallejo. Darlene was heard to say, "I guess he's checking up on me. He doesn't want anyone to know what I saw him do, I saw him kill someone." Four months later, in May, Darlene and her husband Dean Ferrin had an open house. A stranger arrived, uninvited. No one could remember his name but it was "Bob or Joe or Lee, something like that."

On Friday, July 4, 1969, at 11:45 p.m. Darlene went on a date with her friend Michael Mageau. She picked up Michael at his home and when they started to drive away a stranger started to follow them. Darlene tried to elude the stranger but to no avail. As she pulled into the Blue Rock Golf Course the stranger pulled in behind them. He then sped off in his car but soon reappeared. When the stranger returned he stepped out of his car and shined a flashlight into the Ferrin vehicle. (Had this individual carried a flashlight in one hand and a gun in another during a prior assault? If so, then through trial and error, he would have learned that it would be less encumbering to have a flashlight attached to his weapon, thus freeing the other hand to subdue his victim, if necessary. Keep in mind that the Phantom Killer held a gun in one hand and a flashlight in the other.)

The stranger walked up to the passenger side of the Ferrin vehicle where Michael was seated. There was a sound of metal from the gun barrel hitting his window. Without warning, shots were fired. Michael was shot in his jaw and slug passed through his tongue. Bullets hit Darlene. Darlene was shot nine times, two in the right arm, two in the left arm and five times in her back (note 49, page 12). Had Darlene been killed by someone she met years earlier? Perhaps in Texas? There was speculation by the detectives that Darlene Ferrin's killer may have met her at one time or another. The next day on July 5, 1969, her killer called the Vallejo Police Department from a public pay phone and stated. "I want to report a double murder. If you go one mile east on Columbus Parkway to the public park, you will find kids in a brown car. They were shot with a 9mm Lugar. I also killed those kids last year, goodbye." By the time the police had traced the call the man had left the phone booth.

On August 7, 1969, the *Chronicle* received the following letter from the Zodiac:

"Last *Christmass*	**Christmas**	**S**
In that *epasode* the police were	**Episode**	**A**
Wondering as to how I could		
Shoot & hit my victims in the		
Dark. They did not openly state this,		
But implied this by saying it was a		
Well lit night & I could see		
Silowets on the horizon	**Silhouette**	**W,U,T,E & H**
Bullshit that area is *srounded*	**Surrounded**	**U & R**
By high hills and trees. What		
I did was tape a small *pencel*	**Pencil**	**E**
Light to the barrl of my gun. If		
You notice, in the center of the beam		
Of light if you aim it at a wall or		
Ceilling you will see a black or	**Ceiling L**	
Darck	**Dark**	**C**
Circle of light about 3 to 6 in.		
Across		
When taped to a gun barrel, the		
Bullet will strike exactly in the		
Center of the black dot in the light.		
All I had to do was spray them. . .		
No address. (Emphasis added)		

Proposed Solution:

The misspelled words might spell the name: **CHARLES**

(I believe this may be the correct solution because the last letter **S** is the first letter in the first misspelled word and the last letter in the name Charles. The **C** is the last letter in the final incorrect word which is the first letter in the name Charles. However, this is only a guess on my part. There are obviously additional letters that are unaccounted for, namely the letters W, U, T and E.)

CECELIA SHEPARD AND BRYAN HARTNELL
September 27, 1969

Cecelia Ann Shepard and Bryan Hartnell had both attended Pacific Union College in Angwin, California. On September 27, 1969, they decided to go on a date to Lake Berryessa, located north of San Francisco. Bryan drove his 1956 white Karmann Ghia coupe. The couple found a location on a peninsula, laid out a blanket and began to enjoy the day. At around 4:00 o'clock in the afternoon, as they sat on a blanket a man approached them with a gun in hand wearing a square-hooded cloth outfit over his head and shoulders with a white circle and cross-stitched on a tunic that appeared to have been professionally sewed on. It seems to me that the executioner's hood might have been prepared by someone who could have tried this method before. Perhaps in the commission of an earlier assault the assailant had placed a cloth bag over his head and then eventually realized that while committing his crime the bag became more of a nuisance than an effective disguise. That method of concealment was cumbersome, so this time the refined hood might have been constructed so that it fit squarely on his head, allowing for better vision. The stranger wore a lone knife in a wooden sheath on his side hip and several lengths of white plastic clothesline hung from his belt. The man's stomach hung over his belt. Cecelia said to Bryan, "My God, he's got a gun."

The stranger at first demanded their money and keys. The man said he had escaped from prison in Montana, that he had killed a guard in the process, and needed a car in which to escape to Mexico. Soon after, his true intentions became known to Cecelia and Bryan. This person intended to kill them both. He said to Cecelia, "You tie the boy up." When she failed to properly tie Bryan Hartnell with the rope, the stranger took over. He first tied up Cecelia, then Bryan. Once Bryan was securely tied up, their assailant said, "I'm going to have to stab you people." The Zodiac had struck again. He began stabbing Bryan Hartnell in the back with his foot-long knife. Hartnell was stabbed six times in his back, one blow coming within a fraction of an inch of his heart. The man "gave a ghastly, frenzied sound and, letting out a low exhalation, began stabbing the girl in the back." He continued to thrust his bayonet-type knife into her breasts, groin and once in her abdomen. Her aorta had been cut in two places. The next afternoon, Cecelia Shepard died in the hospital from her wounds. Bryan Hartnell survived the attack after crawling over three hundred yards from where the Zodiac first tied him up.

164

The police were able to obtain very few pieces of evidence from the crime scene. Bryan was able to describe his attacker's voice: "It was a remarkably calm voice, a voice that was not high or low pitched, a monotone." Bryan further stated, "That voice…it was like a student's. But kind of a drawl; not a Southern drawl though." Detectives found deep footprints that confirm the Zodiac weighed over 200 pounds. Police determined the Zodiac Killer wore size 10 ½ Wing Walker shoes that may have been purchased under military contract for distribution to the Navy and Air Force on the west coast. It appeared that the Zodiac might be somehow connected to the armed forces when he committed the Lake Berryessa crimes.

At 7:00 p.m., one hour and ten minutes after the knifings, the phone rang at the Napa Police Department. The caller on the line said, "I want to report a murder--no, a double murder. They are two miles north of park headquarters. They were in a white Volkswagen Karmann Ghia." The police traced the call to a pay phone located at 1231 Main Street at the Napa Car-wash. Then the police arrived at the phone booth, the caller had disappeared. The caller left the receiver dangling from the phone. The following facts and clues could be ascertained from this crime:

1. The perpetrator wore a cloth hood over his head that may have been a modification of a cloth hood that had obstructed his vision during a prior crime.

2. The man said he needed a car to escape to Mexico.

3. The man forced the female victim to tie up the male victim.

4. The female victim was not sexually assaulted.

5. After the attack the perpetrator called the police from a pay telephone and in a short message reported a double murder, told the emergency dispatcher where the victims could be found, and then left the receiver dangling from the phone.

6. The man may have had sewing skills as exhibited by the cross stitched on his tunic.

7. The man had a drawl, not a southern drawl, and spoke in a monotone voice.

8. While attacking the female victim the perpetrator gave a "ghastly, frenzied sound and let out a long, low exhalation before he began stabbing the girl" (Note 48, page 71).

October 11, 1969

The official police report submitted by officers Pelisetti and Peda regarding the murder of taxi driver, Paul Lee Stine, who was killed by the Zodiac on October 11, 1969, is written as follows:

Upon responding to the above location officers Peda and Pelisetti found Yellow Cab #912 parked at the northeast corner of Washington St. at the corner of Cherry St. The reporters together with two other witnesses_____, age 14 and_____, age 13, same address and phone as reported, stated that they saw the below described suspect in the front seat of the Yellow cab, mid to the passenger side, with the victim slumped partially over his lap. The suspect appeared to be searching the victim's pockets. (Witnesses never heard a gun shot). The suspect then appeared to be wiping (fingerprints) on the interior of the cab, leaning over the victim to the driver's compartment. The suspect then exited the cab by the passenger side front door, also wiping with a white rag, possibly a handkerchief. The suspect then walked around the cab to the driver's side and proceeded to wipe the exterior of the left door area. The suspect then fled (walking) north on Cherry St. towards the Presidio of S.F. R/Os immediately checked the interior of the cab and found the victim to be slumped over the front seat with his upper torso in the passenger side, head resting on the floorboard, facing north. Ambulance was summoned, Code Three, and other units were requested for an immediate search of the area. Description was obtained from reporters whose observation point was directly across the street (50ft.) and unobstructed. Description was broadcast and numerous units responded to institute a search of the area. P.E.H. ambulance #82 responded, Stewart Dousette, victim was examined and pronounced dead at 10:10 pm.

Inspector Krake responded and summoned dog units and fire department "spotlight" vehicle to assist in the search. R/Os called for Crime Lab Coroner, Yellow cab officials, and a tow.

Assistant traffic manager of Yellow Cab, LeRoy Sweet responded and gave reporting officers the victim's identification. Mr. Sweet further stated the last dispatch given the victim was at 9:45 pm to 500 9ᵗʰ Ave. apt #1. Victim allegedly never arrived at the above location as the dispatch was reassigned to another cab at 9:56 pm. R/Os noted that the meter of the cab was running, indicating that the victim possibly picked up another fare (suspect) en route to the original assignment. (The meter read $6.25 at exactly 10:46 pm.) *A check with Yellow Cab Co. revealed that the victim had arrived at work at approximately 8:45 pm and had only one fare prior, that being from Pier 64 to the Air Terminal.* (emphasis added). Sgt. Falk responded in G #10, Lt. Kiel also responded. The military police headquarters of the Presidio of S.F. was also notified and an intense search of the Julius Kahn area was made by seven dog units, other Richmond and C.P. units--to no avail. The coroner responded, Deputy Schultz and Kindred, and took charge of the deceased. Coroner's receipt attached to this report. Crime Lab responded and took necessary photographs of the preserved Scens-Dagitz and Kirkindal--all physical evidence was retained by crime lab for I.D. The auto, Yellow cab #912 Calif. Lic. Y17413, was towed to the Hall. Impounded for homicide prints, Tow slip attached this report. Room 100 was notified, given description, and advised to have broadcast continuous throughout the morning as per insp Armstrong's direction. Crime lab's initial investigation showed that the victim was devoid of any U.S. currency, nor did he have possession of a wallet; the ignition key for the cab was also missing.

According to the official police report this is the sequence of events:

1. Paul Lee Stine arrives at work at 8:45 pm.
2. Between 8:45 pm and 9:45 pm, Stine picks up a fare at Pier 64 in San Francisco and delivers the fare to the air terminal.
3. A last dispatch to 500 9th Ave. Apt 31 was radioed to Stine.
4. 9:58 pm, the last dispatch was reassigned to another cab.
5. 10:10 pm, Stine is pronounced dead.

When Paul Stine dropped off the fare at the Air Terminal there was a good chance that he may have picked up a new fare at that time. If my theory is correct, Paul Stine may have picked up a fare at the airport and that person may have been the individual who murdered him in San Francisco. The police report indicated that Stine "possibly picked up another fare (suspect) en route to the original assignment."

Unfortunately the police operator made a mistake and reported the perpetrator as a NMA (Negro male adult) instead of the initial and correct identification of the perpetrator as a WMA (white male adult). Did the assailant appear to the witnesses to be a black man when he was possibly a dark-tanned white man?

As later developments would reveal, the Zodiac had disappeared into the shadows of the night in the direction of the Presidio. After an extensive search the police were unable to locate the suspect. The Zodiac killer had vanished into the night.

October 14, 1969

On Tuesday, October 14, 1969, the *San Francisco Chronicle* received the following message:

This is the Zodiac speaking. I am the murderer of the taxi driver over by Washington St & Maple St last night, to prove this here is a blood stained piece of his shirt. I am the same man who did in the people in the north bay area.

The S.F. Police could have caught me last night if they had searched the park properly instead of holding road races with their motor cicles seeing who could make the most noise. The car drivers should have just parked their cars & sat there quietly waiting for me to come out of cover.

School children make nice targ- ets, I think I shall wipe out a school bus some morning. Just shoot out the front tire + then pick off the kiddies as they come bouncing out.

October 13, 1969 letter sent to the *San Francisco Chronicle* in the Zodiac case. (courtesy of Tom Voigt, www.zodiackiller.com)

Two police officers did encounter the Zodiac Killer while searching for the murderer of Paul Lee Stine near the Presidio in San Francisco. A police artist was able to create a new composite drawing of the Zodiac. The following description of the Zodiac was provided: 5'11", thirty-five to forty-five, 200 pounds, short brown hair. The second police composite drawing changes the hair line, widens the jaw, shows a drooping eyelid and opens the mouth of the Zodiac.

WANTED

NO. 90-69   <u>WANTED FOR MURDER</u>   OCTOBER 18, 1969

HAIRLINE

Drooping
eyelid

OPEN MOUTH

ORIGINAL DRAWING   AMENDED DRAWING

Supplementing our Bulletin 87-69 of October 13, 1969. Additional information has
developed the above amended drawing of murder suspect known as "ZODIAC".

WMA, 35-45 Years, approximately 5'8", Heavy Build, Short Brown Hair, possibly with
Red Tint, Wears Glasses. Armed with 9 MM Automatic.

Available for comparison: Slugs, Casings, Latents, Handwriting.

ANY INFORMATION:
Inspectors Armstrong & Toschi
Homicide Detail   THOMAS J. CAHILL
CASE NO. 696314   CHIEF OF POLICE

October, 1969, composite drawing of the Zodiac Killer
(courtesy of Tom Voigt, www.zodiackiller.com)

The Zodiac included a crossed circle at the end of the October 14, 1969, letter to the *San Francisco Chronicle*. No one ever determined exactly what the sign of the Zodiac stood for. I have my own theory.

Look carefully at what the Zodiac wrote in the letter to the *Chronicle* on July 24, 1970:

This is the Zodiac speaking

I am rather unhappy because you people will not wear some nice ⊕ buttons. So I now have a little list, starting with the woeman + her baby that I gave a rather intersting ride fo- a coupple howers one evening a few months back that ended in my burning her car where I found them.

This is the Zodiac speaking

Being that you will not wear
some nice ⊕ buttons, how about
wearing some nasty ⊕ buttons.
Or any type of ⊕ buttons that
you can think up. If you do
not wear any type of ⊕
buttons I shall (on top of every
thing else) torture all 13
of my slaves that I have
wateing for me in Paradice.
Some I shall tie over ant hills
and watch them scream + twich
and sqwirm. Others shall have
pine splinters driven under their
nails + then burned. Others shall
be placed in cages + fed salt
beef untill they are gorged then
I shall listen to their pleass
for water and I shall laugh at
them. Others will hang by
their thumbs + bann in the
sun then I will rub them down
with deep heat to warm

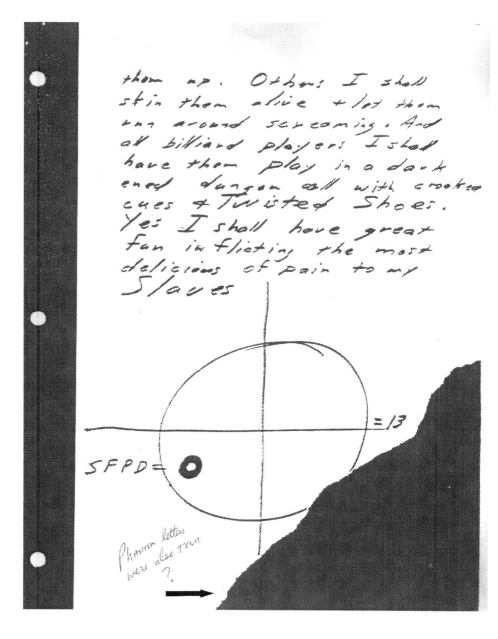

them up. Others I shall
skin them alive + let them
run around screaming. And
all billiard players I shall
have them play in a dark
end dungeon cell with crooked
cues + Twisted Shoes.
Yes I shall have great
fun inflicting the most
delicious of pain to my
Slaves

= 13

SFPD =

Phantom letters
were also fun
?

Portion of the July 24, 1970, letter sent to the San Francisco Chronicle in the Zodiac case.
(courtesy of Tom Voigt, www.zodiackiller.com)

In my opinion the Zodiac was specifically referring to the sign of the Zodiac as a "button." The repeated mentioning of the sign of the Zodiac immediately in front of the word "buttons" suggests, in no uncertain terms, that the sign of the Zodiac was in fact a button. If you take an ordinary sewing button and run thread through the button holes then cut the threads what emerges is the sign of the Zodiac.

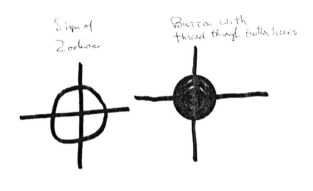

Sign of the Zodiac?

This is the Zodiac speaking
up to the end of Oct I have
killed 7 people. I have grown
rather angry with the police
for their telling lies about me.
So I shall change the way the
collecting of slaves. I shall
no longer announce to anyone.
when I comitt my murders,
they shall look like routine
robberies, killings of anger, +
a few fake accidents, etc.

The police shall never catch me,
because I have been too cleve-
for them.
1 I look like the description
   passed out only when I do
   my thing, the rest of the time
   I look entirke different. I
   shall not tell you what my
   descise consists of when I kill
2 As of yet I have left no
   fingerprints behind me contrary
   to what the police say

176

in my killings I wear trans-
parent finger tip guards. All it
is is 2 coats of airplane coment
coated on my finger tips - gutte
annoticible & very efective.
3 my killing tools have been bought
en through the mail order out-
fits before the ban went into
efect. except one & it was
bought out of the state.
So as you see the police don't
have much to work on. If you
wonder why I was wipe ing the
cab down I was leaving fake clews
fo- the police to run all over town
with, as one might say, I gave
theecops som bussy work to do to
Keep them happy. I enjoy needlling
the blue pigs. Hey bbe pig I
was in the park — you were aseing
fire trucks to mask the sound
of your cruzeing prowl cars. The
dogs never came with in 2
blocks of me & they were to
the west & there was only 2

groups of parking about 10 min apart then the motorcicles went by about 150 ft away going from south to north west. Ps. 2 cops pulled a goof abot 3 min after I left the cab. I was walking down the hill to the park when this cop car pulled up & one of them called me over & asked if I saw any one acting sapicisous or strange in the last 5 to 10 min + I said yes there was this man who was running by waveing a gun + the cops peeled rubber + went around the corner as I directed them & I dissapeared into the park abbot + a half away never to be seen again.

Hey pig doesnt it rile you up to have you noze rubbed in your booboos?

If you cops think Im going to take on a bos the way I stated I was, you deserve to have holes in your heads.

Take one bag of ammonium nitrate
fertlizer + 1gal of stove oil +
damp a few bags of gravel on
top + then set the shit off
+ will positivity ventalate any
thing that should be in the way
of the Blast.

The death machine is allready
made. I would have sent you
pictures but you would be nasty
enough to trace them back to
developer + then to me, so I
shall describe my masterpiece
to you. The nice part of it is
all the parts can be bought on
the open market with no quest
ions asked.

1 bat. pow clock - will run for
    aprox 1 year
1 photo electric switch
2 copper leaf springs
2 6V car bat
1 flash light bulb + reflector
1 mirror
2 18" cardboard tubes black with
    shoe polish in side + oute

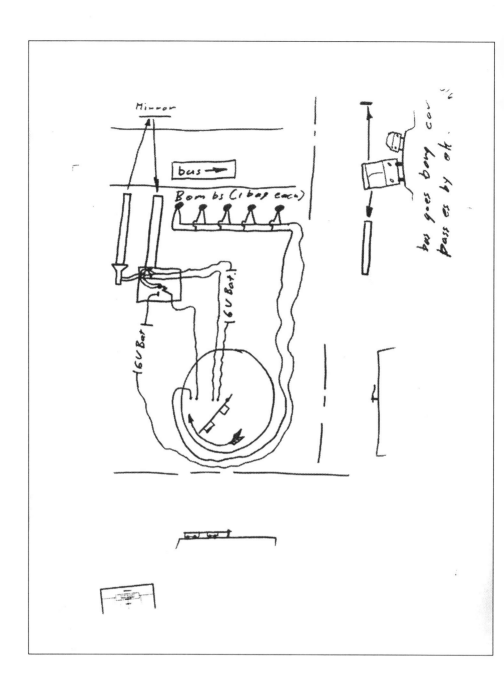

the system checks out from
one end to the other in my
tests. What you do not know
is whether the death machine
is at the sight or whether
it is being stored in my
basement for future use.
I think you do not have the
man power to stop this one
by continually searching the
road sides looking for this
thing. + it would be to re root
+ the schedule the buses bec
ause the bomb can be adapted
to new conditions.
Have fun !! By the way
it could be rather messy
if you try to blast me.

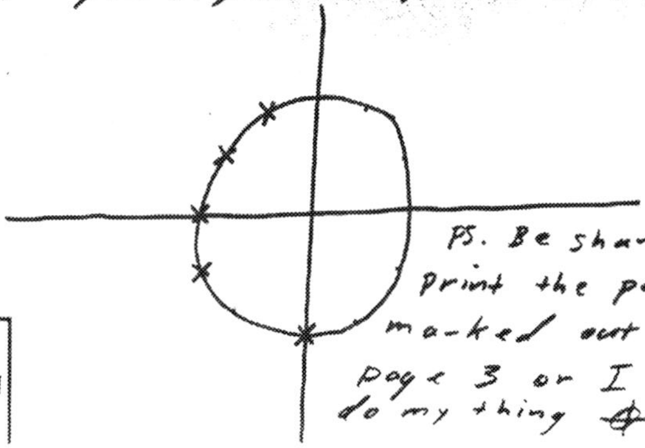

PS. Be shure to
print the part I
marked out on
page 3 or I shall
do my thing ⊕

To prove that I am the
Zodiac, Ask the Valleso
cop about my electric gun
sight which I used to start
my collecting of slaves.

November 9, 1969, letter sent to the *San Francisco Chronicle* in the Zodiac case
(courtesy of Tom Voigt, www.zodiackiller.com)

By November 9, 1969, the Zodiac had already killed at least six individuals, usually in secluded areas. These killings and his taunting, enigmatic letters to police and newspapers generated a great deal of fear in the general public. As though this weren't enough to satisfy his need for publicity and power, he added a new level of terror to his madness. Seldom do serial killers change their pattern or method of killing, including the type of victims. However, on November 9, 1969, the Zodiac threatened to do just that by sending a letter to the *San Francisco Chronicle* together with a drawing of a "bus bomb." The Zodiac indicated that the "bomb" was intended to be used to blow up a school bus full of children. At this point it is important to remember that the Zodiac had his own sense of humor that he wove into his deceptive writings. The Zodiac had written several phrases throughout his various letters that indicated he was having a "good time." For example, on August 7, 1969, he wrote, "By the way, are the police having a good time . . ." On November 8, 1969, the Zodiac wrote in his letter to the *San Francisco Chronicle*, "I thought you would need a good laugh before you hear the bad news." On November 10, 1969, he wrote in another letter to the *Chronicle*, "Have fun." On April 19, 1970, he wrote on a greeting card, "I hope you enjoy yourselves when I have my Blast." The Zodiac seemed to get a great deal of enjoyment, not only writing and taunting the police, but also from fooling them. I believe that for some sort of personal satisfaction, he wrote his "bus bomb" letter intending to instill fear in the public and gain the attention he craved. I also believe he received personal gratification knowing full well that his "bus bomb" was no bomb at all; in my opinion, it may have been a drawing of his sewing machine. To the Zodiac, this was great fun. I am confident that I can establish that the Zodiac's "bus bomb" was in fact a drawing of a sewing machine. Keep in mind that the Zodiac wrote in his November 10, 1969, letter to the *Chronicle*, "If you cops think I am going to take on a school bus the way I stated I was, you deserve to have holes in your head." He may have been referring to his method referred to in his October 14, 1969 letter in which he wrote, "School children make nice targets, I think I shall wipe out a school bus some morning. Just shoot out the front tire & then pick off the kiddies as they come bouncing out." Or, on the other hand, he may have been referring to his "bus bomb" described in his letter of November 9, 1969. In any event let's take a closer look at the Zodiac's "bus bomb" drawing that he included with his November 9, 1969, letter to the *Chronicle:*

Upon close examination, you can see the spool, thread, stitches, pressure plate, needle, shuttle (bus), mirror and side lever that are all parts that are associated with a sewing machine.

Zodiac Map 1

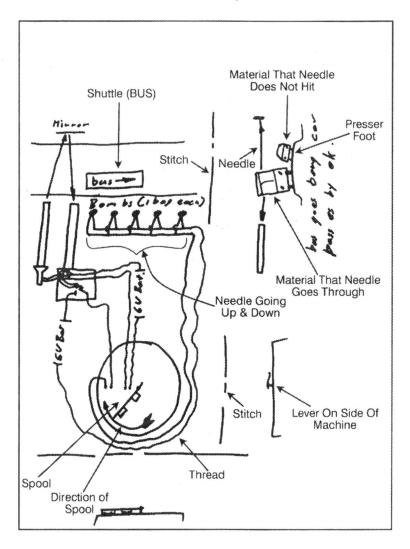

Zodiac's "Bus Bomb" appears to have been a drawing of a sewing machine

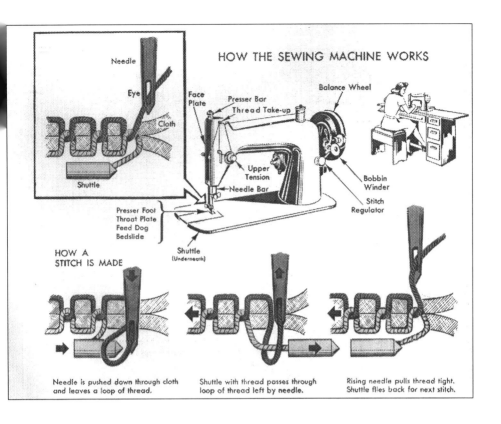

Illustration of a sewing machine from *The World Book Encyclopedia*, copyright World Book, Inc. By permission of the publisher, www.worldbook.com

The Zodiac was proficient at sewing (Note 48, page 320).

In his November 9, 1969, letter, the Zodiac referred to his "bus bomb" as a "**death machine**." He wrote "The system checks out from one end to the other in my tests. What you do not know is whether the **death machine** is at the sight or whether it is being stored in my basement for future use" (emphasis added). If you switch the word "sewing" for the word "death" and then figure the Zodiac used his imagination, while looking at his sewing machine, to concoct his grand story about the construction of a bus bomb it starts to make sense. He then mailed his letter to the *Chronicle* and received the attention he was looking for and personal satisfaction derived by fooling the detectives.

Unless, of course, you believe the Zodiac's version, on its face, that the drawing was in fact a bomb that included "mirrors on the side on the highway that reflects light to photoelectric cells that work only in daylight and cause several separate 'bombs' to go off that will strike a moving school bus (not a truck or other tall vehicle) and that will not strike a moving car. If you believe that, then I have a bridge for sale that you might be interested in purchasing.

CHANNEL SEVEN TALK SHOW

At 2:00 A.M., October 22, 1969, the Oakland California Police Department received a telephone call that may have come from the Zodiac killer. The caller requested a meeting with either attorney F. Lee Bailey or Melvin Belli. The caller wanted one otr the other to appear on a T.V. program known as the Channel Seven Talk Show. The meeting was scheduled; Melvin Belli appeared and received several telephone calls. The first of these calls may have come from the Zodiac Killer. Mr. Belli asked the caller if he could refer to him by a name other than Zodiac. The caller responded "Sam." Belli asked the caller where they could meet and the response was, "At the top of the Fairmont Hotel," a statement that may prove to be important in connection with later developments. It was reported that subsequent telephone calls to Mr. Belli were traced to a mental patient at the Napa State Hospital.

"DEAR MELVIN LETTER"
December 20, 1969

San Francisco attorney Melvin Belli received the following Christmas letter from the Zodiac on December 20, 1969:

Mr. Melvin M. Belli

1228 Mtgy

San Fran Calit

Mery Xmass &
New Year

187

Dear Melvin

This is the Zodiac speaking I
wish you a happy Christmass.
The one thing I ask of you is
this, please help me. I cannot
reach out for help because of
this thing in me wont let me.
I am finding it extreamly dif-
icult to hold it in check I am
afraid I will loose control
again and take my nineth &
posibly tenth victom. Please
help me I am drownding. At
the moment the children are
safe from the bomb because
it is so massive to dig in & the
triger mech requires much work
to get it adjusted just right. But
if I hold back too long from
no nine I will loose complet all
controol of my self & set the
bomb up. Please help me I can
not remain in control for much
longer.

December 20, 1969, letter to Melvin Belli in the Zodiac case.
(courtesy of Tom Voigt, www.zodiackiller.com)

PROPOSED SOLUTION:

In the letter you will notice the following:

"I am **f**inding	I am	**F**	
"I am **a**fraid"	I am	**A**	
The letter contains five words with			
Extra letters:			
Christmas**s**		**S**	
Extre**a**mly		**A**	
Nin**e**th	**E**		
Drown**d**ing			**D**
Contr**o**ol		**O**	
There are three words with missing letters:			
Di**f**icult	**F**		
Po**s**ibly	**S**		
Tri**g**er		**G**	
And the word:			
Vic**to**m	**TO**		

The word "complet" is crossed out and
not finished. All the Zodiac had to do to
finish this word was to add the letter "e,"
instead, he drew a single line through the
unfinished word and continued with the
letters: **ALL**   **ALL**

In my opinion, the word puzzle

might go like this: I AM F A GO TO S E DALLAS

KATHLEEN JOHNS
March 17, 1970

On March 17, 1970, Kathleen Johns was traveling with her ten-month-old baby on Interstate 5 near Bakersfield, California, on her way to Travis Air Force Base. At about midnight, when she turned onto Highway 132, she noticed headlights in her rear view mirror from a car that seemed to be following her. She slowed her vehicle down to let the other car pass. The car didn't pass her. Instead, she noticed blinking lights from the other vehicle. A stranger signaled her that one of her wheels was malfunctioning and to pull over and stop along the road. Kathleen was pregnant and apprehensive. She eventually pulled over and stopped her vehicle on the side of Highway 132. She allowed the stranger to attend to her wheel as she waited in her car. When she again started to drive, the wheel came completely off. The stranger stopped his vehicle and again approached her and offered assistance. "Oh no," he said. "The trouble's worse than I thought. I'll give you a ride to the service station." The stranger offered to drive her to a service station so she could summons help for her disabled vehicle. Kathleen could see the lights of an ARCO station about a quarter mile up the road. Kathleen was reluctant at first to accept a ride with him but then eventually accepted his offer. The stranger drove past the ARCO station and then past two exits. Kathleen's apprehension turned to fear not only for herself but also for her baby. She turned to the unknown driver, "Do you always go around helping people on the road like this?" He responded, "When I get through with them, they don't need any help." Kathleen Johns became totally afraid at this point. She knew she was in trouble. After driving down a lonely dirt road, the man said, "You know I'm going to kill you. I'm going to throw the baby out." Kathleen, although frightened, kept her head. She made a mental note of everything she could about her abductor and the contents of his vehicle. Her heart was pounding when she decided to make a run for it. When the stranger slowed down at a stop sign, Kathleen grabbed her baby and jumped from the moving car. She ran into tall grass and hid until the stranger was run off by a semi-truck driver (Robert Graysmith's interview with Kathleen Johns).

Later, at a local police station, Kathleen identified her abductor as the same person in the composite drawing of the Zodiac. Kathleen and her baby had apparently been riding with the Zodiac killer.

ALTERED PHILLIPS 66 MAP
June 26, 1970

The Zodiac sent a letter to the *San Francisco Chronicle* on June 26, 1970, stating:

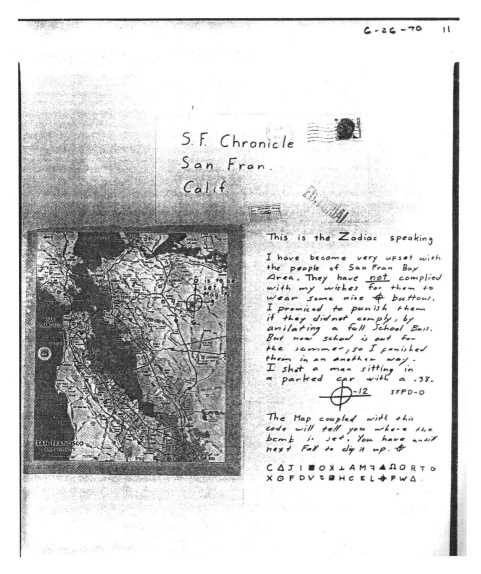

June 26, 1970 Phillips 66 Map in the Zodiac case.
(courtesy of Tom Voigt, www.zodiackiller.com)

A radian is a unit of measurement used by engineers and mathematicians of 57 degrees, 17 minutes, 44 seconds. It is an angle over an arc whose length is equal to the radius of a circle, of which the arc is a part.

The corporate headquarters for Phillips 66 is in the state of Oklahoma. The Phillips 66 sign on the Zodiac's map is located in the Pacific Ocean approximately eighty miles from the center of the sign of the Zodiac on the map. Dallas, Texas, is located approximately eighty miles south of the state of Oklahoma. Could the Phillips 66 decal on the map have anything to do with the solution to the Zodiac's puzzle?

GILBERT AND SULLIVAN'S: THE MIKADO
July 24, 1970

On July 24, 1970 the Zodiac sent his twelfth letter to the *San Francisco Chronicle*. In the letter he paraphrased a portion of Gilbert and Sullivan's *Mikado* from memory.

Here is a copy of the Zodiac's twelfth letter:

As some day it may hapen
that a victom must be found.
I've got a little list. I've
got a little list, of society
offenders who might well be
underground who would never
be missed who would never be
missed. There is the pest-
ulentual nucences who whrite
for autographs, all people who
have flabby hands and irritat-
ing laughs. All children who
are up in dates and (implore)
you with im platt. All people
who are shakeing hands shake
hands like that. And all third
persons who with unspoiling
take thoes who insist. They'd
none of them be missed. They'd
none of them be missed. There's
the banjo seranader and
the others of his race and
the piano orginast I got him
on the list. All people who
eat pepermint and phomphit

in your face, they would
never be missed They would
never be missed And the
Idiout who phraises with in-
thusastic tone of centuries
but this and every country but
his own. And the lady from
the provences who dress like
a guy who doesn't cry and
the singurly abnomily the
girl who never kissed. I don't
think she would be missed
Im shure she wouldn't be
missed. And that nice impriest
that is rather rife the judic-
ial hummerest I've got him on
the list All funny fellows, com-
mic men and clowns of private
life. They'd none of them be
missed. They'd none of them be
missed. And uncompromiseing
kind such as wachamacallit,
thingmebob, and likewise, well-
-nevermind, and tut tut tut tut,
and whatshisname, and you know

who, but the task of filling up the blanks I rather leave up to you. But it really doesn't matter whom you place upon the list, for none of them be missed, none of them be missed.

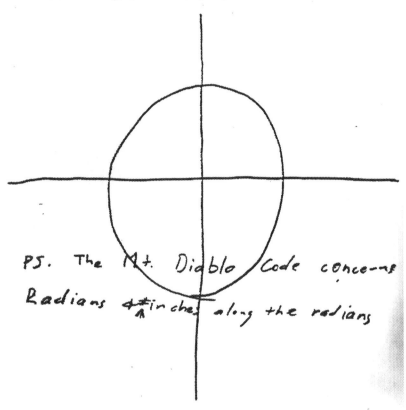

PS. The Mt. Diablo Code concerns Radians & # inches along the radians

June 24, 1970, "Mikado" letter in the Zodiac case
(courtesy of Tom Voigt, www.zodiackiller.com)

One line of the Zodiac's version reads as follows:

"All children who are up in dates and *implore* you with implatt"

The correct verse from the *Mikado* is written as follows:

"All children who are up in dates and *floor you* with em flat. . ."

The Zodiac misquoted the original *Mikado* by using the word "Implore" instead of "floor you." The word "implore" is a word that is not commonly used. John Keats, included the word "implore" in his poem "The Eve of St. Agnes."

"Buttress'd from moonlight, stands he and implores."

If the Zodiac was in fact an admirer of the works of John Keats, it could be possible that he misquoted the *Mikado* by substituting a word from the Keats' poem that was buried in his memory.

ZODIAC'S HALLOWEEN CARD
October 28, 1970

On Wednesday, October 28, 1970, *San Francisco Chronicle* crime reporter Paul Avery received a Halloween card from the Zodiac. The Zodiac enjoyed sending greeting cards and may have been particularly fond of holidays. This could account for the number of murders that took place on holidays that coincide with traditional greeting cards, i.e. St. Patrick's Day, Valentines Day, Labor Day, Christmas and so on. Avery's Halloween card stated in two places "sorry no cipher." This card was not a cipher. In my opinion it was a different kind of puzzle. This time a seek-a-word puzzle. The trick might be to discover his name written in the puzzle.

Here is a picture of the Paul Avery Halloween card:

Zodiac Halloween card. (courtesy of Tom Voigt, www.zodiackiller.com)

The name "FRED" can be found in what might be a word puzzle.

AIRMAIL LETTER

Here are some interesting facts that relate to the Zodiac killings:

a. Practically every one of the Zodiac murders occurred on weekends or on holidays.

b. On February 26, 1969, Darlene Ferrin mentioned to her babysitter, "I heard he was back from out of state." when referring to a stranger who had been parked outside her home at 560 Wallace in Vallejo, California.

c. On September 27, 1969, Bryan Hartnell and Cecelia Shephard were attacked by the Zodiac at Berryessa Lake. Bryan Hartnell told the police:

"That voice... It was like... a student. But kind of a drawl not a Southern drawl though."

d. d.March 22, 1970, another victim, Kathleen Johns, described the Zodiac as follows: "I remember thinking he may be a serviceman."

e. The police had speculated that the Zodiac may have been a Navy man who committed his crimes while docked in San Francisco Harbor. Several eyewitness accounts identified the Zodiac as having a military-style crew cut, that he wore a Navy-type windbreaker, that his pants were pleated and his shoes spit shined.

f. On March 15, 1971, the Los Angeles Times received a letter from the Zodiac. The letter contained this phrase: "The longer they fiddle and fart around the more slaves I will collect for my afterlife" (emphasis added). Author Robert Graysmith argued in his book *Zodiac*, that the term "fiddle and fart around is a phrase used by older people around the state of Texas, most commonly in Lubbock County, Texas."

g. The word "AIRMAIL" took up one third of the envelope used by the Zodiac to mail the March 15, 1971, letter to the Los Angeles Times.

Zodiac's "Airmail letter." (courtesy of Tom Voigt, www.zodiackiller.com)

What this indicates to me is that the Zodiac may very well have been from a state other than California. When he writes the word "AIRMAIL," he is almost shouting out that he air-mailed the letter himself. Several coincidences seem to point to the state of Texas as being the home of the Zodiac. The letters may have been personally air-mailed when the Zodiac was transported to California by military aircraft. The known California murders committed by the Zodiac killer took place between the years 1966-1969, at the same time the Vietnam War was being waged in Southeast Asia. Soldiers and sailors were being transported by the thousands in the United States at that time from one military installation to another. Few restrictions that I know of were imposed to gain access to military flights. There were few, if any, background checks, no metal detectors to go through, just a review of the person's identification, and a thumb print. It was possible for someone to forge the required identification needed to fly "seat waiting" on military aircraft. If the person appeared as an officer, very few questions would be asked. If someone was military personnel, dependent of military personnel, or if that person had forged documents with the necessary picture identification and dressed as an Air Force or Navy man. He could have easily flown from Texas to California on a Friday afternoon and returned to Texas on Sunday night without detection. This person would probably have known that military manifests would be routinely destroyed approximately two years after each flight, thereby eliminating the evidence linking him to his method of transportation from one state to another. California has several Air Force and Naval air stations near the locations of each Zodiac murder.

Kathleen Johns was abducted by a person thought to be the Zodiac while on her way to her mother's house in Petaluma.

March Air Force Base is located near Riverside, California, where Cheri Jo Bates was murdered. The Grand Prairie Naval Air Station (Dallas NAS) was located near Dallas, during this time period. The Carlswell Air Station was located in Fort Worth near Dallas during the Vietnam War. The Grand Prairie Naval Air Station and Carlswell Air Force Base have since either been closed or incorporated into the Fort Worth Naval Air Station in Fort Worth.

DONNA LASS
September 6, 1970

Samuel Clemens once said about Lake Tahoe, "The lake burst upon us, a noble sheet of blue water lifted six thousand three hundred feet above the level of the sea, and walled in between a rim of snow-clad mountain peaks . . . thought it must surely be the fairest picture the whole earth affords."

My brother owned a cottage near the famous Donner Pass just west of Truckee off Highway 89. We vacationed in this area and skied the mountains at Heavenly and Squaw Valley. We also tried our luck at the Boomtown Casino playing black jack, so I became somewhat familiar with this area. This is a beautiful and fascinating part of America, rugged and unforgiving, full of history of the American West, including the story of a group of unfortunate emigrants who, in late fall 1846, found themselves at the foothills of the Sierra Nevada Mountains. They were ill equipped and totally unprepared for the onslaught of one of the worst snowfalls in decades that descended upon them. George Donner, Jacob Donner, James Reed, Charles Graves, Franklin Graves, Lewis Keseberg, their families and several other weary travelers became trapped in what would become, for several in their party, a wintry tomb. Up to twenty feet of snow fell during the first week of their captivity. It wasn't long before food supplies became depleted. Starvation soon followed. The historical account of the plight of the emigrants reflects cannibalism among some of the survivors. After the ordeal was finally over and the survivors rescued in the spring of 1847, Keseberg was tried for the murders of George and Tamzene Donner, Lavinah Murphy, George Foster, Samuel Donner and Mr. Wolfinger. He was acquitted because of lack of evidence.

On Labor Day, September 6, 1970, a twenty-five year old nurse by the name of Donna Lass mysteriously disappeared from a South Lake Tahoe Hotel. The authorities never found her or her remains. There are several remote locations in this vast expanse that have not been explored by humans for years. A body could easily be hidden off a dirt road and never be found. The remains of more than one murder victim have been found in remote areas north of Lake Tahoe over the years. The police were at a standstill, no clues, no body, just a pretty young nurse missing and a family desperate to find her.

On Monday, March 22, 1971, Paul Avery of the *San Francisco Chronicle* received a postcard written in the Zodiac's hand.

200

On the reverse side of the card the Zodiac had glued an advertisement that had run in the *Chronicle* two days before. It was an artist's drawing of the Forest Pines Condominiums Village located near Lake Tahoe. The Avery postcard contains the words, "Pass Lake Tahoe Areas." The first letters of each word in this phrase are **PLTA**. These letters, when switched around, spell "**PLAT**." A plat is a map. Was the Zodiac sending a clue that may include the directions to the body of Donna Lass?

The South Lake Tahoe Police considered the possibility of a connection between the disappearance of Donna Lass and the Zodiac killer. For years the search for Donna Lass went on without any success. On January 30, 1974, nearly three years after her disappearance, the *San Francisco Chronicle* received the following note in the Zodiac's handwriting:

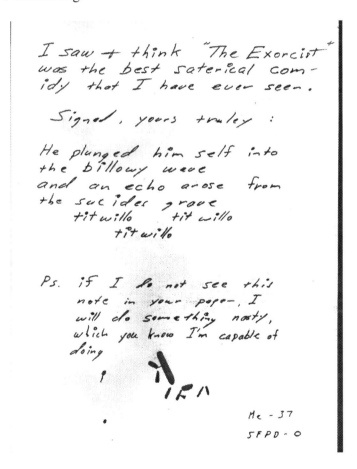

Zodiac's "Exorcist" letter. (courtesy of Tom Voigt, www.zodiackiller.com)

The "Exorcist" was not a satirical comedy; it was a horror movie. The words satirical and truly are misspelled, as are other words.

SAT   eri   CAL

Tru   LEY

These misspelled words may spell **SATLEY, CAL**. Sattley, California, is a small town located on State Highway 89 in Sierra County, north of Lake Tahoe. The symbols that follow the Zodiac's "Exorcist" letter may represent roads leading to Sattley, from Lake Tahoe, California.

The mark on the left side of the map may represent the location of the remains of Donna Lass.

Additional comparisons between the Phantom Killer letters and the Zodiac letters are shown below.

DL #9-616

letter which bears postmark of "June 24, 1946, 3 PM, Texarkana, Ark. Tex.
This letter is typewritten in the lower case. The third letter was also
postmarked during 1946 but the remaining part of the postmark has been
torn off. This letter was received by _____ and is a handwritten letter. The last two letters were mailed in a three cent stamped
envelope of the long type that can be purchased at the Post Office. The
first letter is in a small envelope and the stamp has been placed on the
envelope. These letters are being set forth:

I. "Soon as read no time to lose for lives are in danger·

The writer would like to meet you personally, but every
movement is being watched, on account thinking writer overheard
conversation or least portion of it. Wish you would never give
me away ever if you knew as my life would not be worth any more
to these parties than was of those lately murdered.

"Please believe this, gun of German make, using .45 or 38 caliber,
was borrowed recently for more trouble, so watch this week end
for something or later. They said that had gotten by with so much
_____ is carrier of gun, gotten from _____
_____ they said had 40 or 50 to cover up for
alibis if ever questioned. _____ said like first girl murdered,
well enought no one else not to have her did not mention last
couple, _____ is clever and cunning gotten by with stealing and
rapping and has plenty to help him, as his dad is law on Ark side.

"Said _____ was carrying gun for own protection and would
have good alibi of March 24. This is true and hope you will see
into this as are getting braver please burn this, even tho true,
writer would be killed if ever known, this is valuable to you.
Shake him down. But please burn. Writer will not signname as
want to live."

II. _____

"Some time ago you were written a letter, concerning three different
parties, addressed to you at Texas Police Station, and whether you
got it or not, is not known.

[handwritten margin notes:] FBI Anspakn? Weekend written as two words? See letter to Unique Times Herald pages 108-109 Zodios by Robert Graysmith

- 2 -

(Zodiac letter to Vallejo Times-Herald
August 1, 1969)

(Courtesy of Tom Voight
ZodiacKiller.com)

6

(Zodiac Killer Letter Written 11/9/69)

This is the Zodiac speaking
up to the end of Oct I have
killed 7 people. I have grown
rather angry with the police
for their telling lies about me.
So I shall change the way the
collecting of slaves. I shall
no longer announce to anyone.
when I comitt my murders,
they shall look like routine
robberies, killings of anger, +
a few fake accidents, etc.

The police shall never catch me,
because I have been too (clever)
for them.
1 I look like the description
passed out only when I do
my thing, the rest of the time
I look entirle different. I
shall not tell you what my
descise consists of when I kill
2 As of yet I have left no
fingerprints behind me contrary
to what the police say

(COURTESY of TOM Voight
ZodiAc KIIIeR·com)

205

DL #9-616

(letter cont'd)

"Sometimes letters written like this seem to be maybe to you people not too much importance, but to others possibly would mean their life. This letter referred to was written in time before the Starks' murder and you were given three names and this is another note or letter written in behalf of lives of people who care to live, but cannot come to you. Trusting you are not favoring no certain Ark. Law man or his friend, which is not written in any way, shape or manner, as an accusation of any kind with reference to our laws or you. If you will do some questiong think you will have something, as as what we need in this town is co-operation and no pay off. Talk getting mighty big and brave and time getting ripe, so get busy and watch these people.

"Trust you will keep this confidential as you said you would in the newspaper, is not written with spirit of ralling things up, but with all good intention to help protect the lives of not only one person, but possibly many.

"If you will check Blue two door Sedan, without top, you, of it' had been the findings, no doubt would of been an advantage to you. This Sedan belongs to boy not over 24, North of Texarkana, Arkansas. Has been washed and rewashed, and had two friends to help him, and gun was returned to one of them. Keep that confidential, confidential as it measn the lives of more than one."

III

"As some people have hobbies I have one looking at different license number, especially State licenses and have tried to find you in or on the phone and am told you were out and wish you would keep this confidential. While travelling out highway toward Little Rock noticed car parked near railroad track and it backed out, since then learned car the night Mr. Stark's was murdered was parked close to railroad track, road where told _____ went across to sisters house and this car number _____ and saw it since on trips to Texarkana, but just recently learned the

b6

b7C

- 3 -

in my killings I wear trans-
parent finger tip guards. All it
is is 2 coats of airplane cement
coated on my finger tips — quite
unnoticible + very efective.
3 my killing tools have been bought
en through the mail order out-
fits before the ban went into
efect. except one & it was
bought out of the state.
So as you see the police don't
have much to work on. If you
wonder why I was wipeing the
cab down I was leaving fake clews
for the police to run all over town
with, as one might say, I gave
the cops som (bussy) work to do to
keep them happy. I enjoy needling
the blue pigs. Hey blue pig I
was in the park — you were aseing
Fire trucks to mask the sound
of your cruzeing prowl cars. The
dogs never come with in 2
blocks of me + they were to
the west + there was only 2.

(Zodiac letter written 11/9/69)

groups of parking about 10 min
apart then the motor cicles
went by about 150 ft away
going from south to north west.
ps. 2 cops pulled a goof about 3
min after I left the cab. I was
walking down the hill to the
park when this cop car pulled up
+ one of them called me over +
asked if I saw any one
acting sapicisous or strange
in the last 5 to 10 min + I said
yes there was this man who
was running by waveing a gun
+ the cops peeled rubber +
went around the corner es
I directed them + I dissap —
eared into the park about +
a half away never to be seen
again.
Hey pig doesnt it (rile you up)
to have you noze rubed in your
booboos?
If you cops think Im going to take
on a bos the way I stated I was
you deserve to have holes in your
heads.

(COURTESY of Tom Voight ZodiAC KiLLeR.com)

208

(As some) day it may hapen
that a victom must be found.
I've got a little list. I've
got a little list, of society
offenders who might well be
underground who would never
be missed who would never be
missed. There is the pest-
ulentual nucences who whrite
for autographs, all people who
have flabby hands and irritat-
ing laughs. All children who
are up in dates and (implore)
you with im platt. All people
who are shakeing hands shake
hands like that. And all third
persons who with unspoiling
take thoes who insist. They'd
nene of them be missed. They'd
none of them be missed. There's
the banjo seranader and
the others of his race and
the piano orginast I got him
on the list. All people who
eat pepermint and phomphit

7 (1947, FBI Report on Phantom Killer of Texarkana)

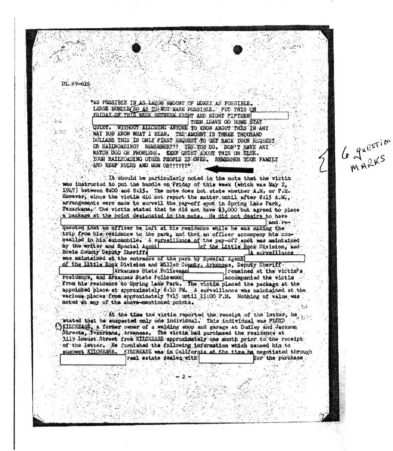

DL #9-616

"AS POSSIBLE IN AS LARGE AMOUNT OF MONEY AS POSSIBLE.
LARGE BUNDLE SO AS TO NOT MAKE POSSIBLE.' PUT THIS ON
FRIDAY OF THIS WEEK BETWEEN EIGHT AND EIGHT FIFTEEN
                                    THEN LEAVE GO HOME STAY
QUIET. WITHOUT ALLOWING ANYONE TO KNOW ABOUT THIS IN ANY
WAY YOU KNOW WHAT I MEAN. THE AMOUNT IS THREE THOUSAND
DOLLARS THIS IS ONLY FIRST REQUEST TO GET BACK YOUR REQUEST
OR RAILROADING? REMEMBER?? YES YOU DO. DON'T HAVE ANY
WATCH DOG OR PROWLERS. KEEP QUIET ABOUT THIS OR ELSE.
YOUR RAILROADING OTHER PEOPLE IS OVER. REMEMBER YOUR FAMILY
AND KEEP RULES AND HIM OR?????"

6 question MARKS

It should be particularly noted in the note that the victim
was instructed to put the bundle on Friday of this week (which was May 2,
1947) between 8:00 and 8:15. The note does not state whether A.M. or P.M.
However, since the victim did not report the matter until after 8:15 A.M.,
arrangements were made to surveil the pay-off spot in Spring Lake Park,
Texarkana. The victim stated that he did not have $3,000 but agreed to place
a package at the point designated in the note. He did not desire to have
                                                          and re-
quested that an officer be left at his residence while he was making the
trip from his residence to the park, and that an officer accompany him con-
cealled in his automobile. A surveillance of the pay-off spot was maintained
by the writer and Special Agent   of the Little Rock Division, and
Bowie County Deputy Sheriff   A surveillance
was maintained at the entrance of the park by Special Agent
of the Little Rock Division and Miller County, Arkansas, Deputy Sheriff
          Arkansas State Policeman   remained at the victim's
residence, and Arkansas State Policeman   accompanied the victim
from his residence to Spring Lake Park. The victim placed the package at the
appointed place at approximately 8:10 PM. A surveillance was maintained at the
various places from approximately 7:15 until 11:00 P.M. Nothing of value was
noted at any of the above-mentioned points.

At the time the victim reported the receipt of the letter, he
stated that he suspected only one individual. This individual was FLOYD
KILCREASE, a former owner of a welding shop and garage at Dudley and Jackson
Streets, Texarkana, Arkansas. The victim had purchased the residence at
3119 Locust Street from KILCREASE approximately one month prior to the receipt
of the letter. He furnished the following information which caused him to
suspect KILCREASE. KILCREASE was in California at the time he negotiated through
          real estate dealer with   for the purchase

- 2 -

210

(Zodiac's "dRipping pen" greeting CARD, Nov 8, 1969)

This is the Z o d i a c s p e a k i n g

I though you would need a good laugh before you hea- the bad news you wont get the news fo- a while yet PS could you print this new cipher- in your front page? I get awfully lonely when I am ignored, So lonely I could do my **Thing!!!!!!!**

and i can't do a thing with it!

(6 ExclAMATioN MARKS)

(6 Lines unde WORD "Thing")

Des July Aug Sept Oct = 7

(CourTesy of Ton Voight ZodiAe Killer.com)

211

AFTERWORD

It is my intention to revisit these cold cases and hopefully rekindle some interest and possibly lead to a resolution of these matters once and for all. If only a portion of my ideas and theories are accurate, then the contents of this book might lead to some evidence that may be used to determine the identity of the killers. The individuals involved in the Cleveland Torso Murders, the murders of Georgette Bauerdorf, Jeanne Axford French, Suzanne Degnan and other murder victims mentioned are probably all dead by now. William Heirens is still alive as of this writing and remains incarcerated by the State of Illinois in Dixon, Illinois. I believe there is a high probability that the Zodiac Killer is still alive and is more than likely incarcerated in a penal institution for some other similar crime. Based on all of the research I have completed, I would suspect that if he is alive the Zodiac is probably incarcerated in the State of Texas. Dr. Donald Schrag wrote in 1979, "All multiple or mass murderers either become incarcerated for life as a common criminal, are declared psychopathic and are placed in a criminal institution or realize the hopelessness of their condition and seek intensive psychiatric assistance (*Wichita Eagle-Beacon*, August 5, 1979). If the DNA of all criminals between the ages of fifty-seven to seventy-five years old currently incarcerated for serial murder could be tested and their DNA compared to the known DNA of the Zodiac, the odds might favor ferreting out the culprit. I selected the representative age group based on possible eyewitness accounts in the Zodiac case. A possible witness in the Cheri Jo Bates murder on October 10, 1966, reported the possible age of her assailant at thirty-five. If this was an accurate report, then the Zodiac would have been born in 1931, and would be seventy-six in 2006. In the Darlene Ferrin case a possible witness indicated the "man at Terry's: thirty-five to thirty-eight in 1969. If this witness report was accurate, the Zodiac's birth date would have been 1931-1934, and he would be seventy-two to seventy-five in 2006. Zodiac witness Michael Mageau (who was not considered to be reliable because of his condition at the time) thought his attacker was between twenty-six to thirty years of age in 1969. If Mageau was correct in his assessment, the Zodiac would be between the ages of sixty-three to sixty-seven in 2006, and would have been born between 1939-1943. A possible witness on October 11, 1969, described the Zodiac as being thirty-five to forty-five years old. If accurate, the Zodiac's date of birth would have fallen between the years 1924-1934, and he would be seventy-two to eighty-two years old in 2006. Possible Zodiac witness, Sandra Betts, described the man as being thirty-eight years old in 1969. If accurate and if see did run into the Zodiac, he would have been born in 1934 and would be 73 years old in 2006.

It is quite possible that the Zodiac is imprisoned for some other offense other than serial murder. With that in mind a prisoner profile could be conducted using certain parameters as guidelines. The study could be narrowed by eliminating all black men and all women because there has never been any indication (other than Mary Jeanne Larey) that the Zodiac was a woman or a black man. The search should concentrate on strong, highly intelligent white male between 5'8" and 6'4" tall, weighing between 180-220 pounds when originally incarcerated, who enjoy poetry and opera. The inmate might have a background in the teaching profession and enjoy sewing. He may be involved in softball or baseball in the prison system. Eliminate from the search any prisoner with an arm or leg missing unless the limb was severed after 1977. Focus on an inmate who was convicted for killing a stranger, not a spouse or relative. Concentrate on inmates who killed women or couples. Look for an inmate who killed at close range either with a knife or gun. Look for an inmate who killed more than one person, who has a large ego and who enjoys mailing greeting cards and postcards. For years the emphasis has been trying to solve the clues sent by the Zodiac. Finding the Zodiac in prison might be the easiest and best route to take.

If the authorities wait too long the same thing might happen to the Zodiac's DNA that happened to author Patricia Cornwell's suspect in the Jack the Ripper case, namely, Walter Sickert. All known DNA of Walter Sickert was destroyed when his body was cremated in 1942 (unless of course DNA from the remains of Sickert's natural mother could be analyzed). Worse yet, if the Zodiac is currently incarcerated, he may someday be freed as a "harmless old man," by an uninformed, sympathetic parole board. At the very least DNA samples of all convicted murderers who fit the Zodiac's profile should be preserved in the event of their deaths as a method of trying to resolve these old cold cases.

Any legal restraints or constitutional issues concerning this method of inmate profiling and DNA testing should be overcome. If the profiling created a reasonable belief that a particular inmate might be responsible for any of the murders mentioned in this text, then in that event DNA testing and comparisons would be appropriate. In a 2-1 decision in 2003, the Ninth Circuit Court of Appeals in San Francisco ruled that a law requiring parolees to give blood for a DNA databank used to investigate crimes violates the Fourth Amendment ban on unreasonable searches and seizures. The reason given was that blood would be extracted from parolees who are not suspected of committing new crimes. The Court, in its decision, did mention that other inmates, like parolees, retain certain rights of privacy. "Even parolees maintain a reasonable expectation of privacy in their own bodies," said Judge Stephen Reinhart in the majority decision. Inmates who are incarcerated for murder and other serious crimes who fit the test of "probable cause" based on a reasonable belief that they may have committed additional felonies should be subject to DNA testing. This is not a difficult or terribly expensive task and should be conducted for the benefit of the victims.

Based on the following clues I would suggest that the prisoner profiling and DNA comparisons begin with inmates in the 57-76-year-old category in the State of Texas:

1. The Phantom Killer wore a cloth-hood over his head and attacked couples on secluded lover's lanes at night.

2. The Phantom Killer attacked and murdered his victims at close range approximately 175 miles from Dallas, Texas.

3. Two of the Phantom Killer's victims were murdered in Texarkana, Arkansas, not far from a night club called Club Dallas.

4. In 1946, the Phantom Killer appeared to be inexperienced at his trade based on the fact that he wore a loosely fitting cloth-hood over his head that probably interfered with his eyesight. The hood had slits for the eyes and mouth but not the nose. He carried a gun in one hand and a flashlight in his other hand. In addition Betty Jo Booker and Jimmy Hollis were playing in a band at a "young people's dance" that might have also been attended by their stalker who also may have been a young person.

5. In different attacks in California in 1969, the Zodiac wore a hood over his head that did not interfere with his vision and he used a rifle with a flashlight attached to the barrel, thus freeing the other hand. The hood had slits for the eyes and mouth but not for the nose.

6. In 1969, the Zodiac wrote in one of his letters "Because the longer they fiddle

and fart around, the more slaves I will collect." The author Robert Graysmith has suggested that this form of slang is used predominately by older people, most commonly around Lubbock, Texas.

7. On August 7, 1969, the Zodiac wrote in a letter, "Bullshit that area is surrounded by high hills and trees." The word "bullshit" is used throughout the United States but quite frequently in the Lone Star State, famous for its Long Horn Steers.

8. Darlene Ferrin and her family visited the Dallas/Fort Worth area in 1962, and gave a stranger their Vallejo, California, address and phone number. When in Texas, Darlene told a man who was with them in a bowling alley to "push off" and in effect snubbed his advances.

9. The Zodiac's "Dear Melvin" letter may provide a clue that indicates that he was from Dallas, Texas.

10. The Zodiac may have, and in my estimation probably did, originate from a state other than the State of California. He killed several individuals in California on weekends and holidays but for some reason not during the week. The murders occurred at a time when the United States was engaged in war in Vietnam and Cambodia. A serviceman, or someone pretending to be a serviceman, dressed like a serviceman and with the proper, forged documents, could easily travel freely throughout the United States on either domestic or military flights.

11. During the Vietnam War there was a military naval air station in Dallas, Texas and a military air station in Fort Worth, Texas. The State of California has several military and naval air stations some of which are located close to the sites where the Zodiac committed his murders.

12. In 1969, Paul Stine was killed by the Zodiac in San Francisco in his taxi. Two hours earlier Stine had been at the airport.

13. One of the envelopes sent by the Zodiac included the words "AIRMAIL" written in large letters. However the letter not sent by the US Postage Service by airmail.

14. On March 17, 1970, Kathleen Johns was traveling to the Travis Air Force Base when she was abducted by a person that fit the description of the Zodiac Killer.

15. In the Phantom Murders and in the Zodiac murders several of the letters

were typed in upper case. Letters were mailed to the stepfather and father of a victim who had been brutally murdered.

16. Nearly all of the Zodiac murders and attacks occurred on weekends and holidays.

17. The Phantom's shoe size was estimated at 9 ½-10 ½. The Zodiac's shoe size was estimated at 10 ½.

Solving the Zodiac murders in California becomes more and more difficult as time passes. Witnesses die; original detectives assigned to the cases retire or pass away; police agencies become burdened with several hundred if not thousands of murders, rapes, burglaries and other crimes that call for more immediate attention. After the murders, people grow older, a new generation emerges, and the general public, although somewhat interested, becomes apathetic towards these cold cases. Those who survive and were directly affected by the acts of terror and brutality never forget. Their lives were forever changed. They became burdened with the great loss and agony suffered as a result of a seemingly senseless crime that touched their lives somewhere in the distant past. Establishing the identity of a killer after years have passed since the crimes took place is a discouraging task, but not an impossible one. With some additional detective work, a little luck and forensics, one or more of these killers may be eventually identified.

SYNOPSIS OF VICTIMS: TORSO MURDERS AND RELATED CASES

DATE	VICTIM
September 5, 1934	A torso of a woman identified as "the Lady of the Lakes" is located near 156th Street in Cleveland.
September 23, 1935	An individual described as Victim No.1 is found at the foot of Jackass Hill in Cleveland. Victim No. 2, later identified as Edward Andrassy, is found near the body of Victim No.1. Both had been decapitated and emasculated.
January 26, 1936	The torso of Victim No. 3, Flo Polillo, is discoved behind Hart Manufacturing Plant in Cleveland.
June 5, 1936	Victim No. 4, known as the "Tattooed Man," is found in Cleveland's Kingsbury Run.
July 22, 1936	Victim No. 5 is found decapitated on Cleveland's west side.
September 10, 1936	Victim No. 6 is found dismembered in Cleveland.
May 5, 1937	Victim No. 7's upper torso is found in Lake Erie off of East 30th Street in Cleveland.
June 6, 1937	The skull of Victim No. 8 is found in Cleveland under the Lorain-Carnegie Bridge.
July 6, 1937	Searchers in Cleveland scour the banks of the Cuyahoga River for the remains of victim No. 9.
July 9, 1937	The lower half of Victim No. 10 is discovered in Cleveland floating down the Cuyahoga.
August 16, 1938	The dismembered torsos of Victim No. 11 and Victim No.12 are discovered at the East 9th-Lake Shore dump site in Cleveland.
1939-1942	At least five more torso victims are found in Pennsylvania.
October 12, 1944	Georgette Bauerdorf is found murdered in her Los Angeles apartment.
June 5, 1945	Josephine Ross is murdered in Chicago.
December 10, 1945	Frances Brown is murdered in Chicago. Her killer leaves a note on her bedroom wall in red lipstick.

January 7, 1946	Twenty-seven days later, 6-year-old Suzanne Degnan is murdered and dismembered in Chicago by someone with the skill of a butcher.
September 4, 1946	Seventeen-year-old William Heirens pleads guilty to the murders of Ross, Brown and Degnan.
September 5, 1946	William Heirens is handed three consecutive life sentences for the murders and one year to life for burglaries and assaults.
January 14, 1947	Almost exactly one year after the murder and dismemberment of little Suzanne Degnan, Elizabeth Short (the Black Dahlia) is mutilated, killed and cut in half, by someone "with the skill of a surgeon" in Los Angeles. The killer calls himself the Black Dahlia Avenger.
February 10, 1947	Exactly 27 days later Jeanne French is murdered in Los Angeles. A note in red lipstick is written on her body.
February 12, 1947	Ica Mable M'Grew is kidnapped and raped in Los Angeles. The Black Dahlia Avenger is a possible suspect.
March 12, 1947	The nude body of Evelyn Winters is found near railroad tracks in Los Angeles. The Black Dahlia Avenger is a possible suspect.
May 11, 1947	Laura Elizabeth Trelstad is found strangled in Long Beach, California. The Black Dahlia Avenger is a possible suspect.
July 8, 1947	Rosenda Josephine Mondragon's body is found near railroad tracks in Los Angeles. The Black Dahlia Avenger is a possible suspect.
February 14, 1948	Viola Norton is savagely beaten by two men near the location where the Black Dahlia's bisected body was found one year earlier. The Black Dahlia Avenger is a possible suspect.
June 13, 1949	Louise Margaret Springer is kidnapped and murdered in Los Angeles. Her assailant violated her with a 14-inch finger-thick tree branch. She worked two blocks from where the body of the Black Dahlia was discovered January 15, 1947. The Black Dahlia Avenger is a possible suspect.

June 12, 1950   Cuyahoga County Coroner Dr. Gerber estimates that forty-four-year-old Robert Robertson was killed on June 12, 1950, the same day he disappeared. Robertson's torso and other body parts were found near Norris Brothers Company Movers at 2138 Davenport Avenue in Cleveland on July 22, 1950. If Dr. Gerber's estimated date of death was correct, then this murder could not have been committed by Jack Anderson Wilson because on June 12, 1950, according to his five-page rap sheet, Wilson was arrested and charged in Los Angeles with suspicion of burglary. Robertson was a suspected homosexual (page 191, *Torso*).

CHRONOLOGY OF THE TORSO MURDERS AND OTHER RELATED MURDERS

August 5, 1920

Birthdate of Arnold Smith, a/k/a Jack Anderson Wilson, whose birthdate is also reported as 8/5/24. Wilson is born in Canton, Ohio, and spends his early years in that state.

September 5, 1934

First torso murder victim found in Cleveland is known as the "Lady of the Lakes."

1935

Elliot Ness becomes Cleveland's Director of Public Safety.

September 23, 1935

Edward Andrassy, Victim No. 1, and Victim No. 2 are found at the foot of Jackass Hill 1in Cleveland. The killer may have tried to burn one of the victims.

January 26, 1936

Body parts of Flo Polillo (Victim No. 3) are discovered behind Hart Manufacturing Plant in Cleveland.

June, 1936

The headless torso of a white male is found in an abandoned box car near New Castle by railroad detectives. The individual may have been killed in Cleveland and later located in a box car that moved by rail to New Castle.

June 5, 1936

The "Tattooed Man" (Victim No. 4) is discovered in Cleveland's Kingsbury Run. His head is wrapped in his pants.

June 27-October 4, 1936

The Great Lakes Exposition takes place in Cleveland. Jack Anderson Wilson attends.

July 22, 1936

The decapitated torso of Victim No. 5 is located on Cleveland's west side.

September, 1936

Detectives Orley May and Emil Musil were told that a woman who had been in the workhouse said that, "Another inmate named Helen O'Leary had identified Jack Wilson, a former butcher who had worked at a

220

meat market on St. Clair, as the murderer of Flo Polillo. Wilson, according to the nameless informant, was a known "Sodomist" who carried a large butcher knife. May and Musil spoke to Detective Cooney, who knew of the deviant former butcher and promised to haul him in for questioning. Whether Jack Wilson was ever questioned is not known, but police were apparently unable to implicate him in Flo Polillo's murder" (Note 36, p. 58).

September 10, 1936	Victim No. 6 is found in Cleveland's Kingsbury Run near East 37th Street.
October, 1936	The decapitated torso of a white male is found along railroad tracks near Haverstraw, New York. The New York Central passes near Haverstraw. The killer used a saw to behead this victim.
March, 1937	The upper half of Victim No. 7 is discovered in Cleveland.
June, 6, 1937	The head of Victim No. 8 is found under the Lorain-Carnegie Bridge in Cleveland.
July 6, 1937	Body parts of Victim No. 8 are recovered from the Cuyahoga River in Cleveland.
July 10, 1937	The lower half of Victim No. 10 is discovered floating down the Cuyahoga River.
April 8, 1938	Body parts of Victim No. 10 are found about three feet from a storm sewer outlet along the Cuyahoga River.
August 16, 1938	The severed bodies of Victims No. 11 and No. 12 are found at the East 9th-Lake Shore dumpsite in Cleveland.
December 29, 1938	Cleveland postal workers find a letter dated December 23, 1938, postmarked from Los Angeles. The author of the letter claims he buried a head of one of his victims between Western and Crenshaw in Los Angeles. A copy of the correspondence is dispatched to Los Angeles police to search for the author of the letter.

-Late 1930's	Glover Loving, Jr., a/k/a Jack Anderson Wilson a/k/a Jack Wilson, surfaces in Los Angeles.
1939-1942	Six additional torso murders occur in Pennsylvania similar to the Cleveland Torso murders. In a torso murder that occurred in New Castle sometime between September and October, 1939, the killer used a saw to separate the victim's head from his torso. Detective Peter Merylo is convinced that the Mad Butcher of Kingsbury Run is back at work by late 1939. The victim's palms had been burned either before or after the killing. Some lawmen theorized that if the burning occurred before the murder, then the killer, by 1939, was torturing his victims. By 1939, was the Mad Butcher of Kingsbury Run changing his method and manner of killing?
1942	Jack Anderson Wilson reappears in Los Angeles.
Mid 1942	Los Angeles detectives tentatively identify the author of the December 23, 1938, letter to Cleveland Chief of Police Matowitz. Detective Merylo dismisses the identified letter as that of a "raving crank."
1943?-April, 1946	Elizabeth Short is not in California (Note 38, p. 95).
March 22, 1943	Jack Anderson Wilson is arrested in Los Angeles for suspected violation of the Selective Service.
August 5, 1943	Jack Anderson Wilson turns 24 years old while in Indianapolis, Indiana. "He is bumbling around the city until a young female, a WAC, is murdered in a downtown hotel. He then immediately leaves Indianapolis and ends up in Los Angeles" (Note 35, p. 200). Indianapolis is located approximately 185 miles from Chicago. Wilson is known to have been in Indianapolis on August 5, 1943.

1944	Jack Anderson Wilson is in the Army for a short time (Jan. 12, 1944-March 15, 1945).
	Pilot Joseph Gordan Fickling meets Elizabeth Short in Southern California.
October 12, 1944	Georgette Bauerdorf is found murdered lying face down in her bathtub in her apartment on Fountain Avenue in West Hollywood. She had been raped as she lay dying. A tall man with a limp dressed like a soldier was seen near her abandoned car shortly after the murder.
November 12, 1944	Elizabeth Short is in Tucson, Arizona.
1945-1946	Elizabeth Short travels by train from Los Angeles to Chicago. She may have taken an interest in the Chicago murder of Suzanne Degnan.
At times during 1945-1946	Elizabeth Short is in Chicago. She meets Pilot Joseph Gordan Fickling, and she meets with a doctor in Hammond, Indiana.
During 1945	Elizabeth Short visits relatives in Medford, Massachusetts. While in Medford, Elizabeth "made collect calls from a pay phone attempting to secure employment—modeling in Miami through Duffy (Duffy Sawyer) or perhaps in Chicago—maybe in Indianapolis" (Note 35, p. 53).
January-June, 1945	Several other women are reported murdered in Chicago, the former home of Elliot Ness. The women are pathologically cleaned by their killer, postmortem.
January 14, 1945	Eunice Rawlings disappears from her Roscoe Street apartment in Chicago. (Rawlings' apartment is located near the Ross and Brown apartments.)
January 17, 1945	A purse containing Eunice Rawlings' name is found on a Lake Michigan beach in Chicago.

June 5, 1945	Josephine Ross is murdered in Chicago. Her killer wraps her head in her dress. A passenger train known as the Red Line runs within one block of her apartment. She is murdered exactly ten years after the "Tattooed Man" was found murdered in Cleveland.
September 2, 1945	Elizabeth Short is in Medford, Mass.
December 10, 1945	Frances Brown is murdered in Chicago. Her killer wraps her head in her pajamas. A large knife is found lodged in her neck by detectives.
January 7, 1946	Six-year-old Suzanne Degnan is murdered and dismembered in Chicago not far from railroad tracks and near Lake Michigan. Her body parts are discarded by her killer in the Chicago sewers. (Several body parts of the victims of the Mad Butcher of Kingsbury Run were discarded in Cleveland's sewer system near Lake Erie.) Her killer leaves a ransom note demanding $20,000, soaked in oil.
February-April, 1946	Elizabeth Short is in Medford, Massachusetts.
May-June, 1946	Elizabeth Short is in Hammond, IN.
June 24-July 12, 1946	Elizabeth Short is in Chicago (Los Angeles D.A.'s files).
June 26, 1946	Seventeen-year-old William Heirens is arrested in Chicago and later charged with the murders of Josephine Ross, Frances Brown and Suzanne Degnan.
July, 1946	A Chicago newspaper reports that Heirens confessed to the murders of Ross, Brown and Degnan.
August 12, 1946	The headless, armless torso of Eunice Rawlings washes up on a Chicago beach. Her death is ruled a suicide.
September 5, 1946	William Heirens is handed three consecutive life sentences for the Chicago murders.
December, 1946	At Elvera French's apartment in San Diego, Elizabeth Short wrote a letter to Gordan Fickling: "I think I'm going to be coming back to Chicago to do some work

(modeling job with "Jack") . . . I am sorry that you feel as you do, and I hope that you can find a nice young lady to kiss every New Year's Eve. I believe it would have been wonderful if we belonged to each other now. I do want you to know that I'll never forget coming West to see you. Even though it has not worked out that you did take me in your arms and keep me there. Honey, it was nice as long as it lasted . . ." (Note 35, p. 109). (Compare to Appleton letter on pages 43-44)

January 14, 1947	Almost exactly one year after the murder/dismemberment of Suzanne Degnan, Elizabeth Short is tortured, killed and severed in Los Angeles. Her killer drains the blood from her body. X's are carved into her upper pubic region. Part of the female organs have been cut out of her body and her mouth has been cut into a grotesque smile.
January 25, 1947	The Black Dahlia Avenger sends a package containing belongings of Elizabeth Short. The package is drenched in gasoline.
January 27, 1947	"Had my fun with police" postcard is mailed by the Black Dahlia Avenger to the *Los Angeles Examiner* by the Black Dahlia Avenger.
January 27, 1947	Letter received by the Los Angeles District Attorney's Office, "Sorry Greenwich Village, not Cotton Club."
January 29, 1947	Three additional notes from the Black Dahlia Avenger are received by Los Angeles police and newspapers: "Dahlia's killer cracking," "I will give up,'" and "We're going to Mexico."

He also wrote on a postcard: "If he confesses you won't need me." (Was he referring to William Heirens or to Daniel Vorhees, who may have confessed to the murder of the Black Dahlia?)

January 30, 1947	The Black Dahlia Avenger sends a note addressed to Captain Jack Donahoe: "Dahlia killing justified."
January 31, 1947	Six additional messages, possibly mailed by the Black Dahlia Avenger, are published by the *Los Angeles Herald-Express*: "Here is the photo of the werewolf" killer's I saw him kill her a friend." (Note the possessive-pasted word "killer's" possibly indicating that the photo of the werewolf killer was intended to be a reference to the writer's). Was the Black Dahlia Avenger alluding to William Heirens who had been called a "werewolf" in the Chicago newspaper six months earlier?
February 3, 1947	Sylvia Horan is raped on Stocker Street between La Brea and Crenshaw Avenue in Los Angeles eight blocks from where Elizabeth Short was murdered January 14, 1947.
February 10, 1947	Jeanne French (Red Lipstick Murder) is killed in Los Angeles.
February 10, 1947	Following the murder of Jeanne French the *Los Angeles Herald-Express* publishes a special edition headline: "WEREWOLF STRIKES AGAIN KILLS L.A. WOMAN WRITES 'B.D.' ON HER BODY."
February 12, 1947	Ica Mabel M'Grew is kidnapped and raped in Los Angeles. Possibly connected to the Black Dahlia murder.
1947 after the murder of Black Dahlia	In Los Angeles, following the murder of the Black Dahlia, there are six additional murders that detectives feel might be related. Gordan Fickling told Charlotte, North Carolina, detectives he had received a final letter from Elizabeth Short dated January 8, 1947, in which she told him not to write anymore at her address in San Diego because her plan was to relocate to Chicago (Note 36, p. 140).

March 11, 1947	Evelyn Winters is murdered in Los Angeles and her body is dumped near railroad tracks. Before the killer left the scene he wrapped the victim's dress around her neck (Note 36, p. 403). The victim's shoes and undergarments were found at commercial and Center Streets, one block from where the body was located. The Black Dahlia Avenger is a suspect.
May 12, 1947	Laura Elizabeth Trelstad is strangled in Los Angeles with a piece of flowered cloth believed to be torn from a man's pair of pajamas or shorts. The Black Dahlia Avenger is a suspect.
July 8, 1947	Rosenda Josephine Mondragon is strangled to death in Los Angeles. Her right breast is slashed. The Black Dahlia Avenger is a suspect.
July 16, 1947	Marian Davidson Newton is strangled to death in San Diego with a thin wire or cord. Two men's handkerchiefs are found near her body. The Black Dahlia Avenger is a suspect.
February 14, 1948	Viola Norton is abducted by two men in Los Angeles and beaten on the head and face with a tire iron. The Black Dahlia Avenger is a suspect.
May 9, 1948	Jack Anderson Wilson is arrested in Los Angeles for vagrancy, lewd behavior.
July 26, 1948	Jack Anderson Wilson is arrested in Los Angeles and charged with battery.
June 13, 1949	Louise Margaret Springer worked two blocks from where the Black Dahlia's body was found on January 15, 1947. Her killer strikes her in the head and strangles her to death with a white sash cord. He then inserts a 14-inch finger-thick length of tree branch into her vagina. The Black Dahlia Avenger is a suspect.
May 23, 1950	Jack Anderson Wilson is arrested in Los Angeles for being drunk.

June 3, 1950	Jack Anderson Wilson is arrested in Los Angeles for being drunk.
June 12, 1950	Jack Anderson Wilson is arrested in Los Angeles and charged with burglary and suspicion of burglary.
June 12, 1950	Robert Robertson disappears from the Wayfarer's Lodge in Cleveland.
July 22, 1950	Robertson's dismembered torso is found behind a factory on East Twenty-Second Street in Cleveland. Police discovered with the body pages 457 and 458 of the Cleveland phone directory which contained listings for the letter "k" (Note 37, p. 191). Cuyahoga County Coroner Dr. Gerber estimates that June 12, 1950, was the date of death. Detective Merylo was convinced that this was the work of the Mad Butcher of Kingsbury Run. In 1947, the Black Dahlia Avenger signed one of his notes "2 k's." If he was in Los Angeles on June 12, 1950, then Jack Anderson Wilson is probably not Robert Robertson's killer.
August 21, 1950	Jack Anderson Wilson is charged with suspicion of armed robbery in Los Angeles.
February 21, 1951	Jack Anderson Wilson is charged with grand theft in Los Angeles.
May 2, 1951	Jack Anderson Wilson is charged with Susp. 487.3 PC (grand theft) in Los Angeles.
July 4, 1957	Jack Anderson Wilson is charged with intoxication in Los Angeles.
1958	Jack Anderson Wilson, while incarcerated in Oakland City Prison, tells an inmate a story about a "queer's head" he'd seen in a glass box in Cleveland. The head was that of the "Tattooed Man." A casting of his head was displayed at the Great Lakes Exposition in Cleveland in 1936.

November 27, 1963	Karyn Kupcinet, daughter of *Chicago Sun Times* columnist Irv Kupcinet, is murdered in Hollywood. Inspectors at the sheriff's department think her murder might be connected to the deaths of the Black Dahlia and Georgette Bauerdorf (Note 38, p. 172).
February 4, 1982	Jack Anderson Wilson dies in a fire at the Holland Hotel in Los Angeles before Detective John St. John has the opportunity to question him.
1991-1992	Cleveland Police Chief Edward Kovacic receives an official request from the Los Angeles authorities to look into a possible connection between the Cleveland Torso Murders and the murder-dismemberment of the Black Dahlia in 1947. Kovacic hands the assignment to Sergeant John Fransen, who quickly disposes of the notion that the same individual could be responsible for the murders in both cities . . ." (Note 34, p. 215).

COMPARISON OF QUOTES FROM EXPERTS

Cleveland Torso Killer

Cuyahoga County Coroner Dr. Samuel R. Gerber suggested that the Mad Butcher of Kingsbury Run could be, among other things, a "prosector butcher" (page 79, *Butcher's Dozen*). Gerber added, "He may have been a doctor or medical student sometime in the past, a butcher, osteopath, chiropractor, orderly, nurse or hunter in order to accomplish the dissection with such perfect finesse." "He is a pervert who sometimes drugs his victims and may lead a normal life when not absorbed with his sadistic passion" (page 168, *In the Wake of the Butcher*).

Detective Merylo was convinced the Butcher was a sexual pervert (page 74, *Butcher's Dozen*).

Cuyahoga County Coroner Arthur J. Pearce: "The killer would have to possess the skill and anatomical knowledge of a surgeon to sever the head from the body so cleanly" (page 71, *In the Wake of the Butcher*).

Cleveland Director of Public Safety Elliot Ness: "The Torso Murderer was a big man with the strength of an ox."

Pathologist Straus: "The killer is apparently a sex maniac of the sadistic type. This is indicated by the condition of his victims. He is probably a muscular man. The slayer definitely has expert knowledge of human anatomy. The incisions of his knife are clean and were made without guesswork. He may have gathered his knowledge as a medical student. Or it is possible that he is a butcher" (page 79, *In the Wake of the Butcher*).

Sergeant James Hogan: "The Butcher had cut the skin around the arms and legs and wrenched them from the socket" (pages 57-58, *In the Wake of the Butcher*).

On July 6, 1937, Dr. Hurbert S. Reichle, head of pathology at City Hospital: After carefully examining the grisly pieces, Reichle declared that, "his department never dissected a body in such a manner but whoever had made the incision in the lower trunk clearly knew something about anatomy" (page 119, *In the Wake of the Butcher*).

230

In December, 1938, Dr. P. R. Heimbold, a coroner's physician in Pittsburgh: The bodies had been cut "by an expert who has some knowledge of anatomy or was a butcher" (page 153, *In the Wake of the Butcher*).

Suzanne Degnan Murder

Dr. Jerome J. Kearns, the coroner's physician: "The killer had to be an expert in cutting meats because the body was separated at the joints. Not even the average doctor could be so skillful. It had to be a meat cutter" (page 49, *William Heirens: His Day In Court*); "a person with a knowledge of anatomy," "motivated by a powerful sex drive" (January 12, 1946, *Chicago Sun*).

Dr. William D. McNally, toxicologist: reported to Coroner Brodie that a sharp knife had been used to dissect Suzanne and that the expertise could only have come from a butcher or a hunter accustomed to the dissection of animals" (page 49, *William Heirens: His Day In Court*).

Chicago Chief of Police Walter G. Storms: "The girl's murderer was either a physician, a medical student, a very good butcher, an embalmer or perhaps a livestock handler" (page 49, *William Heirens: His Day In Court*).

Coroner Brodie: "It was a very clean job with absolutely no signs of hacking as would be evident if a dull tool was used. The bones were intact, carefully wrenched from their sockets (page 49, *William Heirens: His Day In Court*).

The seventy-four pound child may have been carried down a ladder. Police theorized that it may have been the work of two men. Could it have been the work of one very strong, tall man?

Black Dahlia Murder

Detective John St. Johns: "The perpetrator may have had some knowledge of anatomy but he wasn't necessarily in the medical profession" (page 133, *Severed*).

Lieutenant Jess Haskins: "They [the detectives] speculated that the killer was someone who had medical knowledge or who was familiar with anatomy, possibly a mortician" (page 71, *Childhood Shadows*).

Los Angeles Detective Finnis Brown: "Of course it's a sex crime and we're looking for a pervert" (page 121, *Severed*).

If Jack Anderson Wilson was in fact the person who killed the Black Dahlia and also was the Cleveland Torso Killer, then the remarks made by the experts could be combined and compared to the experts' reports in the Suzanne Degnan case. Comparing the reports would then provide the following conclusions concerning the killer:

a. He was very strong.
b. He was a sexual pervert.
c. He was possibly a butcher or meat cutter.
d. He had knowledge of anatomy.
e. He used a large sharp knife.
f. He wrenched the bones from the sockets.

Now compare these clues to additional similar facts identified between the Cleveland Torso murders, Black Dahlia murder and the murder of Suzanne Degnan. In each set of cases the killer:

1. Dismembered a human body during a time period when the known killer was still active at his trade. Suzanne Degnan was dismembered January 7, 1946, and the Black Dahlia was severed on January 14, 1947.
2. Removed the victim from one location, dismembered at a separate location and then discarded the body parts at a third location undetected.
3. Discarded body parts and other evidence in city storm sewers.
4. Killed in cold winter nights in the month of January.
5. Killed on June 5.
6. Used a tub and water in the dismembering process.
7. Dismembered the body in an area that had coal in it.
8. Mopped the floor after the dismemberment.
9. Wrapped a torso in a sugar sack or may have left a sugar sack at the scene of the crime.
10. May have used a balled-up handkerchief to gag his victim.
11. Left a striped pillow cloth or striped pillowcase at the scene of a murder.
12. Left a ransom note following a murder demanding $20,000.
13. Wrote a note in large letters followed by small letters.
14. Wrote a note in red lipstick.

232

15. Burned evidence following a murder.
16. Soaked evidence in either gasoline or oil.
17. May have turned out or broken a yard light before entering the dwelling to commit
    the crime.
18. May have had some musical background.
19. Killed near railroad tracks in a large city.
20. Killed near Lake Michigan or Lake Erie where sewers from the city flow towards the big lake.
21. Wrote letters to newspapers or telephoned someone associated with the crime following a murder.
22. May have sexually assaulted the victim, possibly postmortem.
23. Wrapped an article of clothing around the victim's neck.
24. Wrapped a silk stocking around the victim's neck.
25. May have used a thin wire as a ligature.

The clues and evidence seem to indicate that Jack Wilson might have been at Suzanne Degnan's bedside in the early morning of January 7, 1946 and not 17-year-old William Heirens as the press, police and public hastily concluded in their rush to judgment.

WILLIAM HEIRENS' MURDER CONFESSION: SUZANNE DEGNAN

Mr. Crowley Q: What is your name?

A: William George Heirens.

Q: Where do you live?

A: 4175 Tuohy Avenue.

Q: How old are you?

A: Seventeen.

Q: With whom do you live?

A: I live with my mother and father and brother.

Q: Where do you go to school?

A: University of Chicago.

Q: Now calling your attention to Jan. 7, 1946, early Monday morning, did you on that date kidnap and murder Suzanne Degnan?

A: Yes, sir.

Q: What did you do with the body?

A: The body was—part of that is not clear to my memory, but as things stand I have the knowledge it was deposited in different sewers in the neighborhood.

Q: Did you cut it up before you put it in the different sewers?

A: To my knowledge, yes, it was cut up when it was put in the sewers.

Q: What kind of an instrument did you use to cut it with?

A: A knife was used.

Q: What did you do with the knife?

A: It was deposited on an elevated station—not an elevated station, but the elevated   tracks.

Q: Where?

A: North of Glenlake.

Q: North of Glenlake?

A: Yes.

Q: How far away from Thorndale is Glenlake?

A: A block.

Q: And is it the block north?

A: Yes, sir.

Q: Did you deposit it in a particular place or just throw it?

A: I threw it.

Q: Where were you when you threw the knife away?

A: Down on the bottom of the siding of the "L."

Q: Where were you going?

A: I was going north.

Q: Walking?

A: Yes, sir.

Q: Where did you finally arrive at walking north after throwing the knife away?

A: At the Granville "L" Station.

Q: Then where did you go?

A: Back to school.

Q: How?

A: Back on the Jackson Park Express.

Q: Did you board the train at Granville?

A: Granville "L" Station.

Q: What time did you get back at school?

A: Six o'clock.

Q: In the morning?

A: Yes.

Q: Where did you go when you got back there?

A: I went back to my room.

Q: At that time did you have a roommate?

A: No, sir.

Q: You were living alone at that time?

A: Yes, sir.

Q: What particular location at the university did you live in January of 1946?

A: Snell Hall, it is practically on the corner of 57th and Ellis.

Q: What was your room number?

A: 51.

Q: Did you go to bed?

A: No, I stayed up and studied.

Q: On your ride from the north side to the university did you meet anyone that you knew?

A: No.

Q: Were there other passengers on the elevated train at the time?

A: Very few.

Q: You didn't recognize any of them as persons you knew?

A: No.

Q: How long after you disposed of the last part of the body was it before you threw the knife away?

A: Oh, I would say an hour and a half.

Q: What did you do for an hour and a half after you disposed of the last part of the   body?

A: Well, to my knowledge—well, what I know myself from what I remember myself, the last part of the body was disposed of—I don't know, I think they were the arms, they were disposed of near Broadway, on the other side, on the west side of the "L" Station?

Q: After the cover fell on your finger, when you disposed of the arms, did you then go immediately to the Glenlake "L" Station?

A: No.

Q: What "L" Station?

A: Then I went—I am not sure of this, but I am quite sure I went directly back to the basement, because to my recollection I was in the basement.

Q: What basement did you go back to?

A: To the one where the cutting up was supposed to have taken place.

Q: And do you know where that is located?

A: No.

Q: It is a basement in an apartment building on Winthrop Avenue, is it?

A: Yes.

Q: And would it be in the 5900 block?

A: It is south of the Degnan home.

Q: Just south of the Degnan home?

A: Yes.

Q: But on the block west of the Degnan home?

A: It would be in the 5800 block.

Q: When you got back to the basement, what did you do?

A: When I got back to the basement I seen there was blood in the tub there. I had some inkling of what happened, I realized—I didn't know the exact facts what happened until later I read about it, and it was made known to me that way, but I knew of it, then I realized something terrible happened. I washed up what was there and cleaned it up, and then it dawned on me something must of happened to the child. The last thing I remember I was with the child, and after a while—after I disposed of the bag—I was holding it I remember like that, and while I was there the thing was on the edge and it dropped down, and it caught my finger and it woke me up to the fact.

Q: That is when you were putting the arms in the sewer?

A: Yes.

Q: You knew you were putting the arms in the sewer?

A: No, I didn't know what they were.

Q: Were the arms in the bag?

236

A: Whatever it was was in the bag.

Q: You had made other trips to other sewers before that and put parts of the body in other sewers?

A: That is what I don't know, whether I did or not, but from what I put together, that is what happened. To my knowledge I do not know anything previous to where I dropped that thing on my finger.

Q: You remember writing the ransom note?

A: That was after.

Q: When did you write that note?

A: In the basement.

Q: Was that after you disposed of the body?

A: Yes.

Q: Which basement did you write the ransom note in?

A: The basement where the blood was.

Q: Where the body was cut up?

A: Yes, sir.

Q: Well, now, tell us how you happened to write that ransom note?

A: It came into my head that I had done something as I told you before, and I realized it must have been the child, and I didn't address the note because I didn't know the name of the people, so to relieve the parents in all ways possible I could would be to give them some hope the child was alive and that was the manner in which I wrote it.

Q: In what particular part of the basement were you when you wrote the ransom note?

A: I was in the rear part.

Q: When you wrote it were you standing or sitting?

A: Standing.

Q: Did you have the paper placed against anything?

A: Yes, sir.

Q: Against what?

A: A broken locker door.

Q: Did you have more than one sheet of paper?

A: No.

Q: Was that a full sheet of paper you had at the time you wrote the ransom note?

A: Yes.

Q: Did you tear it at any time?

A: No, I had torn it before I wrote the ransom note.

Q: Where were you when you tore it?

A: Down there.

Q: What did you do with the part of the paper you tore off?

A: I think I either left it there or put it back in my pocket, but it was in my pocket for such a long time that the torn part of it got dirty and I used the clean part, and I tore the dirty part off.

Q: Had you been carrying that sheet of paper around in your pocket?

A: Yes.

Q: Was it folded before you did any writing on it?

A: Yes.

Q: Did you write with a pencil?

A: Yes.

Q: Did you hold the paper up to the wall and write—

A: Yes.

Q: —or standing up? This locker you referred to as a broken locker, do you know whose locker that was?

A: No.

Q: Do you know, of course, how it happened to be broken, don't you?

A: No.

Q: Didn't you break into that locker?

A: No, not to my knowledge, I did not, no.

Q: Not to your knowledge?

A: No.

Q: Didn't you take some rags and some bags out of that locker?

A: No.

Q: Didn't you take some bags out of the locker and place parts of Suzanne's body in the bags?

A: No. Mr. Crowley, I would like you to understand something. I am not repeating or I mean repeating some of the things I had knowledge of from the papers. I shall not repeat anything, just from my own, what I know myself to be actual facts. It will not be anything I read in the papers. The actual thing, I do not know if I broke the lock myself or took a bag out.

Q: Let us go back then. How did you happen to pick out this particular house in which Suzanne Degnan lived as a place to commit a crime?

A: Because of the low windows.

Q: How did you happen to observe those low windows?

A: From passing by.

Q: When was it that you passed by there that you first noticed the low windows?

A: About 2:45 that morning, January 7.

Q: 2:45 A.M.?

A: About that time, yes.

Q: Had you ever noticed that place prior to that?

A: No.

Q: Had you ever been in that vicinity before?

A: Yes.

Q: When was the time prior to January 7, that you had been in that same vicinity?

A: Well, to my knowledge I believed it was, I do not know the name or the time or the person, to my knowledge I believe it was an apartment, or a big apartment building nearby.

Q: You were in an apartment of a man named Gold?

A: Yes.

Q: That apartment building is just north of the Degnan home?

A: Yes.

Q: Did you observe the Degnan home at that time?

A: No.

Q: At 2:45 a.m. January 7, when you observed the low window, what were you doing?

A: Well, I had, shall I start at the beginning? Do you want it in chronological order from the time I left?

Q: Tell it in your own words.

A: I left school. We were drinking. I had about six shots. I had gone to my room. I had taken off my coat, prepared for bed. Then it just came on me to go out, and I went out. I had no intention of doing, I intended to go to the "L" station and get on the "L." I got there all right and I fell asleep until Lawrence Avenue, where I woke up, and after getting my bearings I got off at Thorndale. I walked east until Glenlake. I turned east again. From there I went to the alley, Kenmore and Sheridan alley on Glenlake, and I turned south, and on the right-hand side.

Q: You turned south into an alley?

A: Yes. In the right-hand side, in the back yard, rather, behind a building, I think it was. I do not know how many feet, I say it was about fifty feet off the street in, and there was a ladder lying in the back yard, which I could see over the fence, so I took it. Then I went further down into that big apartment building.

Q: Carrying the ladder with you?

A: Yes.

Q: Where were you going then?

A: I intended to burglarize at the time.

Q: Do you know where particularly you were going?

A: No, there was a large apartment building there, and I entered there and I went, it was on the north side of the large apartment building. I entered there and I tried one of the windows on the first floor, near the front of the building. I could not

239

reach it with a ladder because of my condition at the time, so I gave up that.

Q: Where was that apartment building?

A: It is a big one. I believe it is the Gold Apartment, yes, it would be the Gold Apartment.

Q: In the same building where the Gold Apartment is?

A: Yes.

Q: Go ahead?

A: I took the ladder back, because I could not get in that way. Then I walked for a lower window, when I see the Degnan home. I went to the window that was least lighted. There was a light in the back near the door.

Q: Did you do anything to that light?

A: No, then I went east, north, I went west then, and after I turned that corner going in sort of "Z" corner, I went in and looked for the window that was least lighted, I found it and I entered.

Q: Did you use the ladder?

A: Yes.

Q: Before you entered that room did you do anything to the electric light that was lighted outside?

A: No.

Q: Did you hit the bulb with your hand in order to break it?

A: No.

Q: You went into the room with the electric light on?

A: Yes.

Q: Was it pretty well lit up back there?

A: Yes.

Q: When you entered the window of the Degnan home for what purpose did you enter?

A: Burglary.

Q: By that you mean to steal what you could?

A: Just burglary, that is, went in to steal what I could, just burglary.

Q: When you got in there you intended to take something that did not belong to you?

A: Yes, I guess that would be it, but notice I did not intend to take anything special.

Q: When you got inside the window what next happened?

A: I noticed somebody sleeping on the right-hand side in the bed. Then I went toward the door and as dizzy as I was, I may have awakened whoever it was by brushing against the bed, or something of that sort, but anyway, whoever was there, before

I had reached the door to open it, got up in bed, sat up. It started talking. That is where I got her, I took the person, I did not know it was a child at this time, and did not know until I read it in the paper it was a child. Then I knew it must have been a female because of the long hair, which I seen by the flashlight.

Q: Did you have a flashlight with you?

A: Yes, I had a flashlight with me all the time.

Q: Did you put the flashlight on the person in the bed?

A: Well, yes, I put it on, not directly, but I must have shone it in that direction.

Q: Then you could have seen it was a girl, couldn't you?

A: A female, yes, the long hair. My vision was not too good.

Q: Then what did you do?

A: Then I strangled her.

Q: When you say you strangled her, how did you strangle her?

A: With my fingers.

Q: Around her neck?

A: Yes.

Q: Had the child said something to you before you did that?

A: No. She made some utterances. I do not know what they were, too inarticulate to make out.

Q: How long did you keep your hands on her neck, would you say?

A: About two minutes.

Q: You squeezed as hard as you could?

A: Until everything went limp.

Q: As soon as the body of the child went limp you released your grip on her throat, is that right?

A: Yes.

Q: Then what did you do?

A: Then I got back, so I picked up the body and carried it down. Going down the ladder I believe I stepped my right leg over the first onto the lower rung and I carried her down to the lower. From that position I would be carrying the child in my arms in front.

Q: At the time you got to the ground what did you do with the child?

A: Proceeded to the alley and turned north, and from there on I do not know what happened. I got to the apartment building.

Mr. Tuohy Q: What alley did you proceed to?

A: The alley that I came down when I came down with the ladder.

Q: Between Sheridan and Kenmore?

A: Yes.

Q: And you proceeded north?

A: Yes, after I got past the apartment building I do not know what took place after that. I do not know how, what grounds from or just how everything happened.

Mr. Crowley

Q: You finally took the child into a basement of an apartment building on Winthrop Avenue, didn't you?

A: Not to my knowledge, no. I don't know.

Q: The basement where you wrote the ransom note and cleaned up the blood in the sink, you know where that basement is located?

A: I do not know the number, but I know it is south of the Degnan home.

Q: You remember being there that night?

A: Yes, I was there that night?

Q: Now –

A: That morning, rather.

Q: Yes, that morning, don't you remember cutting up the body?

A: No.

Q: Where did you get that knife?

A: Well, from any number of various places, any burglary that may have been committed by me. I do not know what place it is taken from.

Q: You mean that you had taken that knife in a burglary?

A: Yes.

Q: Do you remember where?

A: No.

Q: Did you take it with you when you left the University of Chicago that night?

A: Yes, it was, it would be in my regular coat pocket.

Q: Why did you carry the knife that night?

A: Well, a matter of prying windows open or anything of the sort.

Q: Then you had the knife with you when you entered the Degnan home?

A: Yes, sir.

Q: And you had it with you when you carried the girl out of the Degnan home?

A: I must have.

Q: And you had it with you when you were in the basement after you disposed of the arms and the body?

A: Yes, sir.

Q: Did you wash the knife off then?

A: It was laying across a basin there and as I washed the tubs I must have washed the knife also.

Q: At that time you knew you had used that knife in cutting up the body, did you?

A: I didn't know what I had cut up.

Q: You knew that you had cut something up, didn't you?

A: I didn't know I was doing cutting up as far as that is concerned, but there was blood in the wash tub and at that time my mind was quite clear—not too clear, but clear enough to realize it must have been used for some purpose of that sort.

Q: So you washed it off?

A: Yes.

Q: And you threw it away?

A: Yes.

Q: Why did you throw it away?

A: On previous times when I realized what happened, like a burglary, I had the habit of throwing things away. Quite a few times I had thrown weapons away when I knew what I was doing.

Q: Well, do you know how many times you were in and out of that basement that night?

A: No, I don't.

Q: Do you know if you were in and out of there more than once?

A: No.

Q: Don't you know how you got into that basement?

A: No, I don't.

Q: Was the door open?

A: When I came back from what I remember, the door was open.

Q: Was the light lit?

A: No, there was no light.

Q: Didn't you have a light at any time in that basement?

A: I had a flashlight.

Q: Do you remember at the time you wrote the ransom note whether the light was lit?

A: Yes, I had the flashlight.

Q: You mean you wrote by using a flashlight for your light at the time?

A: Yes, sir

Q: Well, do you know whether or not when you first entered that basement with the girl's body, whether or not the door was open?

A: No, I don't know.

Q: Do you know whether or not you had to go through any window first and open the door?

A: No, I don't.

Q: Was the girl dead at the time you entered the basement with her body?

A: Presumably, yes. I strangled her in her room.

Q: Well, at the time you carried her out of the room did you believe she was dead then?

A: Yes, I believed it.

Q: Why did you take her out of the room if you believed she was dead at the time?

A: I don't know. In fact, I didn't have the realization of it until going down the stairs. And after that I had the realization. When I got to the alley was the first time I had the realization of it.

Q: Did you use an automobile any time that night?

A: No, not that I know of.

Q: Did you use a wire at any time that night around her neck?

A: I might have because of the fact I carry wire in my pocket of the type they found.

Q: Don't you remember that you did?

A: No.

Q: After you got the girl out of the house and started to go north in the alley between Kenmore and Sheridan Road, don't you remember stopping at any time on the journey with that body?

A: No.

Q: Did you just carry the girl in your two arms?

A: Yes. I carried her until I got to this big apartment building, and I don't know how I carried her after that.

Q: Do you know where the big apartment building is located?

A: Yes.

Q: What is the address?

A: I don't know that.

Q: What Street is it on?

A: It is on Kenmore.

Q: How far from the Degnan home?

A: 150 feet about.

Q: Do you remember stopping at any apartment building on the block west of the Degnan home?

A: No.

Q: And about a block north of the Degnan home?

A: No.

Q: Do you know how you happened to reverse your direction and come back south to the place where the body was cut up?

A: No, I don't know.

Q: Do you remember cutting the girl's head off?

A: No.

Q: Do you remember cutting her torso, the body?

A: No.

Q: Do you remember cutting the arms?

A: No.

Q: Or the legs?

A: No.

Q: Don't you know you did that?

A: No, I didn't know.

Q: Do you know where the head was found?

A: I believe I have knowledge of the fact through what I have read, but personally I don't know where it was found.

Q: Doesn't that refresh your recollection as to where you put the head?

A: No.

Q: Don't you know you put the head in a sewer?

A: No.

Q: Do you know where the left leg was found?

A: No.

Q: Haven't you any idea where you put the left leg?

A: No.

Q: Do you know where the torso was found?

A: No.

Q: That is the part of the body above the waist and below the neck?

A: No.

Q: You don't remember where the buttocks and the right leg were found?

A: No.

Q: Do mean to tell us you can't recollect putting those parts of the body in the various sewers they were found in?

A: No. I don't know what sewers I put them in or anything of that sort.

Q: Do you know how long you were in the basement from the time that you first went there until you were through washing off the knife and washing up the tubs?

A: I think I was in the basement about half an hour washing up the tubs.

Q: That is when you were washing the tub it took you a half hour?

A: Yes.

Q: How long were you in there before you did that?

A: I don't know.

Q: Haven't you any idea?

A: I can't figure it out. I would say an hour.

Q: You would say an hour?

A: Yes.

Q: How do you figure that out?

A: I got back to school at six o'clock and it takes an hour for the trip, and it would put me there at five o'clock and—no, it would be less than an hour and a half because I went to a restaurant to get something to eat, and that took about a half hour. Then a half hour there.

Q: When did you go to the restaurant?

A: After five-thirty, before I boarded the "L" I went to Granville Avenue.

Q: Did you have the knife with you at that time?

A: No.

Q: Had you thrown the knife away before you went to the restaurant?

A: Yes.

Q: Where was that restaurant located?

A: On Granville Avenue.

Q: Do you know the name of it?

A: No.

Q: Were there people in the restaurant at the time you were there?

A: There was a policeman in there and a waitress.

Q: Was the policeman in uniform?

A: Yes.

Q: Did you know him?

A: No.

Q: Did you know this waitress?

A: No.

Q: Was she an elderly lady or a younger lady?

A: Middle-aged.

Q: Had you ever eaten there before?

A: Yes, sir.

Q: How long were you there this particular morning?

A: About half an hour.

Q: What did you eat?

A: Doughnuts and coffee.

Q: Did it take you half an hour to eat doughnuts and coffee?

A: Well, probably yes. It is just a fair judgment of mine how long it was.

Q: And when you left the restaurant where did you go?

A: I went to the Granville "L" Station.

Q: Do you remember how you lifted the sewer cover in which you put the arms?

A: No. But when the thing was up and I was holding it up like that, my fingers were under like that, they had those things in it that went around, and my fingers were through the end.

Q: Then do you remember you lifted it with your hands?

A: No, I got it up, and I was holding it up like that. That is how it fell down and caught my finger.

Q: What hand did you have on the sewer cover?

A: My right.

Q: And what hand got hurt when the sewer cover fell down?

A: My right.

Q: You mean to say your fingers were pinched between the sewer cover and the rim into which it fit?

A: No, it didn't get into the rim, it fell on the ground.

Q: You had taken the sewer cover completely off the hole?

A: Yes.

Q: After it fell down and hurt you fingers, did you put it back on the hole again?

A: Yes, sir.

Q: How were you dressed at the time?

A: I had a tan coat, it was a weather coat, sort of like a raincoat.

Q: Do you still have those clothes?

A: No. As I was coming down the alley, I burned the coat.

Q: In what alley?

A: Down the alley next to the "L" station.

Q: What "L" station?

A: That didn't take long at all, five minutes for that. I burned it. When the alley comes to Granville, it turns and goes up and comes down, it makes a Z-shape turn there, and right in the corner that is where I burned the coat.

Q: How far from where you threw the knife?

A: About a block, I believe, or a block and a half or two blocks.

Q: Is the coat the only thing you burned?

A: Whatever was in the pockets.

Q: Why did you burn the coat?

A: There was some blood on one of the wrists.

Q: Is that the only part that had blood on it?

A: Yes, sir.

Q: Is that the reason you burned it?

A: Yes, sir.

Q: Did you have a gun with you that night?

A: I believe so, yes.

Q: What gun did you have?
A: I think it was—I am quite sure it was the one I threw away on the Loyola tennis courts. I threw it away, I think sometime later.
Q: Sometime after that?
A: Yes.
Q: You didn't throw it away that night?
A: No, it was not in my coat, and it was not so big.
Q: Where did you carry it?
A: In my pocket.
Q: After you threw away your topcoat, did you have a suit coat on?
A: A sweater.
Q: And did you carry the gun in your pants pocket?
A: Yes, sir.
Q: In your back hip pocket? Or the side pocket?
A: Side pocket.
Q: Was it a large gun?
A: It was fairly large, yes.
Q: Do you know what caliber?
A: No, I would say about a .32.
Q: A .32 caliber?
A: Yes.
Q: Where had you gotten that?
A: I don't know where I got that.
Q: This wire that you referred to that you carried with you, did you always carry wire with you?
A: Yes, I had the wire already in my coat pocket.
Q: Do you know where you got that?
A: No, some burglary.
Q: What kind of wire was it?
A: It was picture wire.
Q: Picture wire, used to hang pictures, ordinary light silver-colored wire?
A: Yes, sir.
Q: Did you have any handkerchiefs with you that particular night?
A: No.
Q: None at all?
A: No, I had one big one.
Q: What kind of a handkerchief, white?
A: No, I think it was more on the order of a babushka because after I left the note there and took the ladder away, there was a man coming down the alley and I put

the thing over my head, and tied it all the way down here, so it must have been a big handkerchief.

Q: Did you have your hat with you then?

A: No.

Q: Had you already burned your hat?

A: I never wear one.

Q: You didn't wear one that night?

A: I never wore a hat.

Q: Well, after you washed the tubs and washed the knife and wrote the ransom note, where did you go then when you left the basement?

A: Then I went directly to the home and put the note in and left.

Q: And did you carry the knife with you on that trip?

A: Yes, the knife was with me.

Q: What did you do with the ransom note?

A: Then I pushed it in the window.

Q: Did you climb the ladder to do that?

A: About one rung.

Q: Was the ladder still in the same position it was when you took the girl out of the window?

A: Yes.

Q: Did you do anything with the ladder after you put the ransom note in the room?

A: I took it out to the alleyway.

Q: You took it out to the alleyway?

A: Yes.

Q: You mean the alley just east of the house?

A: Yes.

Q: That is the alley between Kenmore and Sheridan Road?

A: Yes, sir.

Q: Where did you place it?

A: I seen this man coming out of the alley, directly forward—I heard him first and he didn't come into view in the alley, and I dropped the ladder and I put the thing over my head, and I proceeded towards the south cutting across the lawn, but I would say I kept about 150 feet in front of him all the time.

Q: You went south?

A: South, cutting across the lawn of the Degnan home, and went to Kenmore and went north on Kenmore until I got to Glenlake, and he was still behind me, and he turned in a building on the end corner there, and I proceeded to the alley—beside the elevated and disposed of the knife and sheath and went to the alleyway and disposed of my coat and turned the corner and got something to eat.

Mr. Crowley Q: Where was the man when you first noticed him?

A: When I noticed him he was approaching the street lamp.

Q: From what direction?

A: He was coming north.

Q: Coming north in the alley?

A: Yes, sir.

Mr. Tuohy Q: Coming north or coming from the north?

The Witness A: He was coming north-he was coming north-he was coming from the south side of Thorndale in the alley, the same alley that runs straight through.

Mr. Crowley Q: And then you say he followed you west on Thorndale?

A: West on Thorndale until Kenmore and then I turned north keeping on the west hand side of the street, and he stayed on the east side until he got to the corner of Glenlake on the east side, and he went in there and I proceeded west.

Q: Was he a short or tall man?

A: I would say between tall and medium.

Q: Did you just continue walking?

A: I waited for a while.

Q: Where did you wait?

A: To see where he was going.

Q: Where were you when you waited?

A: I went into a doorway there. I started to go west.

Q: Started to go west on what street?

A: Glenlake.

Q: Did you have your gun with?

A: Yes.

Q: Did you take it out?

A: No, I didn't take it out, I had it in my pocket, and there was no need to take it out.

Q: Did you believe the man was following you?

A: Well, the way he—yes, I believed he was following me.

Q: And did you have any idea what you were going to do if he caught up with you?

A: I had no reason to know why he would catch up with me at first. I thought he was a robber.

Q: You thought he was a robber?

A: Yes, he followed me that distance.

Q: Now, in this restaurant did you have any conversation with the waitress?

A: I just asked for my order, that is all.

Q: She didn't ask you where you had been or what you were doing in the neighborhood or anything like that?

A: No.

Q: You didn't talk about anything else to her?

A: No. At the time she was having a conversation with the policeman.

Q: Well, when you got back to the University of Chicago, did you still have the wire?

A: No, that was in my coat. I burned it with the coat or I don't know what happened to it. Whatever was in my pockets was burned.

Q: So that if you didn't use the wire in putting it around the girl's neck, it could have been left in you coat pocket?

A: Yes.

Q: But you could also have used it in putting it around the girl's neck?

A: Yes, sir.

Q: And you could have thrown it away?

A: Yes.

Q: As a matter of fact, didn't you do that?

A: No, not that I know of.

Q: Well, on this journey that you say you don't remember, after taking the child, don't you recollect that you tried to get into a basement at the corner of Glenlake and Kenmore? Do you remember that?

A: No.

Mr. Tuohy Q: Or the east side of Winthrop?

The Witness A: No.

Q: The corner of Winthrop and Glenlake?

A: No, I have no recollection of that.

Mr. Cowley Q: When you were in the Degnan home just before you choked this girl, do you know whether the door from her room leading into the apartment was open or closed?

A: Closed, because I went to open it up.

Q: You say it was closed?

A: Yes.

Q: You didn't close it yourself?

A: No.

Q: Did you know who lived in the apartment at that time?

A: No.

Q: Why were you carrying this particular piece of blank paper in your pocket that night?

A: It is a habit of mine going to school, to carry paper in my pocket, to take notes on short notice.

Q: You don't carry dirty white paper in your pocket for that purpose?

A: It gets dirty in my pocket.

Q: How long had you been carrying it?

A: About a week.

Q: Had you planned on using it as a kidnap ransom note at that time?

A: No.

Q: How did it get oil on it?

A: After I had gone and wrote the ransom note in the basement, then I noticed a can of oil on the floor, and I wanted to disguise anything that had been on it, and I squirted the oil on it.

Q: What kind of oil was that, do you know?

A: It was round can on the basement floor of the locker room where I was writing the note.

Q: How big a can?

A: About so high.

Q: Did you put that can on top of the paper?

A: I may have.

Q: Was that can full of oil?

A: No, just a little bit.

Q: Did you turn the oil can over on the paper and force the oil on the paper?

A: I turned it there and pushed it so the oil would squirt out.

Q: Did it have a long funnel on it?

A: No.

Q: Was it an open can at the top?

A: No, it had a regular oil feeding thing.

Q: What?

A: An oil feed, things that are on 3-in-1 Oil cans, but it was not a 3-in-1 Oil can.

Q: You mean it had a spout out of which the oil comes when you force it?

A: Yes.

Q: Did you put that can on the paper at any time and press it to wipe off some of the dirt and oil off the can onto the paper?

A: No, I was holding the thing up, and I noticed that after I had written the note already and I then squirted it on and I threw it away or burned it with my coat.

Q: The can?

A: Yes.

Q: How big was it?

A: A small one.

252

Q: A small one about an inch in diameter?
A: Yes.
Q: Was it round?
A: Yes.
Q: It was not a large can?
A: No.
Q: Why did you put the oil on?
A: To disguise anything that was on the paper.
Q: What did you expect to be on the paper?
A: My fingerprints for one thing.
Q: And what reason did you say you wrote that ransom note?
A: To get the parents away from the idea their child may have been killed.
Q: What good was that going to do?
A: Lessen the burden for them.
Q: The child was not going to return, you knew that?
A: Yes.
Q: How could you lessen their burden by writing a ransom note?
A: At the time they would get the idea that the child would be kidnapped, and anything might happen and prepare themselves for anything that would happen.
Q: Don't you remember putting a gag in the mouth of the girl?
A: No.
Q: When you were carrying the knife, how did you carry it, in a sheath?
A: Yes.
Q: You would recognize the knife again if you saw it, would you?
A: No.
Q: Does that appear to be the size and kind of knife you had and threw away (Mr. Crowley showing the witness a knife)?
A: It would be about the size, yes.
Q: And about that kind and type?
A: It does not look exactly like that. My memory was not so clear that night anyhow. It is about the size, yes.
Mr. Tuohy Q: Is that the knife?
The Witness A: I don't know for sure, Mr. Tuohy.
Mr. Crowley Q: But in appearance this could be the knife?
A: Yes.
Q: It looks like the knife to you?
A: Yes, sir.
Q: I asked you a little while ago how you were dressed and you told us about your topcoat. What kind of trousers did you wear?

A: I think they were—I don't know what color, I suppose they were my brown trousers.

Q: What kind of a sweater did you have on?

A: Brown.

Q: Do you remember the color of your shoes?

A: I wear brown shoes.

Q: Was it a pull-over sweater?

A: Yes.

Q: A V-neck?

A: You have the sweater. I didn't get it cleaned before that.

Q: The police have the sweater you wore that might?

A: Yes.

Q: And it is a brown sweater?

A: Yes.

Q: Do you remember whether or not at any time you touched the private parts of Suzanne Degnan?

A: No.

Q: Did you attempt to get any sexual satisfaction from taking Suzanne Degnan out of that apartment?

A: No.

Q: Why did you disguise your handwriting or attempt to disguise your handwriting in the ransom note?

A: It was not an attempt to disguise it as much as the thing I was writing on. It was a rough board.

Q: Well, you tried to write some of the letters different, didn't you?

A: Yes.

Q: In other words, you didn't want to be caught, is that right?

A: That is right. I didn't want to be caught.

Q: Then you knew you did something wrong?

A: Naturally I knew I did something wrong.

Q: And you knew you had destroyed this girl's body, didn't you?

A: Well, I didn't know what happened to the girl's body, but the blood was there and it was evident to me what happened.

Q: When you wrote the ransom note so the people would get the idea the child was kidnapped and you would relieve their mind that was the reason you wrote the ransom note, certainly you knew the body was destroyed at the time, is that right?

A: That was evident, yes.

Q: And when you wrote the ransom note you didn't want to leave your normal handwriting there so you would be caught, did you?

A: It was my normal handwriting as far as most of the characteristics, but from what I was writing on, I think there was twice I tried to disguise it, and at the time the handwriting I didn't just—my head was not clear at the time, it was getting clearer, and I began to realize.

Q: How did you conceive of asking for $20,000?

A: It is a most logical amount. It could have been two or any amount for that matter.

Q: Why did you pick twenty?

A: It didn't matter to me, it could have a hundred for that matter.

Q: Why did you say, do not notify the F.B.I. or police?

A: That is usually done in ransom notes.

Q: How did you know that?

A: It is reasonable.

Q: Why did you ask that the money be delivered in five and tens?

A: Well, if it was a ransom note, asking for ransom, they don't want big bills, they want small bills. So, I put medium, five and tens.

Q: If the note was intended to simply placate the parents and help the parents in their grief, at the loss over their child, why were you so particular in writing the ransom note in that fashion?

A: Because I had to make it seem convincing.

Q: Your mind was very clear on how to draft a ransom note and make it convincing, was it?

A: At the time it was clear, yes.

Q: Your mind was very clear then, wasn't it?

A: No, it wasn't very clear then. I was hazy when I left my room.

Q: Did you remove any of the clothes off this girl while you were in the basement there?

A: I don't know.

Q: Did you take any of her clothes home with you?

A: No. I did not have anything of that sort.

Q: Sir?

A: I did not have anything of that sort. It may have been, it might have been in a pocket of my coat or something like that and burned.

Q: Did you attempt at any time that night to rent a room in the Fleetwood Hotel?

A: No.

Q: Are you sure of that?

A: Quite sure, yes.

Q: Are you sure you did not go to a hotel and attempt to register at the hotel and ask a lady there whether or not she had a room that she would rent?

A: No.

Q: This paper on which you wrote the ransom note, did you get that out of your room at the university?

A: No.

Q: Where did you get that from?

A: I got it from Harper's Library.

Q: From where?

A: From Harper's Library.

Q: Where is that located?

A: That is at, off 59th and Ellis, Ellis and University and 59th.

Q: Do you remember when you obtained that particular sheet?

A: It was about quite some time before the incident had happened and it was upstairs in the reference library with a lot of desks, and all long tables rather. It was a plain sheet there and it was near by me, and it was probably left there by some student who had taken notes previously.

Q: Did you just take one sheet?

A: Yes, that is all that was there.

Q: You carried it around with you how long?

A: About a week.

Q: Why did you take this odd piece of paper from a strange location and use that particular piece of paper in the ransom note?

A: That is a habit of mine, to take paper of that sort, when it is, well, when it is convenient, for me, that is all.

Q: At the time you took that piece of paper didn't you have in mind then writing a ransom note on it?

A: No.

Q: You are sure of that?

A: I am sure.

Q: In writing this ransom note, Mr. Tuohy will show it to you. The character "and."Mr. Tuohy: That is a picture of it.

Mr. Crowley Q: It is made on that note, do you notice that?

A: Yes.

Q: Do you remember discussing with Mr. Tuohy the fact that you did not know how to make the character "&"?

A: That is right.

Q: You do know how to make that character, don't you?

A: Made an "S" but I did not know how to make that. I never made that character before in my life.

Q: Before you made that character on that ransom note?

A: Yes.

Q: That is a photostat. No, that is a photograph of the ransom note that was written, that is exactly how you wrote it, isn't it?

A: Yes.

Q: Can you see that?

A: Yes.

Q: That is how you made it, isn't it?

A: Yes.

Q: Where did you write these words on that are on the back?

A: While I wrote the other note.

Q: You mean you wrote that all at the same time?

A: Yes.

Q: With the same pencil?

A: No.

Q: You say no?

A: No.

Q: Did you use a different pencil?

A: Yes. This one here I wrote with a pencil, was on the floor in that locker room where the oil can was too, that one here.

Q: Why did you change pencils?

A: Disguise.

Q: What?

A: For disguise.

Q: How many pencils did you have with you that night?

A: One.

Q: When you wrote the face of the note did you immediately then write the other words on the back of the note?

A: No.

Q: How much time between the time you wrote the face of the note and the time you wrote the back of the note?

A: I read it over once and then I figured it was, that was all right. I wanted to add something and there was no room so I turned it over on the other side.

Q: Why didn't you use the same pencil?

A: I had already put it in my pocket.

Q: Why didn't you take it out of your pocket?

A: Because the other was more convenient. It was lying on the floor.

Q: It was more convenient to pick up a strange pencil off the floor than to take the one you had used out of your pocket?

A: It was more convenient and it was also that I wanted to disguise, too.

Q: How was that going to disguise it?

A: I do not know, two different leads I suppose.

Q: What?

A: Two different types of lead.

Q: Did you have that in mind at the time you wrote it?

A: I thought that would help.

Q: That was an extra precaution you took, is that right?

A: It was not extra. It was, say convenient precaution.

Q: You felt that would make it more confusing if they found it was written by two pencils?

A: I had the pencil in my back pocket and I had the coat over it and I could not get it out so well, and I could not get it out.

Q: Are you sure you wrote the ransom note in the basement?

A: Yes.

Q: Are you sure you are telling us the truth about the ransom note being written that way?

A: Yes.

Q: You did not add those words on that ransom note after you got into the room, did you?

A: No. It was a rough board that I wrote it. It would have left a mark on. Later I left a few marks, the line and the five, it was a rough board.

Q: You know you misspelled the word wait on the note, don't you?

A: Yes.

Q: That is the way you continued to misspell that word, isn't it?

A: No, not all the time.

258

Q: What?

A: Not all the time.

Q: Nearly all the time, isn't it?

A: Most of the time, yes.

Q: You know that when you gave us samples of your handwriting you misspelled it that way, isn't that right? You know you insisted you found it in the dictionary?

A: Yes.

Q: You spelled it "waite", didn't you?

A: I insisted on it, yes.

Q: The word "safety," you misspelled "safety" the way it is spelled on the ransom note?

A: Not all the time. About the only time I spell words wrong is when I am nervous. This word here.

Q: You were nervous when you wrote the ransom note, were you?

A: Yes.

Q: It accounts for your misspelling those words?

A: Yes.

Q: Were you nervous when you gave us samples of your handwriting in the Bridewell Hospital?

A: Yes.

Q: That accounts for the fact that you misspelled it again?

A: The same way, yes, like the comma. I never make the comma like that, never at all, never on anything else.

Q: You did on the samples you gave to us, too?

A: I do not know why I did it. In all my writings at school and all my figures and all, I do not write a comma like that.

Q: Did you have any particular reason for tearing that part of the paper?

A: The other part was dirtier.

Q: Is that the only reason?

A: Yes.

Q: When you were in the room with the little girl did you hear any of the other persons in the house moving around?

A: No.

Q: Did you hear any noise in the house at all?

A: No.

Q: Did you hear any dogs growling upstairs or barking?

A: I did not hear nothing.

Q: Did you know there were dogs in the apartment upstairs?

A: No.

Q: Did you know how many families lived in that building?

A: No.

Q: Did you get any satisfaction out committing this particular crime?

A: No, the only thing I get satisfaction out of is the burglaries.

Q: What kind of satisfaction?

A: Is that necessary?

Q: Yes.

A: Sexual satisfaction.

Q: Will you describe that to us?

A: Well, the time, it all depends on the burglary. If I have an erection, and ejection at the place, then I go out without taking anything. That is the satisfaction I get out of it.

Q: When you say ejection, you mean an emission?

A: Yes.

Q: You mean you go in, and after you get into a place you have an erection?

A: Yes, before I get in.

Q: Even before you get in?

A: Yes.

Q: After you get in you have an emission?

A: Yes, not all the time, though.

Q: Sometimes?

A: Yes, sometimes.

Q: If you have an emission you go right out?

A: Yes.

Q: If you don't, you do something else?

A: Yes, until, but it is only when I, after the emission I realize what is going on and I leave.

Q: Did you have an erection on this particular night?

A: Going in, I did.

Q: Where did that erection take place?

A: It started when I tried to get into the other building.

Q: Did it remain with you all the time?

A: Yes. That is another.

Q: Did you have an emission after you got into the place?

A: No, not that I know of.

Q: How long did the erection continue then?

A: I do not know. I know I dropped this thing on my finger, I did not have it any more.

Q: Did you take the girl for the purpose of having sexual intercourse with her?

A: No.

Q: When you left the university to go back north you did not have any erection then, did you?

A: No. I just had the feeling of it, that's all.

Q: Just the feeling of it?

A: No, no, at the time I did not. From the drink and all I don't know whether I did or not.

Q: Let us get back to that Sunday night, that Sunday afternoon prior to the time you went to the Degnan home, were you at your mother and father's home on Touhy Avenue?

A: Yes.

Q: Had you spent the weekend there?

A: Yes.

Q: What time did you leave your mother and father's home to return to school?

A: On the 7:07 bus.

Q: What is the answer?

A: On the 7:07 bus leaving from Touhy and Keeler, on the corner.

Q: The bus leaves seven minutes after seven?

A: Yes.

Q: Where does it take you?

A: Howard Street.

Mr. Tuohy Q: Howard and what?

The Witness A: Howard.

Q: Howard and Paulina?

A: And Paulina, yes, the "L."

Mr. Crowley Q: Then where did you go?

A: Then I went up and took the Jackson Park Express back to school.

Q: To where?

A: Back to either University or Cottage, University Avenue.

Q: To where?

A: Back to either University or Cottage, University Avenue.

Q: How long did it take you to get from your mother's home to school?

A: A good hour. At that time of the day it would be more than an hour.

Q: So it was sometime around 8:15 p. m., or later, that you arrived at school?

A: About 8:30, because it took the bus a while to arrive. The bus usually arrives at Howard twenty minutes after the hour.

Q: What did you do at 8:30 when you got there?

A: I went up to my room.

Q: How long did you remain in your room?

A: I studied for a while and then I went to the washroom to get a drink of water, and I met Gene in there washing his clothes out.

Q: What time would that be, approximately?

A: About nine o'clock.

Q: Then what did you do?

A: Gene invited me into his room to have some drinks with Joe Costello.

Q: Are you sure that is who you drank with, Gene and Joe Costello?

A: Positive.

Q: Could you be mistaken about that?

A: No, I was sick that night.

Q: How is that?

A: I was sick that night, drank too much.

Q: Don't you know Joe Costello was sick in his room that night?

A: No, because I came out before he came out, I went to my room before he went.

Q: How long did you remain in Gene's room?

A: For about, until 12:30. It was after twelve o'clock.

Q: After twelve o'clock midnight?

A: Yes.

Q: Then where did you go?

A: Then I went to my own room.

Q: Then what did you do?

A: I started undressing. I got undressed and I then laid down for a while, but then I got up and went out.

Q: Did you get up right away?

A: No, not right away.

Q: What?

A: Two minutes or so, until I just lay down, I did not even take the covers off the bed. I just laid down and got up again.

Q: Did you go right out and take the "L" train?

A: Yes, I went right to the "L" train.

Q: What time did you get the "L" train?

A: About one o'clock.

Q: About 1:00?

A: 1:30, rather, because it took me sometime to get dressed, too.

Q: Couldn't it have been earlier than that?

A: No.

Q: How do you fix the time at 1:30?

A: Because I got out of Gene's room. I undressed, and it takes you fifteen minutes or more to walk to the "L" station. I had to get dressed over again. I did not have the same clothes on that I wore that day, when I came home.

Q: How do you fix the time you left Gene's room?

A: It was after twelve o'clock.

Q: How do you know that?

A: I looked at my watch, it was after twelve o'clock, as I said myself.

Q: The drinks had not affected you so that you could tell the time of day?

A: No, it had not affected me at all, not much. I usually know when I get enough.

Q: You were not drunk, were you?

A: No, I would not say I was drunk because I got to my room all right.

Q: You say you became ill?

A: No, I did not become ill.

Q: You were not nauseous?

A: No, not unless I get too much, I fall asleep.

Q: I am talking about this night?

A: No.

Q: Did you look at your watch again at the time you left your room?

A: No, I did not take my watch with me. I took it off that night.

Q: You did not have it with you then?

A: No.

Q: So you had no way of telling the time when you were en route going north?

A: No.

Q: You were just giving us an estimate of your time then?

A: An estimate.

Q: If you did not sleep very long and got right up and dressed, you would have got up north a little earlier than 2:30, is that right?

A: Yes.

Q: You could have been up there much earlier than 2:30, couldn't you?

A: No. No, not much earlier, approximately between 2:00 and 2:30.

Q: Did you see anybody else at the university outside of Gene and Joe that particular evening, Sunday, Jan. 6, 1946?

A: No, not that I remember. There may have been, but I was in my room all the time, and I recall to mind that far back Joe and Gene and me being together.

Q: When you were at your mother's house over the weekend did you have the knife and the gun with you?

A: No.

Q: And the piece of paper?

A: No, the paper may have been with me. I think it was in my other pants pocket.

Q: Well, was it with you or wasn't it?

A: I don't know.

Q: Why did you take the knife and a gun and the wire and a piece of paper with you when you went out that night?

A: Well, in burglaries you take a gun.

Q: Burglaries you take a gun?

A: I always had that wire in my packet because on previous burglaries where I wired the front door.

Q: What was the knife for?

A: The knife was to pry open windows and all. I usually carried a knife. Almost always it was something heavy on the order of a knife that could open something.

Q: Why did you bother with a piece of paper?

A: That was in my pocket. I had no reason for that.

Q: Did you take a pencil with you?

A: Yes. I always carried a pencil.

Q: What kind of pencil?

A: It was an ordinary.

Q: Just an ordinary lead pencil?

A: Yes.

Q: Why did you take it with you?

A: That was in my pocket, too.

Q: The paper and pencil would not help you in any burglary, would they?

A: No.

Q: When you started north, didn't you know that you were going to go to the Degnan home?

A: No, I did not. I remember disputing with myself whether I should get off at Granville or Thorndale, but Granville is too far out. I could have been over there.

Q: Do you know why you picked Thorndale to get off?

A: No, it was just a matter of choice.

Q: You disputed with yourself, what do you mean, disputed between Thorndale and Granville?

A: If I wanted to get off at Thorndale I would have to get up in a hurry before the door closes, before it left the station. I wanted to sit until Granville, so I got up and went out.

Q: Where did you get off at?

A: At Thorndale.

Q: At Thorndale?

A: Yes.

Q: That is the place where you had to hurry to get out?

A: Yes.

Q: Now, to get back to this piece of paper, you say you picked it up about a week before, will you tell us again just where you were when you picked that up?

A: In Harper Library.

Q: What were you doing?

A: I was doing some research work, encyclopedias.

Q: Did you have a notebook with you?

A: Yes.

Q: Where was this piece of paper at?

A: It was laying right near me. I had the whole table to myself.

Q: Was it attached to a pad?

A: No.

Q: Was it lying loose as a single sheet?

A: Yes.

Q: How did you fold that paper?

A: End over end. Just fold it in half and fold it quarter. Then fold it a long quarter and a half.

Q: Will you fold this piece of paper in the manner you say you folded it? (folds paper)

Q: What did you do with that after you folded it that way?

A: Put it in my pocket.

Q: Did you have any idea what you were going to use it for at that time?

A: No.

Q: Yet you had lots of paper in your room at the university?

A: Not too much, enough, though.

Q: One sheet of paper is not very valuable to you?

A: No.

Q: Why would you take all the pains to pick up a single sheet of paper in Harper's Library and fold it so carefully as you folded that piece of paper?

A: Well, because by my taking notes in lectures and any time to take notes.

Q: Couldn't you take a sheet of paper from your own pocket?

A: In fact I did not have it with me. I would not have the paper with me all the time.

Q: You always have it with you if you put it in your pocket?

A: Just like people make it a business to carry a pencil.

Q: If you made it your business to carry a pencil and paper with you, why didn't you have paper with you and not find it necessary to take particular sheet?

A: I had no notebook with me.

Q: You are sure that piece of paper was not attached to any pad?

266

A: Yes.

Q: It was lying there loose?

A: Yes.

Q: You just stuck it in your pocket for note paper?

A: Yes.

Mr. Tuohy Q: Was the pad close by?

Mr. Crowley Q: Do you know who had been using this particular piece of paper before you?

A: No.

Q: When you got off of the elevated at Thorndale Avenue Station where did you go?

A: Then I went east.

Q: East on Thorndale Avenue?

A: Yes, sir.

Q: How far east did you go?

A: To Winthrop, I went down Winthrop.

Q: Then did you turn Winthrop?

A: Yes, then north.

Q: How far north on Winthrop did you go?

A: Glenlake.

Q: Then where did you go?

A: Then I turned east and went to the alley between Kenmore and Sheridan, and turned south in that alley until I came to the back yard, about fifty feet off the main road, Glenlake. Then I seen the ladder and I take the ladder. I proceeded north and I tried to get into one of the windows. From there I proceeded after failure, back to the alley and started south again, and I came to the Degnan home.

Q: Did you at any time cut across Kenmore Avenue in a southeasterly direction from the corner of Glenlake and Kenmore to the east side of Kenmore Avenue?

A: Glenlake? What are the streets again? Glenlake.

Q: And Kenmore. You crossed Kenmore Avenue on Glenlake, you said?

A: Yes.

Q: At any time did you walk from the corner of Kenmore to Glenlake in a southerly direction to the east side of Kenmore Avenue?

A: No.

Q: Did you pass in front of an automobile with the light going on Kenmore Avenue just south of Glenlake?

A: No.

Q: After you took Suzanne Degnan's body out of her room you walked east to the alley between Kenmore and Sheridan?

A: Yes.

Q: Where did you go from there?

A: I went north.

Q: How far north?

A: To my knowledge I went up to the apartment building, the big apartment building where I tried to get into.

Q: Where was that apartment building which you tried to get into?

A: It is going north, it is east, on my east side, I mean my left side.

Q: How far from the Degnan home is that?

A: About two houses.

Q: Did you stop there?

A: No.

Q: Where did you go from there?

A: I don't know. I must have continued north. I do not know where I went from then on, but I was going that direction.

Q: Where did you find yourself when you next recollect your whereabouts?

A: I was near Broadway, on the west side of the "L," on the west side of the "L" tracks. I do not know what street it was. Some place south.

Q: It would be Hollywood?

A: I guess so—no, it was some place south.

Q: The alley west of the elevated?

A: Yes.

Q: Between Ardmore and Hollywood?

A: I don't know the street. It could be up in here (pointing at the plan on the table).

Q: Have you been back in that neighborhood since January 7?

A: I do not think so.

Q: When did you throw the gun on the tennis courts at Loyola?

A: It may have been before, it may have been after, but I know there was snow on the ground.

268

Q: Those tennis courts are located at the head of Winthrop and Sheridan Road, where Sheridan Road runs east and west, isn't that so?

A: Yes the gun was dismantled I believe. I think I took the barrel off, the thing that goes around it and threw it in there and I threw the other part in too.

Q: What time did you get back to the university in the morning of January 7?

A: About six o'clock.

Q: Where did you go?

A: I went to my room.

Q: How long did you stay in your room?

A: I studied until, I listened to the radio about, I would say at least a quarter to nine. No, it was about eight o'clock because I know I went to get something to eat that morning.

Q: Where did you go get something to eat?

A: The cafeteria, Hutchinson College.

Q: How long were you there?

A: I was there about half an hour.

Q: Then where did you go?

A: Then I came back to my room, got my books and went to class.

Q: What time was the first class you attended that morning?

A: Ten o'clock.

Q: What did you do between the time you had breakfast and the time you went to class?

A: Continued to study.

Q: Did you make a telephone call to the Degnan home?

A: No.

Q: During that period. Did you ever make a telephone call to the Degnan home?

A: No, never.

Q: How long did that class last?

A: An hour. Fifty minutes. They give you ten minutes.

Q: It was about ten minutes of eleven?

A: Yes.

Q: What did you do then?

A: At ten minutes to eleven I went to the next class.

Q: What time was that out?

A: That was ten minutes to twelve.

Q: Then where did you go?

A: To my next class.

Q: Where did you go the afternoon of January 7?

A: Went to class.

Q: Till how long?

A: Around five o'clock.

Q: Then what did you do?

A: I went back to my room and studied, as usual.

Q: Were you back in the neighborhood of the Degnan home at any time after five o'clock on January 7?

A: No.

Q: Were you present at any time in the Degnan neighborhood when parts of Suzanne's body were recovered?

A: My classes ended between five and six, and I had not eaten all day, so I must have taken breakfast, too, that was about seven o'clock.

Q: What did you do at seven o'clock?

A: After that I was studying.

Q: Where did you study?

A: In my room.

Q: With whom?

A: With myself, nobody.

Q: Was anybody else there?

A: No.

Q: Did anybody see you that day?

A: Everybody was in class.

Q: Outside of the class hour?

A: I think me and Joe Costello ate the next day. I mean for suppertime, because I know wrestling class ends about five-thirty or so and my afternoon class and lecture at three o'clock ends at four.

Q: Did you learn at any time during the day—

A: No, it was a full day.

Q: —that there had been a kidnapping from the Degnan home?

A: No.

Q: Did you read in the newspapers?

A: No.

Q: Or listen to the radio and hear reports of this kidnapping?

A: No. I did not listen to the radio until, I think it was January 8, because January 7 in the morning I listened to the radio until I went to class, after that I listened to—

Q: When you listened to the radio, did you hear any radio report that Suzanne Degnan had been kidnapped?

A: No.

Q: Did you hear anybody discussing the kidnapping of Suzanne Degnan on the morning of January 7?

A: No.

Q: Did you discuss that kidnapping with any of your friends or associates on the day of January 7?

A: No, I did not.

Q: When did you first learn that parts of the body of Suzanne Degnan had been recovered?

A: It was a couple of days after it happened. I believe January 8 I found out.

Q: How did you find out?

A: From radio reports.

Q: Was there any discussion with any of your friends on January 8 about it?

A: No.

Q: Never?

A: No.

Q: Did you ever discuss it?

A: It may have been mentioned, but I never discussed it.

Q: Did you ever discuss it at home?

A: No.

Q: Did your mother ever ask you if you were the boy that did that?

A: No.

Q: Did you ever know anybody by the name of George Murman?

A: I know the name George, I didn't know the name George Murman.

Q: You didn't know anybody by the name of George Murman?

A: That has all been attached to myself. It was practically the truth all what I told you that evening, except like I always have the habit of doing—it just seems a fight with him and me.

Q: George Murman is in reality a name you concocted for yourself, when you do something that you, Bill Heirens, don't want to admit to?

A: You can say that, yes, but the name was concocted right around the time I was at Gibault, that was about five years ago. No, that is about three years ago, and from then on I just seemed to be in a fight, that is all. To tell me he is real. But when you get down to other people, he is not real.

Q: What do you mean by that?

A: He is as real as anybody else to me.

Q: Does he exist? Does he live in flesh and blood outside of your head?

A: No, he doesn't. I realize he is a concoction of my imagination.

Q: Was it a name you concocted to use as an alias?

A: No.

Q: How did you happen to give him the name Murman?

A: There was no reason for that, just anything that popped in my head when you asked me. George was already in my mind.

Q: That is your middle name?

A: Yes, sir.

Q: And it is your father's name?

A: Yes.

Q: And that is how you happened to use the name George?

A: No, it was not the reason at all. I don't know what brought the name about in my head.

Q: When you talk of George Murman, you mean the same individual as Bill Heirens, don't you?

A: As to you, yes. You can accept George as being me.

Q: Do you think that George Murman and Bill Heirens are two separate individuals within the same body?

A: I don't know.

Q: But he does not exist as a living person that you could bring in and introduce to me, and that you know where he lives?

A: When you questioned me as to where he lived, I could not tell because I didn't know.

Q: But he had no existence outside of your imagination, is that right?

A: Well he seems very real to me. He exists. When I say he brings things for me to use, I actually mean it. He brought things in for me to use and I took it as that. Just like the note I wrote, I thought I had sent him away, he was going to Mexico. I thought he would go like that and I wrote the note to myself.

Q: Did you send the note to him?

A: I kept the note. I wrote a lot of notes.

Q: But you knew in reality you were writing those notes to yourself?

A: Not at the time I wrote them, but after a while they seemed to be different.

Q: Did you ever mail a note to George Murman?

A: No.

Q: Did you ever see him?

A: No.

Q: Did you ever talk to him?

A: A couple of times I had talks.

Q: But he was not physically present?

A: No.

Q: So in reality you were just talking to yourself?

A: Yes.

Q: So there is no person George Murman that you know of, other than Bill Heirens?

A: No, there is no other person.

Mr. Tuohy : Let the Sheriff take Bill Heirens over to Mr. Crowley's office for a moment. His counsel can go with him. (William Heirens left the room at 1 p. m. and returned to Mr. Tuohy's office at 1:05 p. m.)

Mr. Tuohy Q: Bill, have you any recollection of washing off the parts of Suzanne's body after you cut it up in the basement?

A: No, I have not.

Q: Would you have any objection to going out with us and identifying for us the particular window in which you climbed into the Degnan home?

A: No.

Q: Will you go out with us and identify it if we ask you to?

A: Yes.

Mr. Tuohy Q: Does counsel have any objection to that?

Mr. John Coghlan A: No.

Mr. Tuohy Q: Would you have any objection to going to the basement of the apartment building where the body of Suzanne Degnan was dismembered and identifying that for us?

The Witness A: No.

Mr. Tuohy Q: Does the counsel have any objection to that?

Mr. Mal Coghlan A: No.

Mr. John Coghlan A: No objection.

Mr. Rowland Towle A: No.

Mr. Tuohy: I think that is all on this statement.

ANALYSIS OF CLEVELAND TORSO MURDERS, SUZANNE DEGNAN MURDER AND THE BLACK DAHLIA MURDER

In addition to the possible—or as I believe, probable—connections between the central cases and Jack Anderson Wilson already examined in preceding chapters, there are further sources of corroboration and evidence supporting the theory that two or more perpretrators were working together to commit these crimes. One source would be to employ DNA technology and the other appears in various news articles and books that I have found only after completing the main body of the text. These are analyzed and included here.

JACK ANDERSON WILSON'S DNA

The charred body of Jack Anderson Wilson was cremated following his death in 1982. If Wilson's mother, Minnie Buchanan Wilson, was not cremated following her death, then her remains could be exhumed and a mitochondrial DNA analysis could be conducted. Wilson's biological mother would have the same DNA as her son, Jack Anderson Wilson. This DNA could then be compared with the known DNA samples in the Cleveland Torso Murders, the murder of the Black Dahlia and the murder of Suzanne Degnan, if available.

JACK ANDERSON WILSON CLUE

As recently as 1990, the Los Angeles Police Department thought the murder of the Black Dahlia might have been connected to the Cleveland Torso Murders. Cleveland Detective Peter Merylo believed that the Mad Butcher of Kingsbury Run "was responsible for the more recent Black Dahlia murder case in Los Angeles" (page 75, *Greatest Crimes of the Century*, 1954, by A.W. Pezet and Bradford Chambers). Los Angeles Detective John St. John suspected that Jack Anderson Wilson killed the Black Dahlia but did not feel Wilson was involved in the Cleveland killings. St. John's assessment that the murder of the Black Dahlia and the Cleveland Torso Murders exhibited separate and distinct "signatures" was based on incomplete information supplied by the Cleveland authorities. Had St. John received all of the facts concerning the Cleveland Torso Murders, including the fact that more than one of the Cleveland Torso Victims was tortured before being killed, then his assessment of the murders could very well have been consistent with that of Detective Merylo.

I recently found some other information that may be worth mentioning and that may shed some light on this mystery. Note, however, that as of the date of this writing I have not found verification of the following information. I read a book written by Max Allen Collins entitled *Angel In Black*, published by Signet in 2002. Mr. Collins' book is, in his words, "based on history although it is a work of fiction." Before writing his book Mr. Collins and his research associate, George Hagenauer, did extensive research on the Cleveland Torso Murders in Cleveland. Collins' book included three entries that caught my attention:

1. Page 202: "We even had a suspect, a young homosexual who worked in the butcher shop of a St. Clair Avenue grocery . . . but this never panned out."

2. Page 269: "You had a suspect . . . some fag butcher . . ." "A young homosexual, yes, who worked on St. Clair Avenue. Like Watterson, he liked to prowl the skid row sections of town, preying on society's dregs. And his name, as you've guessed, was Arnold Wilson." "Yes, but the description of the St. Clair butcher shop boy was not common: he was a very pockmarked kid, very thin, very tall, Merylo said . . . perhaps as much as six four."

3. Page 317: (Here Collins makes reference to his factual account in *Angel In Black*: "Although my pairing of Wilson and the Mad Butcher of Kingsbury Run may seem fanciful, one of Wilson's aliases is in fact the name of a suspected accomplice of the Kingsbury Run Butcher." This clue and the source of Collin's information are of importance because more than one person may be involved. See: "Two Men and a Female Impersonator Clue" below.

I spoke with Mr. Collins and his recollection was that the information contained in numbers 1, 2 & 3 above was based directly on his and his assistant's research of the Cleveland Torso Murders. I have not personally located the source of this information, but it makes sense that the Cleveland detectives would have followed up on the tip received by Detective Orley May from the woman in the Workhouse. They could have located a young 6'4" sodomist-former butcher who worked for "Sam" on St. Clair Avenue in Cleveland during the time of the Cleveland Torso Murders.

There may very well be a police report or an article in *The Plain Dealer* that expressly identified the sodomist-former butcher fingered by the lady in the Workhouse in 1937. If so, then it appears that the Cleveland detectives were investigating a 6'4" sodomist by the name of Jack Wilson as a suspect in the Cleveland Torso Murders but couldn't pin the murders on him, just as the Los Angeles detectives, years later, identified a 6'4" sodomist by the name of Jack Anderson Wilson (a/k/a Jack Wilson) as a suspect in the murder of the Black Dahlia, but couldn't find the corroborating evidence necessary to make an arrest.

According to his Ohio birth certificate Jack Anderson Wilson was born on August 5, 1920. He would have been fourteen-years-old going on fifteen in 1935, when Flo Polillo was killed and dismembered in Cleveland, and twenty-six-years-old in 1947, when Elizabeth Short was killed and severed in Los Angeles.

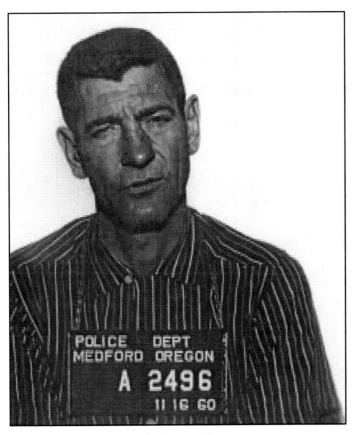

Jack Anderson Wilson

If Wilson had been born in 1920, he would have been 40-years-old in 1960 when his mug shot was taken in Oregon. I have asked several people to look at his photo and guess his age. Everyone indicated that he looks at least 50 or older. His appearance in 1960 could be the result of hard drinking and smoking, or possibly his birth certificate is not accurate. His father's name was altered. Was his date of birth? Note that his birth certificate is on a form that reads 19120. His birth certificates filed in Canton, Ohio, and in Columbus, Ohio, are identical.

Birth Certificate of Jack Anderson Wilson a/k/a Grover Loving, Jr.

On November 10, 1942, shortly after the murders in McKee's Rocks ended, an affidavit was filed at the Canton, Ohio, Department of Vital Statistics. This affidavit appears to have been signed by his mother, Minnie Buchanan Wilson, in the state of North Carolina and lists the name of Wilson's father as Alex F. Wilson.

North Carolina OHIO DEPARTMENT OF HEALTH
COLUMBUS
STATE OF ~~Every~~

COUNTY OF Avery ss.
AFFIDAVIT

I, Mrs. Minnie Buchanan, Wilson being first duly sworn, say that I am the

Mother of Jack Anderson Wilson , and that (h is) original

birth certificate on file with the Ohio Department of Health is incorrect.

The following is a true and correct statement:

NAME Jack Anderson Wilson FILE NO. 80166

DATE OF BIRTH August 5, 1920 PLACE OF BIRTH Canton, Ohio.

NAME OF FATHER Alex F. Wilson

MAIDEN NAME OF MOTHER Minnie Buchanan,

REMARKS

(SIGNATURE OF FATHER OR MOTHER) *Minnie Buchanan Wilson*

Sworn to before me and subscribed in my presence, this 10th day of

November nineteen hundred and 42.

My Commission Expires June 24, 1943.

(SEAL)   OFFICIAL TITLE

V.S. 28   (This affidavit must be typewritten)

THIS IS A CERTIFIED COPY OF THE RECORD ON FILE
IN THE CANTON CITY HEALTH DEPARTMENT

2/4/05   *Robert E Pattison*
DATE   LOCAL REGISTRAR

affidavit signed by Minnie Buchanan Wilson dated November 10, 1942

279

Wilson could have killed Flo Polillo in 1935, in concert with others, when he was fourteen-years-old. Consider the following:

1. In 1935, the United States was in the middle of the Great Depression. The Great Depression began on Black Friday in October, 1929, and didn't end until 1942, after the United States had entered World War II.

2. Little, if any, attention was paid to Child Labor Laws in 1935. It would certainly have been possible for a fourteen-year-old to work in a Cleveland grocery-butcher shop at that time. Keep in mind that this is the era of John Steinbach's *Grapes of Wrath*.

3. Due to the state of the economy in 1935, Wilson was probably forced to work and become a man at an early age. He probably enjoyed a very short childhood.

4. The Cleveland Workhouse included a juvenile section in 1935. (See tip received by Detective Orley May in 1937, from the lady in the Workhouse on page 96 of this text.)

5. If Wilson had been a lust killer he would have had these tendencies at an early age. This is not something that is learned in school or acquired through experience. At age fourteen Wilson would not have been the first young person to commit a murder. Consider the 1874 case of Boston's Jesse Pomeroy. At age eleven he sexually tortured seven young boys and not long after killed and mutilated a ten-year-old girl. A month later he slashed four-year-old Horace Mullen so savagely with a knife that he nearly decapitated him. All of his crimes were committed when he was under the age of fourteen. And what about fifteen-year-old Edmond Kemper who shot and killed both of his grandparents in 1964, in California? Or how about fifteen-year-old Willie Bosket who shot a man in the eye, piercing his brain and then shot the man again in his right temple killing him in a New York subway in 1978? The list of child killers goes on and on. It is not beyond the realm of possibility for Jack Anderson Wilson to have begun killing in Cleveland at age fourteen and to have acquired the ability to "expertly dismember" a human body by practicing his trade carving up dead animals in a local grocery-butcher shop.

According to the woman in the Cleveland Workhouse, who was interviewed by Detective Orley May in 1937, Jack Wilson was a sodomist and "a former butcher who worked for 'Sam'" on St. Clair Avenue. At the Case Western Reserve Historical

Library in Cleveland I located in the *1935 Cleveland City Directory* the following grocery stores located on St. Clair Avenue that were owned by a person with the first name "Sam":

Sam Kaas Grocery, 4034 St. Clair Avenue

Sam Gold Grocery, 9115 St. Clair Avenue

Sam Rocco Grocery, 10819 St. Clair Avenue

Sam Pistollo (Sam Pistitello) Meats, 15808 St. Clair Avenue

Perhaps someone acquainted with one of these businesses can remember a young 6'4" pock-marked employee during 1935-1937, who may have walked with a limp and carried a large butcher knife.

6. At age fourteen Wilson could have already engaged in acts of sodomy. We know that he was charged with sodomy in California in 1948 (See Max Allan Collins' reference to a young homosexual who worked for a butcher shop of a St. Clair Avenue grocery in Cleveland in the "Jack Anderson Wilson Clue" above).

MURDER OF CORPORAL MAOMA RIDINGS

On August 31, 1943, *The Indianapolis Star* reported that a 32-year-old WAC corporal by the name of Maoma L. Ridings was found murdered in the Claypool Hotel in downtown Indianapolis. She was nude from the waist down. Large gashes, "unusually deep" the paper noted, were found in the left side of her neck. "The coroner said also that the autopsy showed the wrists of the victim were slashed some time after she was cut brutally in her throat and face. This indicated that the assailant tried to show Corporal Ridings attempted suicide, the coroner added." "She had been a frequent week-end visitor at the hotel during the last two months, sometimes coming alone and sometimes being accompanied by another member of the WAC from Camp Atterbury." At this same time period Elizabeth Short was living at Camp Cooke in California with a WAC sergeant. There is some question regarding the date Elizabeth Short left her employment at Camp Cooke. Author Mary Pacios wrote in her chronology that "Bette ends her employment at Camp Cooke on August 25, 1943." (She may have ended her employment at a later date.) It is known that Elizabeth Short traveled through Indianapolis on different occasions (See page 173, *Severed*). Now here is what I found to be very interesting: *The Indianapolis Star* also reported on August 31, 1943, that on the day Maoma Ridings was killed "a black- haired woman in black was seen in the room with Corporal Ridings early Saturday night by two bellboys." Following the murder of Maoma Ridings the woman in black disappeared. One of the theories the police developed was that the "woman with black hair, dressed in black" was not a woman but instead a female impersonator. Jack Anderson Wilson was either a female impersonator or he hung out with someone who was a female impersonator. Wilson was in Indianapolis on August 23, 1943, when Corporal Maoma Ridings was murdered. He left town immediately thereafter (Page 200, *Severed*).

MURDER OF SUZANNE DEGNAN

It is known that Elizabeth Short traveled through Indianapolis and Chicago during the mid-1940's. Duffy Sawyer had modeling jobs for her in both of these cities and that is where she met co-pilot Gordan Fickling. Suzanne Degnan was killed and expertly dismembered on January 7, 1946, in Chicago. Elizabeth Short was in Chicago sometime between June-August, 1946. On January 30, 1947, sixteen days after Elizabeth Short was murdered in Los Angeles, the *Los Angeles Examiner* ran the following article:

In Chicago, Freddie Woods, 23, who described himself as a "friend" of the Slain girl, revealed that she was "fascinated" with the brutal slaying of six-year-old Suzanne Degnan, which took place in Chicago a year ago. Woods said he met Miss Short last August when she was in Chicago for 10 days. She told him she was a Massachusetts reporter covering the trial of William Heirens who was convicted of the Degnan kidnapping and slaying. "Elizabeth was one of the prettiest girls I ever met," Woods said. "But she was terribly preoccupied with the details of the Degnan murder."

January 30, 1947, *The Los Angeles Examiner*

It seems too coincidental to me that Elizabeth Short was murdered and expertly severed on January 14, 1947, less than six months after she had been in

Chicago "terribly preoccupied with the details of the Degnan Murder" and pretending to be a reporter from Massachusetts "covering the trial of William Heirens." Did the person responsible for the murder of Suzanne Degnan stalk and eventually kill and expertly sever Elizabeth Short because she was "talking" too much about the Degnan murder? Is that the reason she was so frightened from January 1 through January 8, 1947, the day she was last seen walking towards Sixth Street after she left the Biltmore Hotel in Los Angeles? Did Elizabeth Short's killer cut her mouth, not to present a "grotesque smile" as was commonly thought by the detectives, but rather to send a message to the world that she had a "big mouth" because she was talking too much about the Degnan murder? Author Mary Pacios interviewed retired *Los Angeles Dailey News* reporter Gerry Ramlow concerning the murder of the Black Dahlia. She asked Ramlow about the gashes on Bette's face: "Did he know of other murders in which the victim was cut from ear to ear? 'Usually a low level crook, someone who talked too much,' he said, and looked at me as if he had just realized something" (page 74, *Childhood Shadows: The Hidden Story of the Black Dahlia Murder*).

Why was Elizabeth Short preoccupied with the details of a murder in Chicago where a young girl was killed and expertly dismembered? Did Short know who really killed Suzanne Degnan? In order to answer this question it must first be determined that Elizabeth Short knew Jack Anderson Wilson. Following the murder of Georgette Bauerdorf, an eyewitness reported seeing someone fitting the description of Jack Anderson Wilson near her abandoned automobile. Elizabeth Short and Georgette Bauerdorf worked at the same establishment and Bauerdorf mentioned Elizabeth Short by name in her diary (page 201, *Severed*). Georgette dated a very tall soldier. She saw him several times, but for some reason stopped dating him. She was frightened of him. Detectives at the Los Angeles Sheriff's Department suspected that Jack Anderson Wilson had killed Georgette Bauerdorf, but were unable to prove it. According to John Gilmore's taped interview of Jack Anderson Wilson, Elizabeth Short appeared to have known Wilson because she "got into his car and sat with him for a while" (See page 82 of this text or page 185 of *Severed*).

Now, with this in mind, it seems logical to me that Elizabeth Short may have either known who killed Suzanne Degnan and was reasonably sure that Jack Anderson Wilson was involved with the Degnan murder. Being "preoccupied with the details of the Degnan murder" and "reporting on the trial of William Heirens" may very well have led to Short's murder by Jack Anderson Wilson, the same person who may have been involved in the murder/dismemberment of Suzanne Degnan.

WAS JACK ANDERSON WILSON IN CHICAGO WHEN SUZANNE DEGNAN WAS KILLED?

An article in the January 17, 1982, *Los Angeles Herald Examiner* written by Suzan Nightingale, *Herald Examiner* staff writer, included a statement by author John Gilmore concerning "Mr. Jones," who I believe Gilmore later identified as "Al Morrison." Detective John St. John thought Al Morrison was in fact Jack Anderson Wilson. The article reads in part, "Jones was a shy figure, according to Gilmore, **connected with two deaths** *in Chicago* **before he came to Los Angeles** and 'did jobs' for people" (emphasis added). This information fits into my theory that the same person who killed and expertly severed the Black Dahlia was also responsible for the murder and expert dismemberment of Suzanne Degnan in Chicago. I suspect that one of the two murders Jones claimed responsibility for in Chicago before he went to Los Angeles was the murder of Suzanne Degnan.

Los ANGELES HERALD EXAMINER

Sunday January 17, 1982

Final edition

50 cents

Southern California's Award-Winning Newspaper   (213) 744-8000

id Abscam chief witness lie?

Cowan
ines News Service

ASHINGTON — Justice Department officials have declined to the trial judge alleged in the Abscam case, Melvin lied in some portions of iony.

... gations were said to have de by Weinberg's wife.

Marie, in interviews with a reporter. They have been referred by the Justice Department to Judge George C. Pratt, who presided over the ... Abscam trials in federal court in Brooklyn.

"It's a pending matter before the court," said John Russell, a spokesman for the department. "We're not at liberty to discuss it," he said.

In the Abscam trials, seven members of Congress and other public officials were convicted of accepting money for corrupt purposes from undercover FBI agents. Weinberg played an important role in the investigation and as a witness.

... tant evidence against the defendants was a videotape that showed them talking with the undercover agents and taking money. The agents posed as wealthy Arabs.

It appeared that defense lawyers might try to use Mrs. Weinberg's accusations to support their con-

... tentions that their clients were denied due process during the trials. Officials said the Justice Department was having difficulty ... to be interviewed. Her reported assertions about her husband's testimony were made in interviews with Indy Badwhar, a reporter for columnist Jack Anderson.

"He's been interviewing her over three months," Anderson said yes-

... terday. He said Badwhar spoke to Mrs. Weinberg twice at her Florida home and had also spoken with her by telephone. He said columns by ... berg said had been distributed for publication next week.

Anderson said that "we made transcripts of some conversations" and that "I submitted them to the Justice Department" through Richard Ben-Veniste, a Washington lawyer representing Howard L.

Criden. Criden, ... three other defendants Philadelphia, was ... ate Mrs. Weinberg an aid to defense turn the prosecution said her statement would be "regard rial." He added,

Abscam/A-6, C

LACK DAHLIA

thor claims to have found 1947 murderer

... m Elizabeth Short and sketches of suspected killer as he may have looked in 1947, left, and 1978.

uzan Nightingale
ld Examiner staff writer

he fine, light powder she smoothed over her body may have been the only light thing in Elizabeth Short's life.

She moved in dark shadows, frequented bars, always wore black clothes, and ultimately black secrets.

hey called her the "Black Dahlia."
ho died 35 years ago Friday, and she remains an naic as on that Jan. 15, 1947, when aper headlines screamed about "THE MAN AL WEREWOLF KILLER" who tortured and biected the 22-year-old brunette, abandoning backed torso in a grassy lot on Norton Avenue ween 30th Street and Coliseum Avenue.

Panned by the filming journalistic excesses of day, it was a murder that has horrified and cinated Los Angeles ever since. No motive, no apon and no killer have ever been found.

But John Gilmore — the 13-year-old son of a Los geles cop at the time of the murder — believes has solved the crime that has stumped police for ee decades. After 13 years of research, the thor of books about Charles Manson ("The barbage People") and Charles Schmidt ("The ncson Murders") is convinced the killer is alive and anning a bar in Nevada.

Although he is willing to release composite awings of his prime suspect, Gilmore won't reveal e man's name, calling him instead, "Mr. Jones." ilmore's key source is "Mr. Smith," who knew both ones and Elizabeth Short.

"According to Smith, Jones told him he'd done." Gilmore says, "My source said he sat in the hotel om and drank an entire bottle of whiskey and

"My source said he sat in the hotel room and drank an entire bottle of whiskey and told him in great detail what he'd done."

Author John Gilmore

told him in great detail what he'd done."
Jones was a shady figure, according to Gilmore, connected with two deaths in Chicago before he came to Los Angeles and "did jobs" for people. After holding her against her will in a rented house on 33rd Street, he murdered Elizabeth Short in a fit of frustrated jealousy.

It is the latest theory in a case that has offered as many smoke screens as suspects. The Black Dahlia is, after all, a murder 40 people have confessed to.

"There are people today who confess to the murder even though they weren't born at the time."

But Gilmore, who has talked to "a couple hundred" people in his 13-year quest, is convinced his final piece of the story together building on the collection of shady characters who found their way to Hollywood after World War II.

So certain is Gilmore of his findings, that he took his evidence to the Los Angeles Police Department several weeks ago.

Black Dahlia/A-6, Col. 2

New blast of polar cold in Midwest

Death toll now 253 as much of U.S. shivers

Associated Press

A surge of polar cold nicknamed the Siberian Express blew into the frozen Midwest with paralyzing blizzards yesterday, and the mercury sank to painful lows deep into the Sun Belt.

The frigid winds sent the chill factor to 80 degrees below zero in places and the death toll reached 253 in a wintry assault that began writing weather history last weekend.

"It is one of the most severe outbreaks of cold weather mid-America has seen since the 1800s," said meteorologist Nolan Doule of the National Weather Service in Kansas City.

While temperatures yesterday stopped shy of last weekend's records, such as the all-time low of 26 below in Chicago, readings were close to 30 degrees below zero across parts of Montana, North Dakota and Minnesota, with wind chills below zero as far south as San Antonio, Texas.

More than 120,000 people remained without power in Alabama, Georgia and North Carolina. Freezing rain closed many highways again in north Georgia and snow fell in the Texas Panhandle.

Snow was common from the ...

Weather/A-6, Col. 4

Fog prompts CHP travel advisories and LAX confusion

By Lennie La Guire
Herald Examiner staff writer

Thick, blinding fog enveloped Los Angeles last night, forcing virtual closure of Los Angeles International Airport and blotting out visibility almost completely in some areas, the National Weather Service announced.

The newest return of Billy Jack
Tom Laughlin, the maverick of the movie back to play his real-life role as a crusader this time is rescuing Filmex and running h
Style/E-1

Bruins and Trojans triumph at home
UCLA's Bruins snagged their first confere against Arizona, and guard Dwight Ander points helped the Trojans defeat Arizona
Sports/B-1

Courting trouble for Brown
Conservatives are looking at rulings by state nominee Judge Cruz Reynoso for a use against him — and Gov. Brown.
News/A-3

EDITOR'S REPORT

The newest return	Section B
from Russia — and U.S. automakers	Section D
The same old story	Section E
Comment/F-3	Section F

INDEX
Section B
Section C
Section D
Section E
Section F

January 17, 1982 *Los Angeles Herald Examiner*

The most logical reasons nothing shows up on Jack Anderson Wilson's California rap sheet from 3/22/43-5/9/48 are these:

286

1. He wasn't committing crimes at that time, or was committing crimes and wasn't being caught.

2. He was out of the state of California during most of this time period. In 1944, Wilson was in the military service.

There is reason to believe that he was in Indianapolis in 1943, when Corporal Maoma Ridings was murdered in that city and that he was in Calfornia in 1944 when Georgette Bauerdorf was murdered. According to his taped interview with John Gilmore, Wilson, or at least "Al Morrison," was in California in January, 1947, when Elizabeth Short was murdered. If Wilson or "Al Morrison" was in Chicago during 1945-1946, there may be something like an arrest record, social security or wage payment, telephone number, accident report, photograph, etc., that could establish his presence in that city.

HUMAN EAR CLUE:

Following the murder of Suzanne Degnan in 1946, a human ear was mailed to Helen Degnan, along with a threatening note (page 51,*William Heirens: His Day In Court*). Following the murder of the Black Dahlia in 1947, it was discovered that one of her ear lobes had been sliced off (page 74, *Reporters: Memoirs of a Young Newspaperman*, by Will Fowler). If the person who killed Suzanne Degnan did in fact mail the ear lobe to Mrs. Degnan, this would indicate a signature similar to the ear lobe detail in the Black Dahlia case.

SIMILAR NOTES CLUES:

After Suzanne Degnan was murdered, Chicago's Mayor Kelly received a hastily written note that read:

"This is to tell you how sorry I am I couldn't get ole Degnan instead of his girl. Roosevelt and OPA made their own laws. Why shouldn't I and a lot more? (See page 50: *William Heirens: His Day In Court)*

pretty big sums, as their salaries went, and that Jim indulged in some fancy borrowing to meet creditor claims when pressed.

Could Jim be in debt to anyone of unbalanced mind? Could Jim have turned to less acceptable means of amplifying an income which, though increasing, failed to keep pace with the growth of his tastes? (Incidentally, he is given to gambling for what I'd consider pretty high stakes at cards.) Sinister things can happen to a man who fails to live within his income.

The author offered the names of additional people who knew Jim well upon request.

Questioned by the police about the possibility that Suzanne's death might be an act of vengeance by an unknown enemy, Degnan stated:

> I suppose I have, like anybody else, skeletons in the closet that would be incidents in your life that you would not be too keen to draw out and review, but from the bottom of my heart I can tell you I know of no incident in my life that would not bare full review in a thing like this.

> I have made mistakes that presumably would cause prejudices. I have thought of all the places I have been and all the people I know, and the one thing that has been a tremendous degree of satisfaction to me is that no place I have ever been I can't go back and have a lot of friends. I suppose I have people that don't like me, but nobody that I know of that feuded.

An anonymous note reported:

> Mrs. Degnan is responsible for her child's death. The Degnan child was killed by accident in her room that night.

And yet another note from a "former friend" offered:

> You surely cannot believe the father of the Degnan child is innocent. If you only knew the temper he has. He would do anything when he is in a bad mood....We who know him are not surprised at what happened.

Mayor Kelly received a hastily written note that read:

> This is to tell you how sorry I am I couldn't get ole Degnan instead of his girl. Roosevelt and OPA made their own laws. Why shouldn't I and a lot more?

And Katherine Baker, maid to Marian Murphy of Lake Shore Drive, told police that, according to Mrs. Murphy:

copy of page 50, *William Heirens: HIS DAY IN COURT*
Published with permission by Dolores Kennedy

Now compare the note mailed to Mayor Kelly with the December 21, 1938, letter mailed to Cleveland Chief of Police Matowitz from Los Angeles:

"*I felt bad* operating on those people. . . *What did their lives mean in comparison* . . . In both the note to Mayor Kelly and the letter to Chief Matowitz the writer wrote that he was either "sorry" or "felt bad" followed by a question. Again the pattern is very similar.

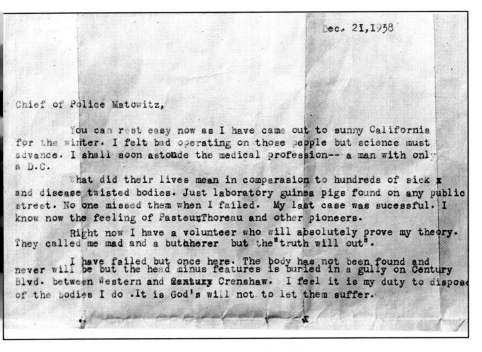

copy of the 1938 letter to Chief Matowitz
(photograph courtesy of Marjorie Merylo Detnz)

CLUE: SIMILAR LETTERS MAILED FOLLOWING A MURDER:

Here is another interesting clue that may help prove that the same person or persons that killed the Black Dahlia may also have killed Suzanne Degnan. Following the murder of Suzanne Degnan on January 7, 1946, Chicago Police Chief Walter Storm received the following enticing communication:

"Why don't you catch me. **If you don't ketch me soon, I will** cummit suicide. There is a reward out for me. How much do **I get if I give** myself

up. When do I get that **20,000** dollars they wanted from the Degnan girl a'
5901 Kenmore Avenue

You may **find me** at the Club Tavern at 738 E. 63ʳᵈ St. known as Charlie the
Greeks. Or at Conway's Tavern at 6247 Cottage Grove Av.

Please hurry now" (emphasis added)

Published with permission by Dolores Kennedy

WILLIAM HEIRENS: HIS DAY IN COURT (51)

It was the work of gangsters and they probably wanted to get revenge on the Flynns because I happen to know that the Flynns run a handbook.

Walter Storms received the following enticing communication:

> Why don't you catch me. If you don't ketch me soon, I will commit suicide. There is a reward out for me. How much do I get if I give myself up. When do I get that 20,000 dollars they wanted from that Degnan girl at 5901 Kenmore Avenue.
> You may find me at the Club Tavern at 738 E. 63rd St. known as Charlie the Greeks. Or at Conway's Tavern at 6247 Cottage Grove Av.
> Please hurry now.

During the succeeding months, cranks surfaced regularly. Notes of confession were found in hallways of apartment buildings. A human ear was mailed to Helen Degnan, along with a threatening note. On May 31, a twenty-eight-year-old Michigan man appeared at the police station in Houston, Texas, announcing that he knew something about the Degnan case. He stated that "I could tell a story that would knock the Chicago cops off their feet," and promptly leaped to his death from an open window in the building.

The police department filtered the information coming in from various parts of the country—trying not to waste their time on worthless leads, while wary of neglecting anything of value.

The investigation became a dragnet of the city of Chicago. So professional was the dismemberment of Suzanne that the police wiretapped the telephone lines of neighboring butcher shops and tree surgeons, hoping to overhear incriminating conversations. Thousands of persons were questioned, especially those with any hint of sexual misbehavior in their past. A variety of busboys, bartenders, postal clerks, cab drivers, doctors, dentists, businessmen, and ex-convicts paraded before the police. Women turned in their husbands, mothers implicated their sons, and a young woman was apprehended because someone had written on the snow which clung to the trunk of her car: "ketch me before I kill."

The most promising suspects were arrested and, upon those arrests, State's Attorney William J. Tuohy and Chief of Detectives Walter G. Storms would tell the press that this time they were certain they had found the killer. Inevitably, the suspect passed the lie detector test, or came up with an alibi, or the police were forced to admit that the fingerprints did not match.

Chief Storms declared publicly that: "In the heat of public anger over this atrocious killing, there is a tendency to condemn the first person seized."

Page 51 from *William Heirens: HIS DAY IN COURT*
Published with permission by Dolores Kennedy

(Remember that Jack Anderson Wilson was an alcoholic, spent a great deal of time in bars, met with author John Gilmore in seedy bars over a period of three years, and in both cases the killer demanded the exact amount of money, $20.000.)

Now compare the letter to Chief Storm to the letter received by the *Los Angeles Herald Express*, in January, 1947, following the murder of Elizabeth Short:

"To Los Angeles Herald Express
I will give up
In Dahlia Killing **if I get**
10 years
Don't try to **find me**" (emphasis added)

copy of January 28, 1947 *Herald-Express* article

In each letter not only were the exactly the same words used by the writer but also note that the order of the words in each communication was very similar:

First:　　"I will"
Second:　"If I get" and "I get if"
Third:　　"find me"
Fourth:　"give myself up" and "give up"
Fifth:　　a number, either 20,000 or 10

I am certainly not an expert in forensic linguistics. I did submit the notes to Alan M. Perlman, PhD, an expert in forensic linguistics analysis. He indicated that "The occurrence of similar words in the two texts means nothing in itself. The longer text has some interesting properties, but the other is too short for meaningful comparisons. I find no evidence of similar or different authorship."

I had another expert (John Pahl, a professor of English and technical writing at Northwestern Michigan College) give his opinion on these two letters. He wrote, "I don't think the wording similarities are all that surprising, at least not the very brief phrases that, in normal English, are almost necessarily the words that one would use to express these thoughts. So I'd look more to the attitudes or psychological tone expressed by the letters, that and their intended effect. There are some similarities here: Both indicate a dare—i.e., Why can't you catch me? (a challenge, a dare) and Don't (you dare) try to find me. Both raise the possibility of giving himself up, if certain conditions are met. Both are looking for some pay-off, in a lighter sentence or in cash. Having said that, I see real differences, too: The first letter provides two places to look for the writer, as though anxious to be caught or at least to be seen among a group of people. The other doesn't want to be caught, but is willing to turn himself in if the punishment is on his terms. Perhaps the most obvious contrast is that the first letter seems to represent a very incoherent train of thought, while the second, though its request for a lighter sentence is totally unrealistic, is logical and straight forward. So there are some striking similarities in what might be called the needs on the part of the writer, but some significant differences, as well, in style and logic. There's no reason they couldn't be the same writer. Even the differences could be a result of the writer behaving or feeling differently after quite different slayings in terms of the two victims or the locations, that and his increasingly urgent state of mind. It's hard to say."

Keep in mind that there were very few communications received by the authorities following the Degnan and Short murders. Each communication was very brief. The chances of two individuals writing the same words, in the same order, would seem to me to be extremely unlikely. If nothing else, one thing is for sure: William Heirens could not have written the above mentioned letter to the *Los Angeles Herald Express* in 1947, because he had been incarcerated in Chicago since July, 1946. Was Elizabeth Short silenced because she knew the real killer of Georgette Bauerdorf and Suzanne Degnan? There were reports that she was extremely afraid of someone shortly before she was murdered. Was her killer concerned that she would talk too much and tip off the authorities? Consider this, on Wednesday, January 29, 1947, fourteen days after the Black Dahlia was murdered, Federal Inspectors at the Terminal Annex Post Office in Los Angeles received the following note:

"A certain girl is going to get same as E.S. got if she squeals on us. We're going to Mexico City—**catch** us if you can.
2k's" (emphasis added)

The person who wrote this note appears to have been concerned about someone squealing on him. Did the same person(s) kill Elizabeth Short because they were concerned that she was going to "squeal" on them? The writer also used the word "catch" in the communication, the same word that was written in the "red lipstick message" by the person who killed Francis Brown, December 10, 1945, in Chicago:

"For heavens
Sake **catch** me
BeFore I kill more
I cannot control myself" (emphasis added)

And in the enticing communication to Chicago Police Chief Walter Storm following the murder of Suzanne Degnan:

"Why don't you **catch** me. If you don't **ketch** me soon. . ."
(emphasis added)
(See page 51, *William Heirens: His Day In Court*)

CLUE: ENVELOPE PUNCTUATION

The 1938 letter to Cleveland Chief of Police Matowitz mailed from Los Angeles contains the same odd punctuation marks that were included in the January, 1947 letter that may have been mailed by the Black Dahlia Avenger to the Los Angeles District Attorney. Here is a copy of the 1938 envelope that was mailed from Los Angeles:

copy of the 1938 Envelope. *Photo courtesy of Marjorie Merylo Dentz*

The 1947 envelope containing the note that may have been mailed by the Black Dahlia Avenger is addressed as follows:

District Attorney,
Hollywood, California.
(See page 170, *Black Dahlia Avenger*)

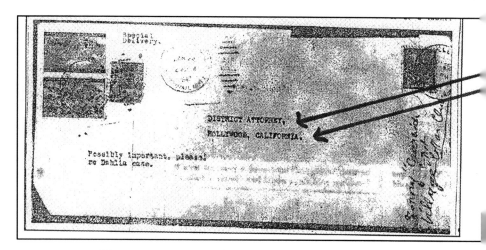

copy of January 28, 1947 envelope mailed to the *Los Angeles Examiner*

On both envelopes the first line is followed by a comma, and the last line, after the name of the state is completely spelled out, is followed with a period. Most writers would not put a comma after the first line on an envelope and most writers would not put a period after a non-abbreviated name of a state on the envelope's last line. Yet on an envelope associated with the Cleveland Torso Murders and an envelope associated with the murder of the Black Dahlia someone did exactly that. This may simply be a coincidence, but then again when considered with all the other coincidences, it might not be. The envelopes may have been addressed by the same person.

CLUE: MURDER OF THE BLACK DAHLIA

On January 18, 1947, six days after Elizabeth Short had been murdered, the *Los Angeles Examiner* ran the following article:

MISS SHORT SOUGHT HELP IN EARLIER PLIGHT, says Taxi Stand Manager

—Monterey Park, Jan. 17.

"Elizabeth Short came to my hack stand last December 29. Her clothes were torn. She told me a man she worked with had tried to attack her." These statements were made by Cab Stand Manager Glen Chandler this morning at his office, 115 North Garfield Avenue. "It was about 7 p.m. when some people dropped her off at my stand," Chandler said. "She looked wild-eyed and hysterical. Blood came from her knees. I didn't know whether she was cut or bruised. Her clothes were torn and she didn't have any shoes on.

She told me the well-dressed man who worked with her wanted to take her to Long Beach and cash her weekly pay check for her.

"Instead, he parked his car on a lonely road just south of Garvey Boulevard near Garfield Avenue. There, she told me, was where he tried to attack her.

"She fled from the car and got a ride to my stand. I put her in a cab and drove her to a hotel at 512 South Wall Street.

"I waited outside for her to come down to pay my fare. When she came down she was all dolled up. She said she didn't have the money and I figured then that I wouldn't get it.

"I don't know where she worked," Chandler said, "but she said she was a waitress.

"I'm positive that she was Elizabeth Short," he concluded.

Notice that Chandler said in this report that the man "who worked with her" tried to attack her. This would have been seventeen days before she was murdered.

January 18, 1947, *The Los Angeles Examiner*

If she had been attacked, as indicated by Chandler (and not otherwise discounted by the Los Angeles detectives) then it seems to me, in all likelihood, that the same person who attacked her two weeks before she was murdered was probably the same person who killed her less than seventeen days later. Assuming the taxi stand manager was correct and he did see Elizabeth Short on December 29, 1946, then ask yourself this question: How often is a girl beaten up by one person and two weeks later tortured and killed by a totally unrelated person? Elizabeth Short's friend and andlady Elvira French recalled that on or about January 2, 1947, "Some people came to our door and knocked. There was a man, a woman, and another man was waiting in a car parked on the street in front of the house. Beth became very frightened—she seemed to get panicky, and didn't want to see the people or answer the door. They finally went back to the car and drove away. Even our neighbors thought all of this was very suspicious."

CLUE: "WAITRESS"

Jack Anderson Wilson mentioned in his taped message to John Gilmore, "This is what he had in mind for the **waitress**" (See page 85 of the text).

Cab stand manager Glen Chandler is quoted in the January 18, 1947, *Los Angeles Examiner* as follows:

"I don't know where she worked," Chandler said, "but she said she was a **waitress**."

Was Elizabeth Short working as a waitress? If so, where and who was she working with during the last weeks in 1946, and the first week in 1947? Was Jack Anderson Wilson working in the same establishment?

CLUES FROM AUTOPSY REPORT

Dr. Victor CeFalu assisted Chief Surgeon Dr. Newbarr in the autopsy of Elizabeth Short. The autopsy report contained in part the following information:

There were multiple lacerations to the midforehead, in the right forehead, and at the top of the head in the midline. There are multiple tiny abrasions and lacerations. The trunk is completely severed by an incision, which is almost straight through the abdomen. There are multiple crisscross lacerations in the suprapublic area, which extend through the skin and soft tissues. There are lacerations of the intestine and kidneys. The uterus is small and no pregnancy is apparent. The tubes, ovaries, and cul-de-sac are intact. Within the vagina and higher up there is lying loose a small piece of skin with fat and subcutaneous tissue attached. On this piece of loose skin there are several crisscrossing lacerations. Smears for spermatozoa have been taken. The anal opening is markedly dilated and the opening measures 1" in diameter. There are multiple abrasions. Smears for spermatozoa have been taken. The stomach is filled with greenish brown granular matter, mostly feces and other particles, which could not be identified. All smears for spermatozoa were negative. It appeared as though many of the lacerations, including the dilation of the anal opening were done after the woman's death.

One of the photos of Elizabeth Short taken at the Los Angeles County Morgue shortly after her murder shows possible bruising near her left knee. If the autopsy report makes mention of the bruising and/or lacerations to her knees, this would tend to verify the report given by taxi stand manager Glen Chandler.

See also, for comparison, the photo of victim No.9 on page 16 of this text. His anal opening is markedly dilated. The anal sphincter muscle that closes the anus no longer functions in a dead body. It appears that victim No.5 was either penetrated sexually or with a foreign object after he was killed.

CLUE: "DESPERATELY NEEDED MONEY"

I am going to mention a few other known facts concerning the last days of Elizabeth Short's life that may shed a light on her killer's identity. Keep in mind that in the Cleveland Torso Murders some of the victims were drugged before being murdered. ("An addict named Al may have supplied Torso victim Flo Polillo with drugs.") Let me preface this information by stating that I believe Elizabeth Short was a beautiful young lady whose life and aspirations spiraled down a dark path out of her control into the web of a vicious predator.

A review of known facts concerning the Black Dahlia covering the time period of December 29, 1946, through January 9, 1947, reveals the following:

1. She was broke and virtually penniless. She could not afford cab fare.
2. She could not afford to rent an apartment and was allowed to live at Elvira French's home for $1.00 per day. According to Los Angeles Detective Joel Lesnick, "Elizabeth was on a hard road, couldn't seem to land a job and having to mooch off friends. . . She wasn't following through with long-range plans, I believe, and bounced from situation to situation; hence the number of apartments

and rented rooms she was in. Was she a true friend to the drunks and downtrodden, or was it part of an act?"

3. Her teeth were decaying and she could not afford to go to a dentist. (At some point in time did someone offer her some form of addictive pain medication for her tooth aches?)

4. She "desperately needed money." On January 8, 1947, her friend, Gordan Fickling, wired $100.00 to her from North Carolina. (Keep in mind that $100.00 in 1947, would have been the equivalent of approximately $1,000.00 in today's dollars.)

5. She owed Elvira French rent money in San Diego but did not pay her out of the money wired from Fickling.

6. According to Dorothy French, daughter of Elvira French, Elizabeth Short was "down and out."

7. She needed new shoes but instead had Red Manley get her old shoes repaired.

8. She was having mood swings and was "flighty and nervous," according to Elvera French.

9. Elvera French said Beth became very "frightened" she seemed to get "panicky."

10. She was down to her last pair of stockings but didn't purchase new ones out of the $100.00 wired from Fickling.

11. Mrs. French said "she was in constant fear of someone" and "frightened when anyone came to the door."

12. "She had chills all night January 8, 1947, at the motel with Red Manley."

13. "She had scratch marks on her arms," Manley said and that "one of them seemed to be bleeding." Short explained that the scratch marks were from a "jealous boyfriend." The marks on her arms were "on the outside, above the elbows."

14. On January 9, 1947, she got all "dolled up," according to Manley, who dropped her off at the Biltmore Hotel in Los Angeles. Manley had asked her where she wanted to be dropped off. He said, "At the Biltmore?" and her response was, "Yes, at the Biltmore." In her financial condition it seems very unlikely that her intended stay was the Biltmore Hotel. She made telephone calls to someone from the Biltmore.

15. On the evening of January 9, 1947, a doorman at the Biltmore last saw her walking towards Sixth Street and into history.

16. Elizabeth Short's remains are buried at the Mountain View Cemetery in Oakland, California.

Los Angeles Examiner January 27, 1947

Teaches Us Today
(See Editorial Page)

VOL. XLIV—NO. 47   LOS ANGELES, MONDAY, JANUARY 27, 1947   CCC

Two Women Tell Dahlia's Fear of Mysterious Trio

Benefactors Reveal Fright Over Visit

KENNEY WARNS OF NORTH POLE ATTACK ON U.S.

Egypt, British Talks Fail

Pact Meet Collapses; Students Riot

GANG KIDNAPS BRITISH BANKER IN JERUSALEM

25 Million Casualties in First Day, Air General Predicts

Victim Taken to Ancient Moslem Cemetery After Being Beaten

Grace Moore, Prince, 20 Others in Fiery Air...

PRINCE DEAD

Man Plunges 86 Stories

HEART OF CITY

SUPER WEAPONS

Stromberg Junior Weds in Raleigh

Chairman Named by YMCA Board

CALLS FOR HELP

Housing Short Price Drop

SINGER MEETS DE...

Allis CIO Wins Bargaining Vote

Teaching Control Newest Jap Strike

Texas Quad Girls to Mark Birthday

U.S. Ship Aground Off French Coast

22 Stolen Autos in 216 Crimes
In the past 24 hours

Byrd to Lead

copy of *Los Angeles Examiner* article dated Jan. 27, 1947

CLUE: TWO MEN AND A FEMALE IMPERSONATOR

In all three cases, the Cleveland Torso Murders, the murder of Suzanne Degnan and the murder of the Black Dahlia similar reports appear concerning three individuals. The most likely suspects to me are the individual named "Eddie" who is mentioned in the murder of Cleveland Torso Victim, Edward Andrassy and in association with Jack Anderson Wilson (see *Severed*, page 180); a person by the name of Al Morrison, who is named as the killer of the Black Dahlia in Jack Anderson Wilson's taped message to John Gilmore; more than likely the same person by the name of "Al" who is mentioned in the Cleveland Torso Murders as having supplied Cleveland Torso Victim Flo Polillo with drugs; and of course Jack Anderson Wilson. Remember that Wilson refers to a female impersonator in his taped message and the Indianapolis police suspected a female impersonator may have been connected with the murder of Corporal Maoma Ridings.

Now, with that in mind, look at the facts that arose from each case:

Cleveland Torso Murders

First: In the Cleveland Torso Murders Detective Peter Merylo suspected more than one person was involved in the murders. He surmised that it would have been too difficult for one man to carry the heavy bodies undetected into Kingsbury Run and deposit them. On July 23, 1936, *The Cleveland Press* ran the following article:

POLICE SEEKING THRILL SLAYERS

"A GROUP OF THRILL-SEEKERS IS RESPONSIBLE FOR Cleveland's grisly series of decapitation murders, detectives believed today as they puzzled over the fifth headless body found in the last 11 months."

POLICE SEEKING THRILL SLAYERS

Fifth Headless Victim Found Indicates Homeless Pursued by Murderers

A group of thrill-killers is responsible for Cleveland's grisly series of decapitation murders detectives believed today as they puzzled over the fifth headless body found in the last 11 months.

Coroner A. J. Pearse, after exhaustive tests, today established that blood was on the nearby clothing of the middle-aged man, dead at least two months, whose body was found yesterday in a gully near the Baltimore & Ohio tracks a half-mile south of the Industrial Rayon Corp.

Dr. Pearse, although he still had not been able to determine how the victim's head was removed from the body, discovered that the right sleeve of the dead man's coat had been slashed as by a knife.

There were no identifying marks on the clothing or papers of any kind in the pockets.

What puzzled Dr. Pearse was how the head could have been removed. It was separated from the spine at the juncture of two vertebrae and gave no signs of having been cut. The skill and anatomical knowledge of a surgeon would have been required to perform a job so neat without leaving evidence of cutting, Dr. Pearse said.

Indications increased that the slayers pick on homeless men not likely to be identified. The latest victim, a man of about 40, had extremely long hair, indicating he probably was a transient.

Likewise the last body—that of a youth of 27—never was identified, despite the presence of numerous tattoo marks all over his body which would have been recognized by friends if he had been a Clevelander.

The youth's body, lying 100 feet from the Kingsbury Run gulch, where his head lay wrapped in his trousers, was found June 6.

Six months before, in January, various portions of the decimated body of Mrs. Florence Sawdey Polillo, 47, began to turn up in lower East Side spots, although her head was never found. In September of last year the headless bodies of Edward Andrassy, 47, and an older man never identified were found in Kingsbury Run not far from where the June victim was found.

PRIEST NAMED AS 3D ARBITER

Msgr. Smith Chairman of Board Settling Street Railway Union Dispute

The Rt. Rev. Msgr. Joseph F. Smith, vicar general of the Catholic Diocese, today was named impartial chairman of the arbitration board to settle the dispute between the Cleveland Railway Co. and the Street Car Men's Union.

He was agreed to at a conference today between William H. Boyd, attorney, arbiter for the company...

CLEVELANDERS PASS OHIO PHARMACY TEST

Cincinnati Man Tops List With 92 Per Cent Grade

Press State Service

CEDAR POINT, O., July 23.—Sixteen Clevelanders today were granted certificates for registration as pharmacists by the Ohio State Board of Pharmacy in session here.

The successful Clevelanders were: Louis E. Golenberg, Charles W. Nevel, Marjorie Loesch, Robert J. Remezyl, Gene W. Johnston, Gustav C. Kostell, Joseph E. Dudas, Maurice Fishman, Meyer H. Kassoff, Benjamin Goldman, Harry Grushow, Joseph E. Huber, Samuel J. Cantor, V. C. Sidkovich, Alex Saferin, Ann J. Donnelly and Jerry R. Bassichus.

Passing grades were won by 72 of 88 applicants who took the state examinations in Columbus June 16 and 17. S. A. Micali of Cincinnati was high with 92 per cent.

COLONIAL HOTEL OPENS CLUB BAR

Fixtures, Ornaments From Original Rooms Used in New One

Completion of a new "club bar" executed after the traditions of years ago was announced today by the Colonial Hotel, 323 Prospect avenue.

In contrast with the trend toward modernism displayed in similar spots, the new bar is decorated with old bronze pieces and paintings from the estate of the original Colonial Hotel valued at $30,000 by the management.

Two of the old bartenders in Cleveland, Harry Cushing and Bill Carey, will preside. The "club bar" has a capacity of 46 persons, and both food and drinks will be served.

SPECIALIZATION

When men ceased making their own shoes and building their own houses, standards of living improved because specialization increased efficiency.

CLEVELAND PRESS July 23, 1936 P. 14

July 23, 1936 *The Cleveland Press* article

In the case of Cleveland Torso Victim No. 8, Rose Wallace, "A woman identified only as Mrs. Carter of Hazen Court reported seeing her in a car with three white man, but after that, Rose Wallace simply vanished" (page 115, *In the Wake of the Butcher*).

John Bartlow Martin wrote in *Butcher's Dozen* on pages 60-61:

Captain J.C. Van Buren of the Nickel Plate police believes he carried them along the lee of an embankment a quarter of a mile from East 37th Street; others argue he would have deposited them in a safer jungle of bushes closer to 37th Street and, moreover, that they were too heavy to be carried so far. Van Buren replies that perhaps there were two murderers.

Murder of Suzanne Degnan

Cecelia Flynn remembered hearing two men arguing in the street below at or about the time Suzanne Degnan was kidnapped from her parents' home in Chicago (page 47, *William Heirens: His Day In Court*).

Witness Robert Reisner told police of a dark-gray car parked on Thorndale with a bareheaded, heavy-set man behind the wheel (page 47, *William Heirens: His Day In Court*). Several taxi drivers reported that they saw a man and a woman driving up and down Thorndale Avenue the night Suzanne was murdered.

William Heirens' "confession" mentioned that he wore a babushka over his head. Was the "confession" concocted in such a way that it in effect presents William Heirens as a female impersonator? Again the reports from witnesses, when taken together, may indicate the presence of three individuals, one of which may have been a female impersonator.

Look again at the Heirens "confession" and compare it to the facts of the Suzanne Degnan murder.

Bill Heirens' "confession" includes the following dialog:

Q. Do you remember how you lifted the sewer cover in which you put the arms?

A. No, I got it up, and I was holding it up like that. That is how it fell down and caught my finger.

Q. What hand did you have on the sewer cover?

A. My right.

Q. And what hand got hurt when the sewer cover fell down?

A. My right.

Q. You mean that your fingers were pinched between the sewer cover and the rim which it fit?

A. No, it didn't get into the rim, it fell on the ground.

Q. You had taken the sewer cover completely off the hole?

A. Yes.

Q. After it fell down and hurt your fingers, did you put it back on the hole again?

A. Yes, sir.

It was also suggested that Heirens used the .32 caliber revolver to pry open the storm sewer covers. Again, I don't believe this is possible. The sewer covers are approximately two inches thick and are constructed of heavy gauge solid-iron. If you have a .32 caliber, make sure it is unloaded and give it a try. You won't be able to open the subject storm sewer covers with one. Here is a photo of a .32 caliber:

photo of .32 caliber

I believe that it is nearly physically impossible for the crime to have been committed by one person as explained in the "confession" of William Heirens. In 1946, as they are today, Thorndale Avenue, Winthrop Avenue, Kenmore and Admore Avenues in Chicago were densely populated areas. Separate body parts were located in storm sewers and catch basins off alleys between Winthrop Avenue and Kenmore Avenue, in an alley between Kenmore Avenue and Sheridan Avenue, in a sewer on Admore Avenue, and in an alley near Hollywood Avenue. I personally retraced the route that was taken by the killers and located each separate storm sewer where Suzanne Degnan's body parts were discarded. Each storm sewer and catch basin is covered by an extremely heavy iron cover that is virtually impossible to remove with your bare hands. They are noisy if moved without assistance. Yet a total of five separate storm sewers, catch basins and sewers were used by the killer(s) to dispose of the body parts. In my estimation no one person could have or would have embarked on such a task. It would have been nearly impossible. It makes no sense. A lone killer would have either left the gory, blood-soaked body parts where he dismembered her, in the laundry room, or in a waste receptacle, or in the first storm sewer he managed to open, and then fled the highly populated area before being detected.

If the sewer cover fell on his fingers as indicated in the Heiren's "Confession" (see page 155 of this text), they would have been crushed, not hurt. As I recall, the storm sewer in the alley where the arms were deposited is a hard surface, so a falling iron storm sewer cover could cause serious injury to a person's fingers. I suspect that William Heirens hurt his fingers when he was hit on the head with a flower pot following an attempted burglary.

A more logical explanation of the way Suzanne Degnan's body parts were discarded would go like this:

The killers knew where the storm sewers were located in advance of the crime. They must have because the crime took place late at night and the alleys and streets were dimly lit in 1946. The January evening was cold and wet, as were the heavy iron sewer covers. Without gloves they would have been uncomfortable to handle. The killers had to have a tool similar to a pick to pry open the heavy sewer covers. One of them acted as a lookout while the covers were removed and the body parts transported. Timing was all important so that the crime would go undetected. The murder, dismemberment and discarding of a child's body parts in seperate storm sewers were committed with the intended purpose of shocking and horrifying the community just like in the Cleveland Torso Murders and the murder of the Black Dahlia. In the Suzanne Degnan murder her body was "expertly" dismembered, a ransom note in the amount of $20,000 was left by the killers, clothing was burned, oil applied to the ransom note, body parts were deposited in storm sewers, the floor of the crime scene was mopped. This murder-dismemberment shocked the nation. In the murder of the Black Dahlia, her body was "expertly" severed, a ransom note demanding $20,000 was found in a murder case associated with the murder of the Black Dahlia (according to Jack Anderson Wilson's taped message to John Gilmore), clothing was burned following the murder, her purse was found soaked in gas. And, again according to Wilson's taped message to Gilmore, evidence was put into storm sewers and the crime scene floor was mopped. Her murder, too, shocked the entire nation.

In order to prove that I am correct, the Chicago Police Department should attempt to recreate the way Suzanne Degnan's murder took place—this time using a live animal of similar size and weight and following these steps:

1. Have a seventeen-year-old strong, able-bodied boy carry a seventy-four pound live, sedated animal from 5943 Kenmore Avenue to the laundry room at 5901 Winthrop Avenue.

2. Have the boy dismember the animal in the unlit laundry room with the assistance of a flashlight and a "knife" he carries in his pocket.

3. Have the boy move the head, legs and torso of the animal from the laundry room at 5901 Winthrop Avenue at 1:00 a.m. (Make sure the street lights are dimmed to reflect the lighting present in 1946).

4. Have the boy carry the individual animal parts to the storm sewer in the alley at 5907 Kenmore, to the storm sewer at Admore & Kenmore, to the storm sewer in the alley at 5900 Kenmore, and to the storm sewer in the alley at 5838 Kenmore Avenue.

5. Have the boy lift and remove the heavy, cold storm sewer covers with his bare hands and/or the butt of a .32 caliber revolver (At least one of the storm sewer covers is screwed shut so be sure to remove the screws).

6. Have the boy deposit individual animal parts in the storm sewers, returning each time to 5901 Winthrop Avenue to retrieve the other animal body parts.

7. Drop the last storm sewer cover located at 5701 Broadway Avenue on the boy's right hand fingers.

8. Have the boy then return to the laundry room at 5901 Winthrop Avenue, mop the floor and write a ransom note with an injured hand.

9. Have the boy deliver the ransom note to 5901 Kenmore Avenue—all without being detected. (The Degnan home is no longer at that address.)

I can assure you that the seventeen-year-old boy will not be able to complete the process. Neither could William Heirens or anyone else for that matter, because the fact is—it is next to impossible for one person, acting alone, to complete all of the steps that were followed in the Suzanne Degnan murder. If you don't believe me, give it a try. I guarantee it can't be done the way it is described in the Heirens "confession."

Black Dahlia Murder

After January 1, 1947, a little more than one week before she disappeared, Elizabeth Short was seen in the company of three individuals, two men and a woman. Dorothy French recalled "a couple of days later some people came to our door and knocked. There was a man and a woman and another man was waiting in a car parked on the street in front of the house." (The woman may have been a female impersonator.)

CLUE: $20,000 RANSOM NOTE

On January 7, 1946, the killer of Suzanne Degnan left a ransom note on the window ledge of her bedroom demanding $20,000. On February 11, 1947, in Los Angeles following the murder of Jeanne Axford French, a ransom note was found in the glove compartment of Los Angeles taxi driver Charles Schneider's taxicab demanding $20,000. Detectives thought that the person who killed French also killed the Black Dahlia.

"ITALIAN" CLUE

John Barlow Martin wrote in *Butcher's Dozen* in 1945, on page 65, the following excerpt concerning the murder of Cleveland Torso Victim, Flo Polillo:

About six weeks before she was murdered, Flo Polillo had returned to the hotel, this time with "an unknown Italian described as twenty-seven-years-old, five feet eight or nine, 135 pounds, dark complexioned wearing a dark cap, a description that nearly matched the description of Andrassy's friend "Eddie." And there was an Italian named "Al" who was a drug addict and also furnished Florence Martin with drugs.

In the case of Cleveland Torso Victim, Edward Andrassy:

Andrassy told his sister that he had stabbed an Italian in a fight at East 9th Street and Bolivar "and that the gang was after him." He stayed close to home. There was no police report on such a fight. An informer said he had concealed Andrassy for three days, until an Italian drove up in a Dodge touring car, invited the informer to go for a ride (he declined), and took Andrassy away.

On page 60 Martin wrote:

Andrassy left home for the last time at 8:00 P.M. on September 19th, 1935, not saying where he was going. Nobody ever admitted having seen him thereafter. This was a Thursday. The coroner thought he probably was killed Friday. On Monday his body was found below Jackass Hill, a spot he was never known to have frequented. On Friday morning a neighbor had seen two young shabbily dressed Italians park an old Ford coupe at the top of Jackass Hill and walk down towards the spot where the bodies were later found.

In 1991, Will Fowler wrote in his book *Reporters: Memoirs of a Young Newspaperman,* on page 84, the following concerning the Black Dahlia:

Manley said Elizabeth had an Italian boyfriend with black hair "who was intensely jealous of her."

Gladys, a neighbor of Elizabeth on the fifth floor of her apartment building,   said:

"her boyfriend was jealous and he was chasing her."

GANG CLUE

A "gang" is mentioned in the Black Dahlia case that included an Italian by the name of Bobby Savarino. One of the last persons seen with Cleveland Torso Victim, Rose Wallace, was a dark- skinned white man named "Bob." A "gang" was mentioned in the case of Cleveland Torso Victim Edward Andrassy.

CLUE: SIMILAR KIDNAPPING OF YOUNG GIRL IN LOS ANGELES

On January 23, 1947, nine days after the Black Dahlia was murdered, *The Los Angeles Herald Express* ran the following in an article entitled "Werewolves Leave Trail of Women Murders in L.A."

On Feb. 15, 1946, Rochelle Gluskoter, a smiling child not yet six with long chestnut curls was seen talking to a man who had stopped his black coupe near her home at 1125 East Eighty-Seventh Street. The little girl nodded and smiled as if in answer to his questions. Then she climbed into his car which drove away. A prolonged manhunt ended with the official announcement that little Rochelle must be dead, the victim of the unknown in the black coupe.

copy of *Los Angeles Herald Express* dated January 23, 1947

Interestingly, Suzanne Degnan was six-years-old when she was kidnapped from her parents' home in Chicago on January 7, 1946, thirty-nine days before Rochelle was kidnapped in Los Angeles. I have absolutely no other information regarding the kidnapping of Rochelle, other than the above-mentioned article, and add this clue, for what its worth. By april 8, 1946, a suspect by the name of William E. Railey was

312

n custody of the Los Angeles County sheriff's office. He was apprehended just as he collected the ransom money in the Rochelle Glusketer kidnapping case.

ADDITIONAL SIMILARITIES BETWEEN THE MURDERS

In the Cleveland Torso Murders, the murder of the Black Dahlia and the murder of Suzanne Degnan certain undisputed facts emerge:

A. The victims in each case were moved from point "A" (safe haven) to point "B," where they were killed, to point "C" (where their body parts were discarded).
B. The victims were all "expertly" severed and/or dismembered by someone with "knowledge of anatomy." *The Cleveland Press* reported on July 23, 1936, that "The skill and anatomical knowledge of a surgeon would have been required to perform a job so neat without leaving evidence of cutting." In the Black Dahlia case it was reported that she was severed by someone with the "finesse of a surgeon."
C. Following each murder the killer(s) "taunted" the police.
D. In the Cleveland Torso Murders and the murder of the Black Dahlia, blood was drained from the bodies by the killer(s) before the bodies were moved.

In the annals of crime there is no question that several people have been killed and dismembered over the years. However, in order for someone to commit a crime similar to the Cleveland Torso Murders, the murder of the Black Dahlia, and the murder of Suzanne Degnan, the person or persons would have to meet all of the following requirements:

1. They would have to want to kill and dismember someone.
2. They would have to possess the fortitude to stomach the gross dismemberment/ bisection of a human being.
3. They would require similar expertise to professionally sever and/or dismember a human body.
4. They would require the ability, patience and sleuth to transport a person from one location; move, kill, dismember and/or sever a body; and dispose of the body parts by posing the corpse in a third location, usually in a large, populated city, without being detected.

5. They would have to know how to contact and have the mindset to taunt the police after committing the horrifically gory crime without being apprehended.

If someone other than the Cleveland Torso Killer murdered the Black Dahlia and Suzanne Degnan, and if someone other than the person who killed the Black Dahlia murdered Suzanne Degnan, then one would have to conclude that three separate individuals met the requirements mentioned in the list above within a time span of twelve years (unless, of course the same person(s) were responsible for the murders in two incidents but not the third; then there would have to be at least two separate individuals who met all of the requirements presented above). It is extremely rare to hear about a person who commits a murder/dismemberment and all of the requirements of numbers 1-5 above are met. The likelihood of this occurrence is again significantly reduced when the relatively short time frame (1935-1947) is brought into the equation. The odds that the above-mentioned requirements were met by two or three separate killers or groups of killers is a long shot by any stretch of the imagination.

I have not personally found any statistics regarding the above-mentioned events, but it seems highly unlikely to have two individuals or sets of individuals in addition to the Cleveland Torso Killer, during this relatively short time span, who had similar professional skill and could accomplish what the Cleveland Torso Killer accomplished. Therefore, it would seem logical that, based on the known facts, the Cleveland Torso Killer may have also been responsible for the murders of the Black Dahlia and the murder of Suzanne Degnan.

How many times since the date of the Black Dahlia's murder on January 14, 1947, has a killer fulfilled the requirements listed in items 1-5? If the answer is never, then one would suspect that during the 1935-1947 time frame there might have been one set, and only one set, of killers capable of and responsible for the Cleveland Torso Murders, the murder of Suzanne Degnan and the murder of the Black Dahlia.

Is it reasonable to dismiss Cleveland's sodomist "Jack Wilson" as a different person than Los Angeles' convicted sodomist "Jack Anderson Wilson, who was originally from Canton, Ohio?" The possibility of two separate individuals having the same expertise to sever a human body during this relatively short time span, who was also a sodomist is so far beyond the realm of possibility that the notion becomes an absurdity. The "Jack Wilson" mentioned in conjunction with the Cleveland Torso Murders was more than likely the same "Jack Wilson" who murdered and severed the Black Dahlia. And it is also very likely that he didn't act alone.

314

SUMMARY

Discovering the killer of the Black Dahlia and the Cleveland Torso Killer may be purely academic at this time but uncovering the true identity of the killer of Suzanne Degnan, Josephine Ross and Frances Brown is more than an exercise in historical study. Suzanne Degnan was surgically dismembered by someone with a great deal of expertise and knowledge of human anatomy. She was kidnapped, strangled, possibly sexually molested, and dismembered in a laundry room with running water and functioning sink. Coal dust was found embedded in her pajamas. Her body parts were discarded in separate storm sewers and catch basins. She was murdered close to a train tract near Lake Michigan on January 7, 1946. The *modus operandi* of the killer(s) and the evidence in the Degnan case parallels the *modus operandi* and evidence in the Cleveland Torso Killings. The method of murder in the Josephine Ross and Frances Brown cases closely parallels the 1943 method of murder in the of Corporal Maoma Ridings case.

Jack Anderson Wilson a/k/a Jack Wilson appears to have been a participant in the Cleveland Torso Murders, the murder of Suzanne Degnan, the murder of the Black Dahlia and several other murders including Corporal Maoma Ridings, Georgette Bauerdorf, Jeanne Axford French, Josephine Ross and Frances Brown. It is highly unlikely that whoever was responsible for the Cleveland Torso Murders stopped killing and dismembering victims after the carnage ended in Cleveland. Similar murders and expert-dismemberments that followed in McKee's Rocks, Youngstown, West Pittsburgh, New Castle, Chicago and Los Angeles all point towards the same perpetrators. There is absolutely no reported indication that Bill Heirens had any experience dismembering animals or human bodies. There is nothing that indicated that Bill Heirens was capable of expertly dismembering Suzanne Degnan. Heirens has been a model prisoner since his incarceration in 1946, and has not exhibited any traits expected of a person who would kidnap, strangle, expertly dismember a six-year-old girl, deposit her body parts in separate storm drains and then taunt the police. On the other hand these are the exact same propensities exhibited by the Cleveland Torso Killer(s) and the person(s) that killed the Black Dahlia.

The Black Dahlia was murdered and expertly severed less than six months after Bill Heirens was incarcerated in Chicago. For some reason Elizabeth Short was "terribly preoccupied with the details of the Degnan murder." She was pretending

315

to be a reporter from Massachusetts covering the trial of William Heirens sometime between June-August 1946, when she was in Chicago. Less than five months later she was murdered and expertly severed in Los Angeles by means that closely matched the Cleveland Torso Murders. Elizabeth Short was expertly severed in Los Angeles the same city that the suspicious letter was mailed from on December 22, 1938, to Cleveland Chief of Police Matowitz concerning the Cleveland Torso Murders.

Law enforcement should pursue this line of investigation to secure the release of William Heirens. I agree with crime writer Craig Rice, who, in 1946, said of William Heirens: "I said that I believe him innocent—and I think I am right." I will go one step further and say that William Heirens did not kill Suzanne Degnan and that the murder of Suzanne Degnan is directly connected to the murder of the Black Dahlia and the Cleveland Torso Murders. And now, with the additional evidence presented in this revised epilogue, the strong connections between all three cases also suggests two or more perpetrators, one of whom seem most certainly to have been Jack Anderson Wilson.

—William T. Rasmussen
Attorney at Law

FURTHER ANALYSIS OF CLEVELAND TORSO MURDERS, SUZANNE DEGNAN MURDER AND THE BLACK DAHLIA MURDER

Since the first revision of what I called the original epilogue in *Corroborating Evidence* I have uncovered additional clues and evidence that tend to establish connections between the Cleveland Torso Murders, the murders of Suzanne Degnan, the Black Dahlia and others. These are analyzed and included herein. I have also added two chapters, one on the Phantom Killer of Texarkana and the other on the Zodiac Killer.

WERE JACK ANDERSON WILSON, AL MORRISON AND MAURICE CLEMENT IN CLEVELAND DURING THE CLEVELAND TORSO MURDERS (1935-1938)?

According to Jack Anderson Wilson's taped message to author John Gilmore, a person by the name of Al Morrison was involved in the murder of Elizabeth Short. I, along with Cleveland's detective Peter Merylo, am of the opinion that whoever was responsible for the Cleveland Torso Murders also killed Elizabeth Short. (I have not found in any of the Cleveland Torso police reports any mention of the Suzanne Degnan case.) With this in mind I contacted the Western Reserve Historical Society in Cleveland, Ohio, and requested a search of the names "Jack Anderson Wilson a/k/a Jack Wilson a/k/a Grover Loving, Jr."; "Alex Morrison, a/k/a Al Morrison"; and "Maurice Clement, a/k/a Eddie Clement." Western Reserve returned a search that included the US Federal Census (1920/1930), the Ancestry-Library Edition Index, Cleveland City Directories (1928-1952) and Cleveland telephone Directories (1926-1952), Cleveland Necrology File, and Cuyahoga Marriage Records. The results of the search revealed that a person by the name of "J.A. Wilson" and another person by the name of "Alex Morrison" lived in the same Cleveland neighborhood in 1936. As of the date of this writing it has not been determined if they were the same individuals associated with the Black Dahlia Murder in Los Angeles. The information has been sent to the respective police agencies for their review.

HEAVY SET MAN WITH GRAY HAIR

Cleveland Torso Murders:

In 1950, "a **heavy**, fiftyish-looking man with **thinning gray hair** came to Norris Brothers Company Movers at 22138 Davenport Avenue every day for six weeks and sunbathed for about twenty minutes on a year-and-a-half-old pile of steel girders at the west end of the company's property. Then one day he stopped coming.' Shortly after workmen found the dismembered torso of a white male (Note 39, page 161).

Suzanne Degnan Murder:

In 1946, in Chicago, a witness by the name of Robert Reisner "told police of a dark gray car parked on Thorndale with a bareheaded, **heavy-set** man behind the wheel." Chicago Chief of Police Walter G. Storms advised the public that "A man was observed in the driver's seat of this car. He was bareheaded and has **gray hair**" (Note 42, pages 47-48).

UNDERGROUND AND OUT OF SIGHT

In the Cleveland Torso Murders Edward Andrassy's headless body was found at the foot of Jackass Hill on September 23, 1935. He was killed and the blood drained from his body at a different location. Detectives questioned as to how he was transported and deposited without anyone noticing anything. Unexplained items were located near Andrassy's body, including pieces of rope, a railroad torch and a two gallon water bucket containing car engine oil (Note 39, page 32).

On a bitterly cold winter-night on January 26, 1936, the dismembered body parts of Victim No. 3, Flo Polillo were discovered in baskets behind Hart Manufacturing Company. No one saw the person or persons who delivered the gruesome packages. The headless body of Victim No. 4, the Tattooed Man, was found in Kingsbury Run on June 5, 1936. The next day, according to Railroad detective Dudley A. McDowell, items of clothing, including worn oxfords, striped socks and a dirty, oily cap were found in the same location. None of these items had been there the day before (Note 39, page 62).

In the case of Torso Victim No. 6 police found "at a point where the water emerged from a large tunnel into a twenty-foot-deep pool, some small bits of human flesh adhering to a ledge, apparently where the killer had thrown the pieces over the edge into a creek" (Note 39, page 76). Lieutenant Harvey Weitzel stated,, "It is my opinion that the missing parts were not thrown into the creek when the torso was thrown in."

Torso Victim No. 7 was found near the foot of East 156th Street in Lake Erie. Two storm sewers emptied into the lake nearby. Detectives Merylo and Zalewski, a Cleveland City Sewer Department employee and a newspaperman, explored a ten-mile stretch of storm drains (Note 39, page 104). During the cold winters in Cleveland during the 1930's, storm drains would not only provide protection from the weather but also an underground passageway where someone could traverse undetected, unseen from street level and patrolling detectives. Someone who knew the streets of Cleveland might also know how to maneuver in the labyrinth of subterranean tunnels that snake under the city. Were Andrassy and Victim No. 2 pulled on a cart through the storm drains? This might explain the rope burns on Edward Andrassy's wrists, the ropes and railroad lantern found near Andrassy's headless body. The railroad torch could have been used to light the way through the storm drains. Use of a railroad torch would have been seen if the body had been transported above ground. The storm drains with their running water could have been used as the killer's abattoir. There, out of sight, the Butcher could have taken time to perform the grisly dismemberments. See Page 22 for photo of Cleveland Storm Sewer.

You will recall that I questioned why and how someone would lift a total of five extremely heavy storm sewer and catch basin covers as described in the William Heiren's "Confession." The City of Chicago, Department of Water Management provided me with information that indicates "there has been little or no change to the subject catch basins and storm drains in the area requested from 1946, to present." Here is a copy of a drawing of the 120 lb. manhole and catch basins provided by the city of Chicago, Department of Water Management:

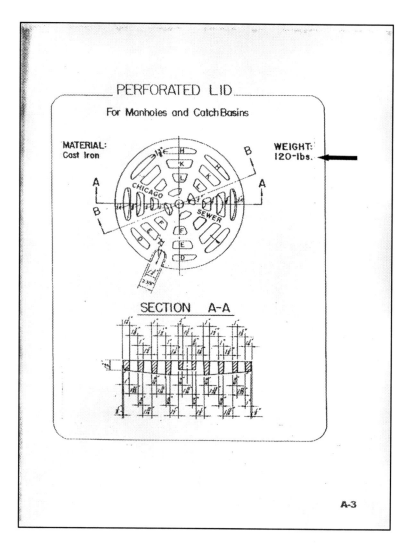

(Courtesy of the City of Chicago Department of Water Management)

320

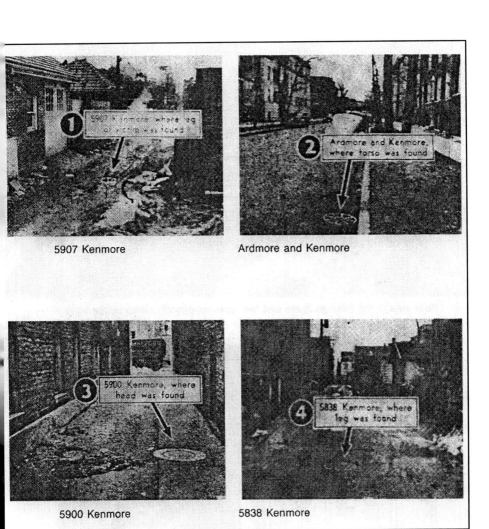

5907 Kenmore	Ardmore and Kenmore
5900 Kenmore	5838 Kenmore

Four locations where body parts of Suzanne Degnan were found
(courtesy of Dolores Kennedy)

THE LEFT LEG

According to author John Gilmore, Jack Anderson Wilson walked with a limp and had "one leg shorter than the other (Note 40, page 212). On page 196 of *Severed*, Wilson is referred to as a person "with a crippled leg."

Crime writer Aggie Underwood got a tip that the person seen walking away from 25th and San Pedro where Georgette Bauerdorf's car was found proceeded with a "halting gait" (Note 40, page 156). My question is, Was Jack Anderson Wilson's left leg either crippled or shorter than his right leg? If so, then consider the following:

a. In the case of Edward Andrassy it looks as though a *severed* penis is positioned close to his left knee (See headless photo of Edward Andrassy on page 31, *In the Wake of the Butcher*).
b. In the Cleveland Torso Murders the left foot of Victim No. 11 appears to have been sliced from the body

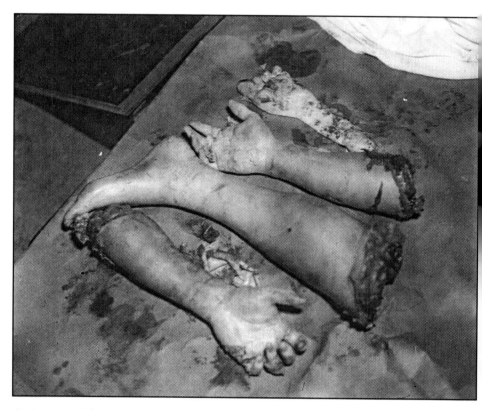

Body parts of Cleveland Torso Victims (possibly parts of Victim No. 11) including a left leg and a left foot. (photo courtesy of Marjorie Merylo Dentz).

c. In the Black Dahlia murder her killer cut a chunk of flesh out of her left leg.

On August 18, 1952, a letter was written by C.H. Ebbert, Chief of Investigation to Walter R. Creighton, Chief Bureau of Narcotic Enforcement. Here is a copy of the subject letter that I located at the Los Angeles District Attorney's file on the Black Dahlia:

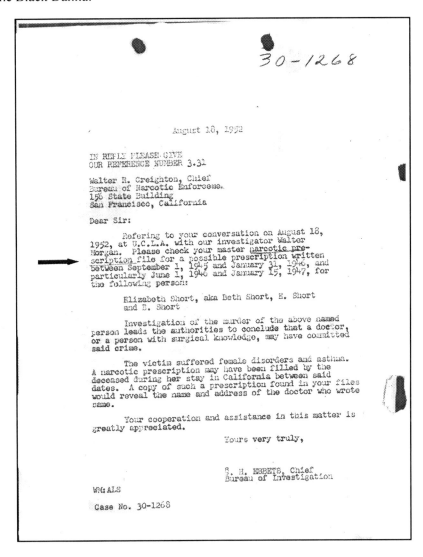

August 18, 1952, letter from C.H. Ebbets to Walter R. Creighton in Los Angeles District Attorney's file on Black Dahlia.

The letter requested an investigation for narcotic prescriptions (not just any type of prescription) that may have been written by a doctor for Elizabeth Short during 9/1/45-1/31/46 and 6/1/46-1/15/47. the letter appears to have been written for one o two possible reasons: Either the detectives were trying to associate a doctor who may have prescribed a narcotic prescription to the person with "surgical knowledge," o because at the time of her death the autopsy may have revealed Elizabeth Short had narcotics in her tissue, fluids or organs, and they were trying to find the doctor who may have prescribed the drug who in turn may have committed the murder. If the autopsy of Elizabeth Short did in fact reveal the presence of narcotics, this would be similar to the findings in more than one of the autopsy reports in the Cleveland Torso Murders. It was determined that the Cleveland Torso Killer drugged at least one of his victims before the dismemberment. (Note 39, page 131). I also call your attention to the 1938 letter mailed from Los Angeles to Cleveland Chief of Police Matowitz. In that letter the writer wrote in part: "It is God's will not to let them suffer" (See page 30 and 87 of this text): "as much as possible, you understand, well . . . there was a purpose to this in such a way though a person undergoes so much it's possible that this person has to be, what you call—anesthesia. It's a word in a crossword puzzle." In both cases the reference may have been to the administration of narcotics prior to the murder/dismemberment.

OHIO LICENSE

A memorandum in the Black Dahlia case that I found at the Los Angeles District Attorney's office dated January 26, 1950, provides the following information in # 14:

> Identified picture of soldier sitting on_____of chev. Coupe Ohio license # E-640V-4

> "name unknown" a new character. As man with Short at Hansen's house in Nov. 46."

Subject: CONNIE STARR -- and Francis Starr (Mother)
          427 So. Mariposa St.
          Apt. 310
          DU 9-2535

1. Connie is Ann Toth's girl friend.

2. Connie stated that she was invited to dinner at Mark Hansen's by
   Ann Toth on Saturday January 11, 1947;

3. that the three of them had dinner together and shortly after dinner
   about 9:00 PM, Beth Short and her boy friend, a young kid with brown
   hair, arrived;

4. that it was a very cold night and Beth Short did not have a coat and
   was dressed in a cotton or gingham dress with a pink top bodice and
   did not have a coat; did not have stockings on;

5. that Beth Short complained of being cold and frozen;

6. that Mark Hansen seated Beth Short on the davenport near the fire-
   place, put a blanket around x her shoulders, placed a pair of his
   socks on her feet, put his slippers on her feet

7. that Mark Hansen asked her xx where she had been, that Beth Short
   stated that they had been to a movie, that Mark asked if they had
   been to his theater, that she answered no, that she had seen the
   picture at his theater and that they caught an early movie elsewhere;

8. CONNIE stated that she was home when she read of Beth Short's murder
   and immediately remarked to her Mother that is was just the other
   day that she just met Beth Short at Mark Hansen's home when she was
   there for dinner:

9. Connie and her mother should be questioned separately xxxxxxxxxxxxx
   xxxxxxx for purposes of corroboration.

10. Connie is an extra-player who obtain's most of her employment by
    request calls and a small portion through Central Casting.

11. Connie's moral xxxxxxxx reputation is not too good, xxxxxxxxxxx

12. Connie also stated that she understood that Beth Short had spent the
    previous night, Friday, January 10, 1947, at Mark Hansen's home, and
    was planning to spend Saturday night there also.

13. Please date as just before Ann went to Modesto
    after they worked together on "arc of triumph"

14. Identified Picture of Soldier sitting on hood
    of Chev. coupe Ohio Lic. # E-640V-4
    "name unknown" - a new character.
    as man with Short at Hansons in Nov. 4/

January 26, 1950, Los Angeles police memorandum in the Los Angeles District Attorney's
file on the Black Dahlia that identifies an Ohio license number.

WRITING ON CHEST OF VICTIM

In the Cleveland Torso Murders on May 3, 1940, three bodies were found at McKee's Rocks in Pennsylvania. Detective Merylo thought the murders were connected to the Cleveland Torso Murders. A size-twelve footprint was located at the scene and a mark made either by a peg leg or a woman's high heel and near it the butt of a cigarette that detective Merylo said had been rolled with marijuana. A single strand of blond hair was found near one of the victims. The word "NAZI" had been carved vertically into the victim's chest from breast to stomach. The letters were crude capitals, the "Z" reversed (Note 39, page 92).

In the Black Dahlia case, Jeanne Axford French was "stomped to death by a fiend who crudely printed an obscene phrase (Fuck You) on her chest." The letters "BD" were written in red lipstick in capital letters vertically from her breasts to her stomach. (For photo see page 195, *Black Dahlia Avenger* by Steve Hodel.)

THE LETTER "K"

Cleveland Torso Murders

At the Norris Brothers crime scene in Cleveland detectives found the dismembered corpse, missing head, no sign of blood at the scene, sports pages from a May, 1949, issue of the *Cleveland News* under the body, and abandoned bits of clothing nearby--though it was not clear if any of it belonged to the dead man. This time, however, there was something new: two pages from the phone book covering the letter **K**" (Note 39, page 161)

Black Dahlia Murder

On Wednesday January 29, 1947, Federal inspectors at the Terminal Annex Post Office in downtown Los Angeles received a fifth note that might have been mailed by the Black Dahlia Avenger. The note read:

A certain girl is going to get same as E.S. got if she squeals on us
We're going to Mexico City-catch us if you can.

2K's

Note 41, page 173)

Maurice Clement

A Maurice Clement was a suspect in the murder of Elizabeth Short.

Here is a copy of the suspects in the Black Dahlia Murder found at the Los Angeles District Attorney's Office:

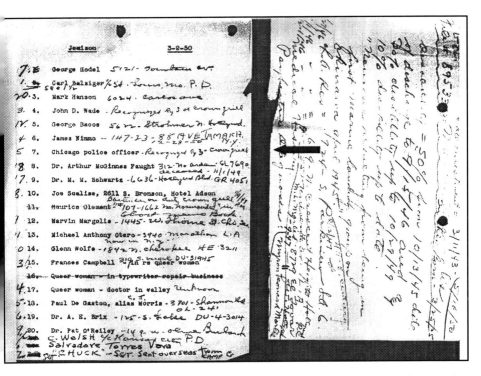

March 12, 1950, list of possible suspects in the Black Dahlia Case found in the Los Angeles District Attorney's file on the Black Dahlia Murder.

In 1946, in Los Angeles, Maurice Clement was described as follows:

1. Short, dark complexioned in his late 30's
2. 5' 6" tall, medium build, little fellow about 35-40 (Note 41, page 116)
3. Slight, dapper, olive-skinned man (Note 41, page 130)
4. A procurer for the syndicate call girl ring run by notorious Hollywood madam, Brenda Allen
5. Worked for the talent department at Columbia Studios
6. Elizabeth Short "knew Maurice and was one of the girls he chauffeured" (Note 44, page 120).
7. Based on witness reports, Maurice Clement would have been between 24-29- years-old in 1935. That being the case, he would have been born between 1906-1911.

In the Cleveland Torso Murders a person by the name of "Eddie" was associated with more than one of the Torso Murders. "Eddie" was described by witnesses as follows:

1. 28-30-years-old in 1935
2. Good looking, good set of teeth
3. 5' 6" tall
4. 15 lbs.
5. Was a chauffeur for a wealthy woman in suburban Lakewood (Note 43, page 60)
6. Based on witness reports, if alive, Maurice Clement would have been between 39-41- years-old in 1946. That being the case, he would have been born between 1905-1907

If Maurice Clement mentioned in conjunction with the Black Dahlia had a letter "E" for a middle initial, could his middle name have been "Edward" or"Eddie," and if so, then was the chauffeur driver by the name of "Eddie" mentioned in the Cleveland Torso Murders, the same chauffeur driver by the name of Maurice Clement who was associated with the murder of the Black Dahlia?

On January 7, 1946, at about 2 A.M., the morning of the kidnapping of Suzanne Degnan in Chicago, a woman was seen on Thorndale Avenue between Sheridan Road and Kenmore Avenue carrying a bundle in both arms. She was seen to get into a car parked on Thorndale Avenue. This woman was described as about 130 pounds, 5' 6" tall, wearing a gray coat with a dark fur collar and a small hat" broadcast to the public by Chicago Chief of Police, Walter G. Storms, January), 1946, Note 42, page 48). The description of this "woman" closely matched the description of Maurice Clement in the Black Dahlia case and "Eddie" in the Cleveland Torso Murders. Jack Anderson Wilson was affiliated with a female impersonator.

CLOSE PROXIMITY OF LOS ANGELES CRIMES

I suspect that the same person or persons who killed 6-year-old Suzanne Degnan in Chicago on January 7, 1946, may have also been responsible for the kidnapping of 6-year-old Rochelle Gluskoter on February 15, 1946, in Los Angeles.

Four locations are in the same general area in the city of Los Angeles:

1. The location between 39th and Coliseum on Norton Avenue where the severed body of Elizabeth Short was posed by her killer(s) on January 14, 1947
2. The location, according to the 1938 letter addressed from Los Angeles to Cleveland Police Chief Matowitz, where a head was buried between Crenshaw and Western on Century Boulevard
3. 1113 East 85th Street where 6-year-old Rochelle Gluskoter was kidnapped on February 15, 1946
4. The residence of Jack Anderson Wilson in the early 1940s

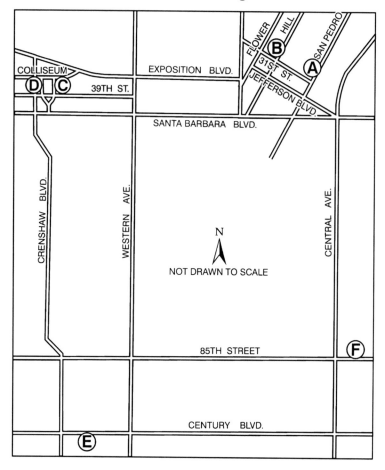

A Portion Of Los Angeles

A. "Chinaman's" house in the 200 block no East 31st Street (See page 83 of text).

B. Jack A. Wilson may have lived on Hill Street.

C. Degnan Boulevard

D. Location of Elizabeth Short's severed body on Norton Avenue.

E. A head may have been buried between Crenshaw Boulevard & Western Avenue on Century Boulevard.

F. 1113 East 85th Street — where 6 year old Rochelle Gluskoter was kidnapped on February 15, 1946.

A portion of Los Angeles showing possible crime scene locations.

PERSON DISPLAYING A CHICAGO POLICE OFFICER'S BADGE

Within a few days before Elizabeth Short disappeared a man displayed a Chicago police officer's badge to allow Short to enter the Columbia Broadcasting Studio. Here is a copy of the letter from H. L. Stanley Chief Bureau of Investigators Los Angeles to Mr. John C. Prendergast, Commissioner of Police, Chicago, dated January 31, 1950:

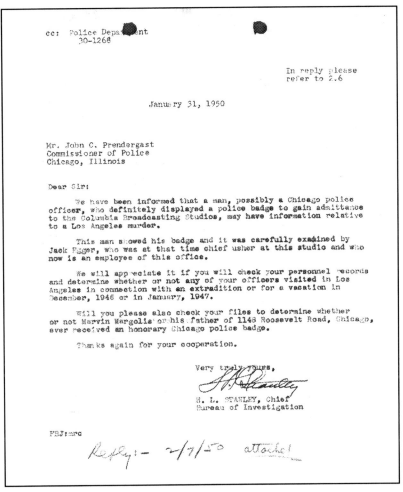

January 31, 1950, Los Angeles District Attorney's file letter from H.L. Stanley to Mr. John C. Pendergast commissioner of the Chicago Police Department regarding a suspect in the Black Dahlia Case.

Detective Division   February 6, 1950

From: Chief of Detectives

To: Commissioner of Police

Subject: Attached communication from H. L. Stanley, Chief, Bureau of Investigation, District Attorney's Office, Los Angeles, Calif.

Report of: Sgt. John T. Martin, Chief Clerk

1.   With reference to the attached communication the records of the Detective Bureau and States Attorney's Office do not disclose any police officers of the City of Chicago being in the City of Los Angeles, California during the months of December 1946 and January 1947, on extradition matters. In response to teletype message #5287 sent through the department received one reply from Sgt. William Barron 14th District stating that while on a disability furlough, he visited some retired Chicago Police Officers in suburban Los Angeles, California, in the latter part of January 1947, but at no time during his visit did they attend a Broadcasting Studio.

2.   Upon inquiry of the Chicago Police Pension Board, informed by Miss Kersten, that there are 69 retired Chicago Police Officers residing in California, 20 of whom reside in Los Angeles.

3.   Records at the office of the Secretary of Police were checked, and same do not show anyone by the name of Margolis as ever applying for or receiving any Chicago Special Police Badge. The Chicago Police Department does not issue "Honorary" badges.

4.   As you will note in the attached communication, same refers to a badge, supposedly a Chicago Police Badge. No further description of this badge is given, as to whether it was the shape of a star, or otherwise. Police Officers of the City of Chicago, as well as numerous other departments of this city and county, are issued stars of various sizes, with the name of their particular department inscribed thereon. Also, previous to Feb. 1st, 1947 retired police officers were issued a replica of their service star, with the word "Retired" inscribed thereon.

5.   This department through the Secretary of Police and with the approval of the Commissioner of Police issues "Special Police" badges. These badges are issued only to corporations such as Banks and Utilities, who employ guards, messengers, etc. These employees are carefully checked through the various units of the Chicago Police Department before such badges are issued. This badge is described as an oblong shield, chrome-plated, with a spread-eagle across the top, and a boxband underneath reading "Chicago Special Police Patrolman" - a seal, the Letter Y in center and raised copper numerals underneath.

6.   This department is now corresponding with Mr. H. L. Stanley, Chief, Bureau of Investigation, District Attorney's Office, Los Angeles, California, re: Marvin Margolis, Detective Bureau File #50-0304.

/s/ John T. Martin

APPROVED:

/s/ Andrew Aitken
Andrew W. Aitken
Chief of Detectives

February 6, 1950, Los Angeles District Attorney's file letter in the Black Dahlia case from John T. Martin to Commissioner of Police.

Keep in mind that Elizabeth Short was in Chicago in July, 1946, "pretending to be a reporter from Medford, Massachusetts," and "terribly preoccupied with the details of the Degnan murder." The week before she was killed she was scheduled to return to Chicago.

The following individuals knew and came in contact with Elizabeth Short while she was in Chicago in July, 1946:

    a. Shg Diamond, a newspaperman whose residence was Park Row Hotel. He claims to have seen Short over a ten-day period and has stated that he had intercourse with her and said that she was always talking about murder cases.

    b. Lou Paris, feature writer for the *Chicago Daily Times*, who knew Short and talked with her, at which time she was keenly interested in the famous Heirens Chicago murder case.

    c. John Giampa, 3421 West Lexington, who was a mailer for the *Chicago Herald American*. He knew her and said Short knew a Chicago detective who worked on the Heirens' case.

    d. Jan Jensen a reporter on the *Chicago Daily News*, who stated he knew the victim in Chicago.

Elizabeth Short was definitely talking in Chicago in July, 1946, about the William Heirens case and about the murder/dismemberment of Suzanne Degnan. Suzanne Degnan was expertly dismembered. Her body parts were placed in separate storm drains and catch basins. Less than six months after being in Chicago, Elizabeth Short was killed and expertly severed in Los Angeles. Her blood was drained from her body. More than one of the Cleveland Torso Victims had their blood drained from their bodies and the body parts of at least one of the Cleveland Torso victims was placed at separate times in Cleveland sewers. Elizabeth Short's face was cut to make it appear that she had a big mouth and was talking too much.

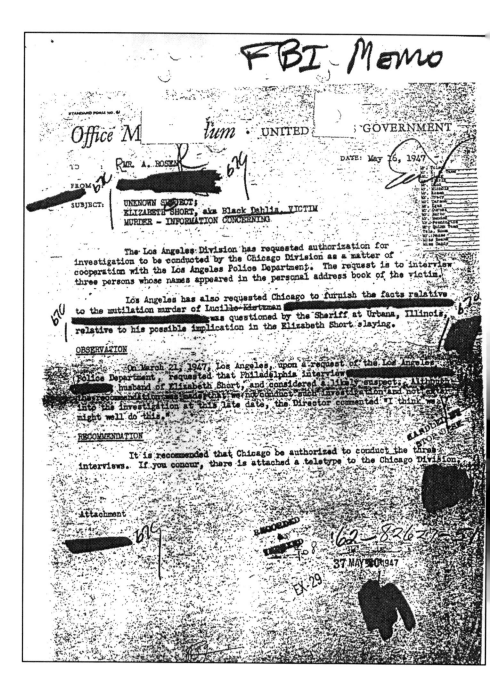

FBI Memo

Office Memorandum • UNITED STATES GOVERNMENT

DATE: May 16, 1947

TO: MR. A. ROSEN

FROM: [redacted]

SUBJECT: UNKNOWN SUBJECT;
ELIZABETH SHORT, aka Black Dahlia. VICTIM
MURDER - INFORMATION CONCERNING.

The Los Angeles Division has requested authorization for investigation to be conducted by the Chicago Division as a matter of cooperation with the Los Angeles Police Department. The request is to interview three persons whose names appeared in the personal address book of the victim.

Los Angeles has also requested Chicago to furnish the facts relative to the mutilation murder of Lucille Kirtman [redacted] was questioned by the Sheriff at Urbana, Illinois, relative to his possible implication in the Elizabeth Short slaying.

OBSERVATION

On March 21, 1947, Los Angeles, upon a request of the Los Angeles Police Department, requested that Philadelphia interview [redacted] husband of Elizabeth Short, and considered a likely suspect. Although [redacted] we conduct such investigation and not go into the investigation at this late date, the Director commented "I think we might well do this."

RECOMMENDATION

It is recommended that Chicago be authorized to conduct the three interviews. If you concur, there is attached a teletype to the Chicago Division.

Attachment

RECORDED
62-82627-

37 MAY 20 1947

EX-29

Federal Bureau of Investigation memorandum dated May 16, 1947, concerning three persons included in Elizabeth Short's personal address book with ties to Chicago.

CARVED LETTER "D"

Some people believe that the "D" cut in the shaved pubic region of Elizabeth Short is the same type of lettering as found on the body of the French woman. Facts reveal that the pubic region of Elizabeth Short's body was not shaved. Experts in handwriting have stated that it would be impossible to determine any type of handwriting from the so-called "D" cut into the pubic region of Elizabeth Short's body. Did the letter "D" cut into the pubic region stand for the "D" in Degnan?

2nd and 3rd LUMBAR VERTEBRAE

In the Black Dahlia Grand Jury investigation LAPD detective Harry Hansen stated: "I think a medical man was involved—a very fine surgeon. I base that conclusion on the way the body was bisected . . . It was unusual in this sense, that the point at which the body was bisected is, according to eminent medical men, the easiest point in the spinal column to severe (between the second and third lumbar vertebrae) and he hit the spot exactly. Dr. Newbarr told Hansen, that the surgery was meticulous and 'couldn't have been done in fifteen minutes, half hour or even an hour.'" The report goes on to state "the murderer had some training in the dissecting of bodies" (Note 44, pages 135-136). "The cut was straight through the narrowest part between the bottom of her ribs and navel" (Note 40, page 4). The FBI Report stated, "It is felt that the murder was committed indoors, where water, drainage facilities and perhaps medical equipment was available" (FBI Report Re: Elizabeth Short, February 15, 1947).

Whoever killed the Black Dahlia and Suzanne Degnan did have plenty of experience in dismembering human bodies. One thing is for certain: William Heirens was in prison in Illinois on January 14, 1947, when the Black Dahlia was killed and expertly severed in Los Angeles.

HANDWRITING COMPARISONS

I don't claim to be a handwriting expert. Usually the best source for making handwriting comparisons with pressure points and spacings are the originals writings. I don't have access to original documents and even if I did I would leave the analysis to the experts. Hopefully all of the known writings in these various cases will be reviewed by handwriting experts. In order to encourage this endeavor, I would like to point out certain similarities for whatever value they may have.

Here is a copy of the ransom note in the William Heirens case concerning the murder of Suzanne Degnan.

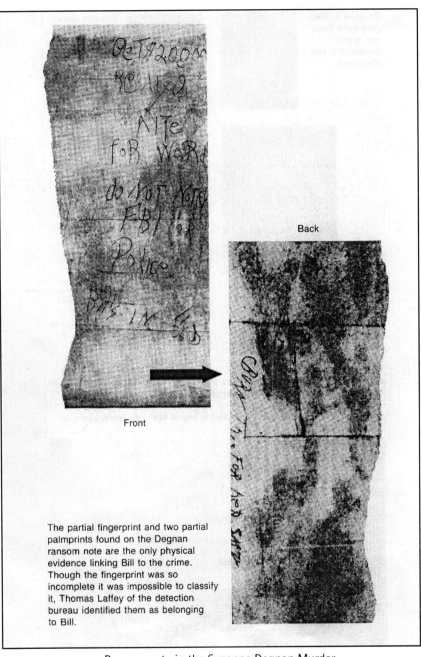

Back

Front

The partial fingerprint and two partial palmprints found on the Degnan ransom note are the only physical evidence linking Bill to the crime. Though the fingerprint was so incomplete it was impossible to classify it, Thomas Laffey of the detection bureau identified them as belonging to Bill.

Ransom note in the Suzanne Degnan Murder
(photo courtesy of Dolores Kennedy).

Now compare the following letters:

The Letter "U"

1. Suzanne Degnan Ransom Note in the word: B*u*rn
2. Black Dahlia Case in Exhibit 28 (*Black Dahlia Avenger*,
   by Steve Hodel) in the words;   cl*u*e, n*u*t and b*u*ilding
3. Mimi Boomhower case:
   In the words: fo*u*nd and Th*u*rsday
4. In the words: f*u*ck and yo*u*
   written in red lipstick on the chest of Jeanne French
   (Note 41, page 195)

Headlines in *The Mirror*, August 26, 1949, including photo of Mimi Boomhower's purse (Copyright, 1949, *Los Angeles Times*. Reprinted with permission).

The Letter "P"

1. In the ransom note in the Suzanne Degnan case in the word: *Police*
2. In the Black Dahlia case on Exhibit 23 on page 175 of the
   Black Dahlia Avenger in the word: Ex*press*

The Letter "R"

1. In the Suzanne Degnan Ransom Note in the word: *R*eddy
2. On Mimi Boomhower's purse in the word: Thu*r*sday

You should also note that the writing on the Boomhower purse reads as follows:

> POLICE.
> DEPT.-
> WE   FOUND **THIS**
> AT   BEACH
> THURSDAY NIGHT(emphasis added)

The reverse side of the Suzanne Degnan note reads as follows:

> BURN **This** FoR heR SAfTY   (emphasis added)

In the Black Dahlia case Federal inspectors at the Terminal Annex Post Office in downtown Los Angeles received the following note:

> A certain girl is going to get same as E.S. got if she squeals on **us**
> **We're** going to Mexico-catch **us** if you can. **2 k's**   (emphasis added)
> (Note 41, page 173)

The written note on Mimi Boomhower's purse reads in part:

> **WE** FOUND THIS AT BEACH . . .   (emphasis added)

On August 24, 1949, plump, 48-year-old socialite, Mimi Boomhower of 701 Nimes Road, Los Angeles, disappeared. She had lived alone in a 10-room Spanish style mansion following the death of her millionaire, inventor husband N.E. Boomhower, in 1943. On August 25, 1949, Walter E. Chaney of 3939 Longridge Avenue, Van Nuys, California found her purse in a phone booth. The next day the *Los Angeles Mirror* reported that Boomhower had pawned a diamond-studded wrist watch for $100.00 in Beverly Hills on July 8, 1949. When she pawned her watch Mrs. Boomhower was wearing a 7 ½ karat solitaire ring valued at over $5,000.00.

August 26, 1949, article in *The Mirror* in the Mimi Boomhower case (Copyright, 1949, *Los Angeles Times*. Reprinted with permission).

The *Mirror* further reported on August 26 that several anonymous phone callers reported tips regarding the disappearance of Mimi Boomhower. One anonymous caller "described himself as an ex-policeman and said he saw Evans with Mrs. Boomhower in the bar of the Hollywood Roosevelt Hotel last week."

The *Mirror* further reported:

> Sgt Ferges said today, "It could be that the purse was found on the beach or it could be a hoax. We don't know. But we do know that the purse belongs to Mrs. Boomhower." Missing persons bureau at Los Angeles said it had received an anonymous call from a man who said he saw the widow and a gambler known to the police "last Thursday or Friday morning." Police said Mrs. Boomhower's companion, if the call stands up, is a known **narcotics** addict and gambler. They are checking out the call.

Now compare these clues to the murder of the Black Dahlia:

a. Shortly before she was murdered the Black Dahlia desperately needed $100.00

b. One of the suspects in the Black Dahlia murder, listed in the Los Angeles District Attorney's file, was a person who flashed a Chicago police officer's badge.

c. In his taped interview with author John Gilmore, Jack Anderson Wilson mentions the Hollywood Roosevelt Hotel:

> They drove further south, to another hotel near 29th Street, also called the Roosevelt Hotel, but not connected to Hollywood's Roosevelt Hotel. (See page 185, *Severed* and page 83 of this text.)

The Hollywood Roosevelt Hotel is a very famous landmark in Hollywood that has been around since 1927. It is known as the birthplace of the academy awards. In his taped message Wilson had already given street directions that placed the Roosevelt Hotel in Los Angeles several miles from the Hollywood Roosevelt Hotel in Hollywood. Was the Hollywood Roosevelt Hotel on Wilson's mind for some other reason other than to make such an insignificant comparison to not being connected with the Roosevelt Hotel near 29th Street?

REVISIT THE CHICAGO CASE OF EUNICE RAWLINGS (See pages 69, 114, 115, 132 and 133 of text).

Rawlings disappeared January 14, 1945, in Chicago. Her headless, armless body washed ashore on a Lake Michigan beach August 12, 1946. On Monday August 12, 1946, *The Chicago Times* reported that a purse containing "the girl's name on a slip of paper was found on the lake shore rocks near Addison." Her death was ruled a suicide. A suicide note was found a dresser in her apartment. Was she forced to write the suicide note? She disappeared on January 14, 1945 exactly two years before Elizabeth Short was murdered in Los Angeles. When her body washed ashore her head and arms were missing. Was she dismembered before she entered Lake Michigan? Her apartment was located close to the apartments of Frances Brown and Josephine Ross, two of the victims in the William Heirens case. I find it very difficult to believe that a 17-year-old girl who, immediately prior to her demise was actively seeking employment, would choose to end her life by jumping into the frigid waters of Lake Michigan in January. According to an expert I spoke with regarding the Rawlings case, the cold waters of Lake Michigan would act as a refrigerator and preserve the body. Wave action and a myriad of other lake effects could cause an eventual dismemberment, so who knows? Eunice Rawlings' "suicide" and surrounding circumstances just seems peculiar to me.

NOTES

CHAPTER 1: The Torso Murders
(1) Badel, James Jessen. *In the Wake of the Butcher: Cleveland's Torso Murders*

CHAPTER 2: The Case Against William Heirens
(2) Badel, James Jessen. *In the Wake of the Butcher:Cleveland Torso Murders*
(3) *Chicago Daily Times*, August 7, 1946
(4) *Chicago Daily Times*, August 12, 1946
(5) *Chicago Daily Tribune,* January 8, 1946
(6) *Chicago Daily Tribune*, January 12, 1946
(7) *Chicago Daily Tribune*, January 12, 1946
(8) *Chicago Daily Tribune*, January 15, 1946
(9) *Chicago Daily Tribune*, January 17, 1946
(10) *Chicago Daily Tribune*, January 18, 1946
(11) *Chicago Tribune Press*, January 7, 1946
(12) *Chicago Sun*, January 12, 1946)
(13) *Chicago Sun*, January 8, 1946
(14) *Crimelibrary.com*
(15) Gilmore, John. *Severed: The True Story of the Black Dahlia Murder*
(16) Hodel, Steven. *Black Dahlia Avenger*
(17) Kennedy, Dolores. *William Heirens: His Day In Court*
(18) Martin, John Bartlow. *Butcher's Dozen and Other Murders*
(19) Nickel, Steven. *Torso: The Story of Elliot Ness and the Search for the Psychopathic Killer*

CHAPTER 3: Georgette Bauerdorf, Elizabeth Short (The Black Dahlia), Jeanne Axford French (The Red Lipstick Murder) and Other Los Angeles Victims
(20) Badal, James Jessen. *In the Wake of the Butcher: Cleveland's Torso Murders*
(21) *Chicago Daily Tribune*, January 15, 1946
(22) *Chicago Daily Tribune*, January 18, 1946
(23) *Chicago Sun*, January 10, 1946
(24) *Chicago Sun*, January 12, 1946
(25) *Chicago Times*, August 12, 1946
(26) *Crimelibrary.com:The Cleveland Torso Murders, Elliot Ness Serial Killer Case*

(27) Gilmore, John. *Severed: The True Story of the Black Dahlia Murder*

(28) Hodel, Steven. *Black Dahlia Avenger*

(29) Kennedy, Dolores. *William Heirens: His Day In Court*

(30) Martin, John Bartlow. *Butcher's Dozen and Other Murders*

(31) Nickel, Steven. *Torso: The Story of Elliot Ness and the Search for the Psychopathic Killer*

(32) Pacios, Mary. *Childhood Shadows: The Hidden Story of the Black Dahlia Murder*

(33) *Cleveland Plain Dealer*

CHRONOLOGY

(34) Badal, James Jessen. *In the Wake of the Butcher*

(35) Gilmore, John. *Severed: The True story of the Black Dahlia*

(36) Hodel, Steven. *Black Dahlia Avenger*

(37) Nickel, Steven. *Torso: The Story of Elliot Ness and the Search for the Pathological Killer*

(38) Pacios, Mary. *Childhood Shadows: The Hidden Story of the Black Dahlia Murder*

SECOND REVISED EPILOGUE

(39) Badal, James Jessen. *In the Wake of the Butcher*

(40) Gilmore, John. *Severed*

(41) Hodel, Steve. *The Black Dahlia Avenger*

(42) Kennedy, Dolores. *William Heirens: His Day In Court*

(43) Martin, John Martin. *Butcher's Dozen*

(44) Wolfe, Donald F. *The Black Dahlia Files*

CHAPTER 4: THE PHANTOM KILLER OF TEXARKANA

(45) *Crime Library*

(46) *Texarkana Gazette*, 1996

(47) *The Kansas City Star*. Sunday, June 2, 1946

CHAPTER 5: THE ZODIAC KILLER

(48) Graysmith, Robert. *Zodiac*

(49) *True Crime-Time Life Books*. 1993

BIBLIOGRAPHY

BOOKS

Badel, James Jessen. *In the Wake of the Butcher: Cleveland's Torso Murders*. Kent State University Press, 2001.

Celebrity Murders. Edited by Art Crockett. Pinnacle Books, Windsor Publishing Corporation, 1990.

Chambers, Bradford and Pezet, A. W.. *Greatest Crimes of the Century*, 1954

Collins, Max Allen. *Angel In Black*. Signet, 2002

Douglas, John and Mark Olshaker. *The Cases that Haunt Us*. New York, Lisa Drew Books/Scribner, 2000.

Ellroy, James. *The Black Dahlia*. Warner Books, Inc., 1987.

Fisher, Jim. *Hopewell: Setting the Record Straight in the Lindbergh Case*. Southern Illinois University Press, 1999.

Fowler, Will. *Reporters:Memoirs of a Young Newspaperman*. Roundtable Publishing, Inc., 1991

Gilmore, John. *Severed: The True Story of the Black Dahlia Murder*. San Francisco: Zanja Press, Amok Books, 1994.

Graysmith, Robert. *Zodiac*. Berkley Publishing Group, 1976

Hodel, Steve. *Black Dahlia Avenger*. New York: Arcade Publishing, Inc., 2003

Kennedy, Dolores. *William Heirens: His Day in Court/Did an Innocent Man Confess to Three Grisly Murders?*.Chicago: Bonus Book, Inc., 1991.

Martin, John Bartlow. *Butcher's Dozen and other Murders*. New York: Harper & Brothers, 1950.

Nickel, Steven. *Torso: The Story of Elliot Ness and the Search for the Psychopathic Killer.*Winston-Salem, N.C.: John F. Blair Publisher, 1989.

Pacios, Mary. *Childhood Shadows: The Hidden Story of the Black Dahlia Murder*. 1st Books, revised 5/23/00.

True Crime.Time Life-Books, 1993.

Wolfe, Donald H.,*The Black Dahlia Files*. Regan Books, 2005.

World Book Encyclopedia

INTERNET REFERENCES

www.crimelibrary.com. Court TV. Serial Killers, Sexual Predators/William Heirens/ Lipstick Killer.

www.zodiackiller.com, Tom Voigt

NEWSPAPERS

Chicago Daily News
Chicago Daily Times
Chicago Daily Tribune
Chicago Defender
Chicago Herald American
Chicago Sun
Chicago Tribune Press
Dallas Morning News
Kansas City Star
Los Angeles Herald Examiner
Los Angeles Mirror (The Mirror)
Los Angeles Times
Riverside Press-Enterprise
San Francisco Chronicle
San Francisco Examiner
Texarkana Gazette
The Chicago Times
The Cleveland News
The Cleveland Plain Dealer
The Cleveland Press
The Indianapolis Star
Washington Times-Herald
Wichita Eagle-Beacon
Vallejo Times-Herald

MAGAZINES

Martin, John Bartlow. "Butcher's Dozen: The Cleveland Torso Murders." *Harper's Magazine*, November 1948:55-69.

INDEX

Printed in the United States
70656LV00005B/8

9 780865 345362